THE HARMONY GUIDE TO
100'S MORE CROCHET STITCHES

Lyric Books Limited

© 1992 Lyric Books Limited
PO Box 152, Mill Hill, London NW7, England

North American Edition
First Published in 1992

ISBN 0 7111 0073 X

Printed in Belgium by
Proost International Book Production

Compiled by
Barbara Devaney, Lesley Kidacka and Jacqueline Lassauzet
with special thanks to Barbara Tennant for the Tunisian section

Graphics by
Stefanie Paradine, Beryl Kempner and Julian Jones

Photography by
Richard Kempner

Layout and Typography by
Debra Mountford

Series Editor
Beryl Kempner

CONTENTS

Introduction

About Crochet

Traditionally crochet was worked almost exclusively in very fine cotton yarn to create or embellish household items such as curtains, table cloths or place mats. Crochet was often added as decoration or trimming on collars and fine lawn handkerchiefs. The frill on the front of a man's shirt was often crochet work.

With the increase in the availability of yarn in a wide variety of textures and colours we are no longer limited to just these articles when we consider ways to use the craft of crochet. The samples in this book were worked in a fine mercerised cotton, but may take on a totally different appearance if different yarns are used. The lacier stitches probably look their best in these smooth threads, but some of the all-over stitches and many of the Afghan (Tunisian) stitches can be more interesting when worked in tweedy or textured yarns.

Equipment

Crochet Hooks

Crochet hooks are usually made from steel, aluminium or plastic in a range of sizes according to their diameter. As each crochet stitch is worked separately until only one loop remains on the hook, space is not needed to hold stitches and the hooks are made to a standard convenient length.

Holding the Hook and Yarn

There are no hard and fast rules as to the best way to hold the hook and yarn. The diagrams below show just one method, but choose whichever way you find the most comfortable.

Due to the restrictions of space it is not possible to show diagrams for both right and left handed people. Left handers may find it easier to trace the diagrams and then turn the tracing paper over, thus reversing the image, alternatively reflect the diagrams in the mirror. Read left for right and right for left where applicable.

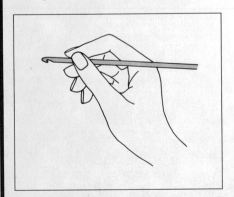

The hook is held in the right hand as if holding a pencil.

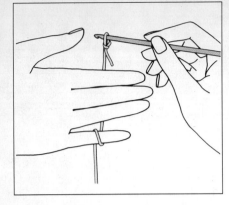

To maintain the slight tension in the yarn necessary for easy, even working, it can help to arrange the yarn around the fingers of the left hand in this way.

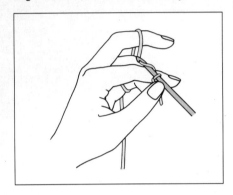

The left hand holds the work and at the same time controls the yarn supply. The left hand middle finger is used to manipulate the yarn, while the index finger and thumb hold on to the work.

To Start

Almost all crochet begins with a base or starting chain, which is a series of chain stitches, beginning with a slip knot.

Slip Knot

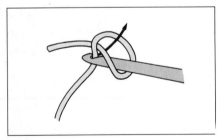

Make a loop then hook another loop through it. Tighten gently and slide the knot up to the hook.

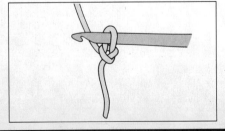

Yarn Over (yo)

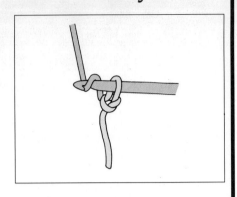

Wrap the yarn from back to front over the hook (or hold the yarn still and manoeuvre the hook). This movement of the yarn over the hook is used over and over again in crochet and is usually called 'yarn over', abbreviated as 'yo'.

Chain Stitch (ch ○)

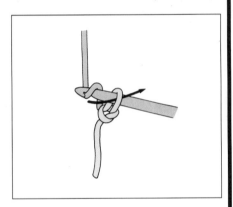

Yarn over and draw the yarn through to form a new loop without tightening up the previous one.

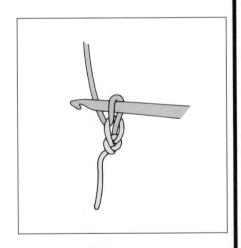

Repeat to form as many chains as required. Do not count the slip knot as a stitch.

Note: Unless otherwise stated, when working into the starting chain always work under two strands of chain loops as shown in the diagram.

Basic Stitches

All the crochet patterns in this book are produced using combinations of the following basic stitches. They are shown in the diagrams worked into a starting chain but the method is the same whatever part of the work the stitch is worked into.

Slip Stitch (sl st •)

This is the shortest of crochet stitches and unlike other stitches is not used on its own to produce a fabric. It is used for joining, shaping and where necessary carrying the yarn to another part of the fabric for the next stage.

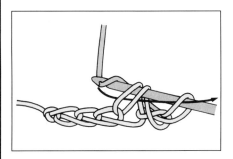

Insert the hook into the work (second chain from hook in diagram), yarn over and draw the yarn through both the work and loop on the hook in one movement.

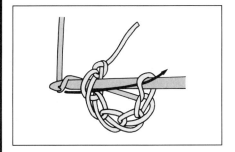

To join a chain ring with a slip stitch, then insert hook into first chain, yarn over and draw through the work and the yarn on the hook.

Single Crochet (sc +)

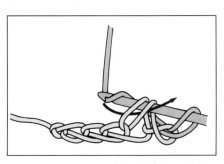

1. Insert the hook into the work (second chain from hook on starting chain), *yarn over and draw yarn through the work only.

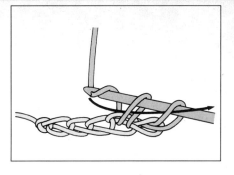

2. Yarn over again and draw the yarn through both loops on the hook.

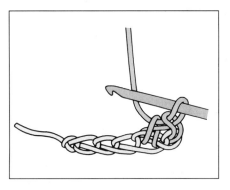

3. 1sc made. Insert hook into next stitch; repeat from * in step 1.

Half Double Crochet (hdc ⊤)

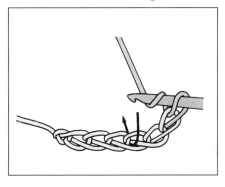

1. Yarn over and insert the hook into the work (third chain from hook on starting chain).

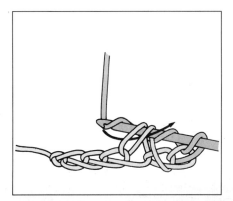

2. *Yarn over and draw through the work only.

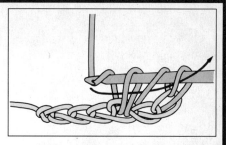

3. Yarn over again and draw through all three loops on the hook.

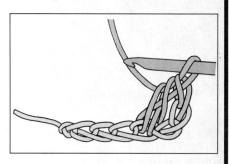

4. 1hdc made. Yarn over, insert hook into next stitch; repeat from * in step 2.

Double Crochet (dc ⊤)

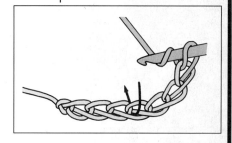

1. Yarn over and insert the hook into the work (fourth chain from hook on starting chain).

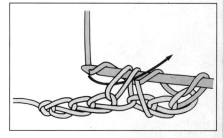

2. *Yarn over and draw through the work only.

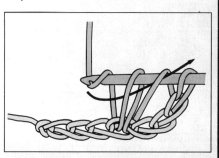

3. Yarn over and draw through the first two loops only.

Making Crochet Fabric

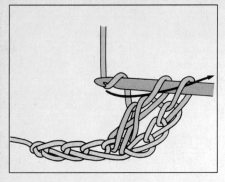

4. Yarn over and draw through the last two loops on the hook.

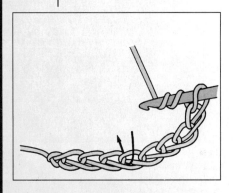

5. 1dc made. Yarn over, insert hook into next stitch; repeat from * in step 2.

Treble (tr ⧫)

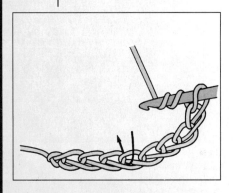

1. Yarn over twice, insert the hook into the work (fifth chain from hook on starting chain).

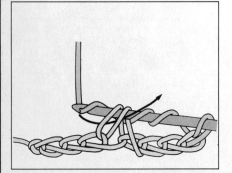

2. *Yarn over and draw through the work only.

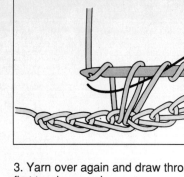

3. Yarn over again and draw through the first two loops only.

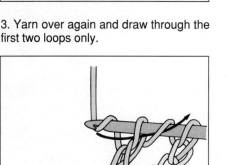

4. Yarn over again and draw through the next two loops only.

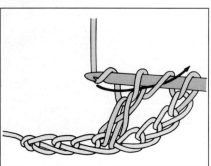

5. Yarn over again and draw through the last two loops on the hook.

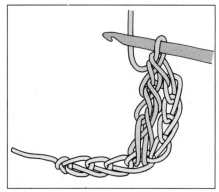

6. 1tr made. Yarn over twice, insert hook into next stitch; repeat from * in step 2.

Longer Basic Stitches

Double treble (dtr), triple treble (ttr), quadruple treble (quadtr) etc. are made by

wrapping the yarn over three, four, five times etc. at the beginning and finishing as for a treble, repeating step 4 until two loops remain on hook, finish with step 5.

Making Crochet Fabric

These are the basic procedures for making crochet fabrics.

Starting Chain

To make a flat fabric worked in rows you must begin with a starting chain. The length of the starting chain is the number of stitches needed for the first row of fabric plus the number of chain needed to get to the correct height of the stitches to be used in the first row. All the patterns in this book indicate the length of starting chain required to work one repeat of the design. See 'Starting Chains and Pattern Repeats' on page 11.

TIP

When working a large piece it is sensible to start with more chain than necessary as it is simple to undo the extra chain if you have miscounted.

Working in Rows

A flat fabric can be produced by turning the work at the end of each row. Right handers work from right to left and left handers from left to right. One or more chain must be worked at the beginning of each row to bring the hook up to the height of the first stitch in the row. The number of chain used for turning depends upon the height of the stitch they are to match as follows:

single crochet = 1 chain
half double crochet = 2 chain
double crochet = 3 chain
treble = 4 chain

When working half double crochet or longer stitches the turning chain takes the place of the first stitch. Where one chain is worked at the beginning of a row starting with single crochet it is usually for height only and is in addition to the first stitch.

Basic Dc Fabric

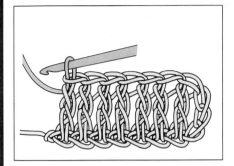

Make a starting chain of the required length plus two chain. Work one double crochet into fourth chain from hook. The three chain at the beginning of the row form the first double crochet. Work one double crochet into the next and every chain to the end of the row.

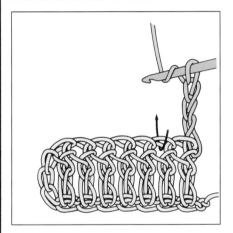

At the end of each row turn the work so that another row can be worked across the top of the previous one. It does not matter which way the work is turned but be consistent. Make three chain for turning. These turning chain will count as the first double crochet.

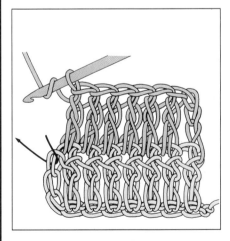

Skip the first double crochet in the previous row, work a double crochet into the top of the next and every double crochet including the last double crochet in row, then work a double crochet into third of three chain at the beginning of the previous row.

Note: Unless otherwise stated when working into the top of a stitch, always work under two strands as shown in diagram.

Fastening Off

To fasten off the yarn permanently break off the yarn about 5cm (2 ins) away from the work (longer if you need to sew pieces together). Draw the end through the loop on hook and tighten gently.

Joining in New Yarn and Changing Color

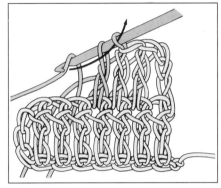

When joining in new yarn or changing color, work in the old yarn until two loops of the last stitch remain in the old yarn or color. Use the new color or yarn to complete the stitch.

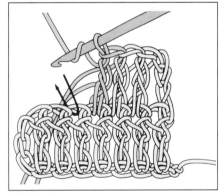

Continue to work the following stitches in the new color or yarn, as before.

If you are working whole rows in different colors, make the change during the last stitch in the previous row, so the new color for the next row is ready to work the turning chain.

Do not cut off any yarns which will be needed again later at the same edge, but continue to use them as required, leaving an unbroken 'float' thread up the side of the fabric.

If, at the end of a row, the pattern requires you to return to the beginning of the same row without turning and to work another row in a different color in the same direction, complete the first row in the old color and fasten off by lengthening the final loop on the hook, passing the whole ball through it and gently tighten again. That yarn is now available if you need to rejoin it later at this edge (if not, cut it).

Stitch Variations

Most crochet stitch patterns, however elaborate, are made using combinations of basic stitches. Different effects can be created by small variations in the stitch making procedure or by varying the position and manner of inserting the hook into the fabric. The following techniques are used frequently to build up crochet fabric.

Note: Terms such as 'group', 'cluster', 'picot', 'shell', 'fan', 'flower', 'petal', 'leaf' and 'bobble' do not denote a fixed arrangement of stitches. Exactly what they mean may be different for each pattern. The procedure is therefore always given at the beginning of each set of instructions as a Special Abbreviation.

Groups or Shells

These consist of several complete stitches worked into the same place. They can be worked as part of a pattern or as a method of increasing.

Five Double Crochet Group

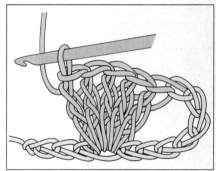

Work five double crochet into one stitch.

Summary of Common Groups or Shells

On diagrams the point at the base of the group will be positioned above the space or stitch where the hook is to be inserted.

2, 3 and 4 half double crochet group

Work 2(3,4) half double crochet into same place.

2, 3, 4 and 5 double crochet group

Work 2(3,4,5) double crochet into same place.

2, 3, 4 and 5 treble group

Work 2(3,4,5) treble into same place.

Stitch Variations

Clusters

Any combination of stitches may be joined into a cluster by leaving the last loop of each temporarily on the hook until they are worked off together at the end. Working stitches together in this way can also be a method of decreasing.

It is important to be sure exactly how and where the hook is to be inserted for each 'leg' of the cluster. The 'legs' may be worked over adjacent stitches, or stitches may be skipped between 'legs'.

Three Dc Cluster

(Worked over adjacent stitches).

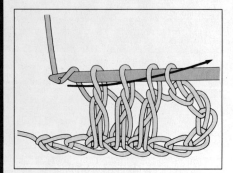

Work a double crochet into each of the next three stitches leaving the last loop of each double crochet on the hook.

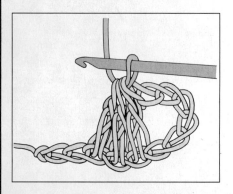

Yarn over and draw through all four loops on the hook.

Summary of Common Clusters

(Worked over adjacent stitches).

On diagrams each 'leg' of the cluster will be positioned above the stitch where the hook is to be inserted.

3, 4 and 5 double crochet cluster

Work a double crochet into each of the next 3(4,5) stitches leaving the last loop of each on the hook. Yarn over and draw through all loops on hook.

3, 4 and 5 treble cluster

Work a treble into each of the next 3(4,5) stitches leaving the last loop of each on the hook. Yarn over and draw through all loops on hook.

Bobbles

When a cluster is worked into one stitch it forms a bobble.

Five Dc Bobble

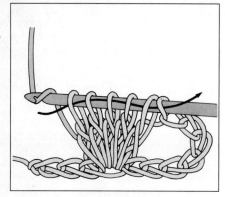

1. Work five double crochet into one stitch leaving the last loop of each on the hook.

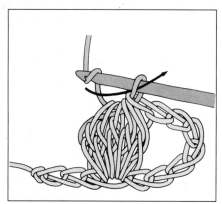

2. Yarn over and draw through all the loops on the hook.

More bulky bobbles can be secured with an extra chain stitch. If this is necessary it would be indicated within the pattern.

Summary of Common Bobbles

Follow instructions as if working a cluster but for each 'leg' insert the hook into the same stitch or space.

3, 4 and 5 double crochet bobble

4, 5, 6 and 7 treble bobble

Popcorns

Popcorns are groups of complete stitches usually worked into the same place, folded and closed at the top. An extra chain can be worked to secure the popcorn.

Five Dc Popcorn

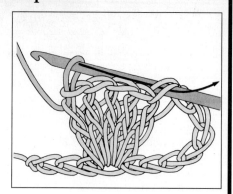

1. Work five double crochet into one stitch. Take the hook out of the working loop and insert it into the top of the first double crochet made, from front to back.

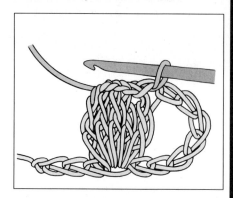

2. Pick up the working loop and draw this through to close the popcorn. If required work one chain to secure the popcorn.

Summary of Common Popcorns

On diagrams the point at the base of the popcorn will be positioned above the space or stitch where it is to be worked.

3 and 4 half double crochet popcorn

Work 3(4) half double crochet into the same place, drop loop off hook, insert hook into first half double crochet, pick up dropped loop and draw through.

3, 4 and 5 double crochet popcorn

Work 3(4,5) double crochet into the same place, drop loop off hook, insert hook into first double crochet, pick up dropped loop and draw through.

3, 4 and 5 treble popcorn

Work 3(4,5) treble into the same place, drop loop off hook, insert hook into first treble, pick up dropped loop and draw through.

Puff Stitches

These are similar to bobbles but worked using half double crochet, into the same stitch or space. However because half double crochet cannot be worked until one loop remains on the hook, the stitches are not closed until the required number have been worked.

Three Half Double Crochet Puff Stitch

(Worked into one stitch).

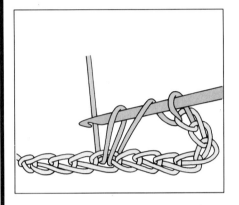

1. Yarn over, insert the hook, yarn over again and draw a loop through (three loops on the hook).

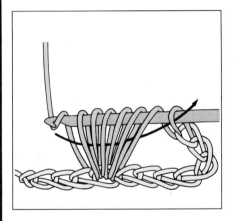

2. Repeat this step twice more, inserting the hook into the same stitch (seven loops on the hook); yarn over and draw through all the loops on the hook.

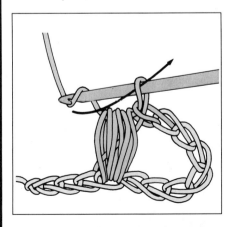

3. As with popcorns and bulky bobbles an extra chain stitch is often used to secure the puff stitch firmly. This will be indicated within the pattern if necessary.

A **cluster** of half double crochet stitches is worked in the same way as a puff stitch but each 'leg' is worked where indicated.

Picots

A picot is normally a chain loop formed into a closed ring by a slip stitch or single crochet. The number of chains in a picot can vary.

Four Chain Picot

(Closed with a slip stitch).

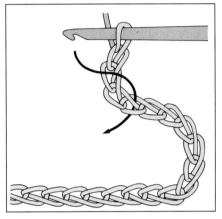

1. Work four chain.

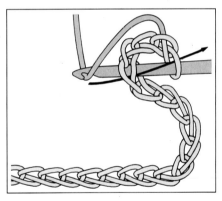

2. Into fourth chain from hook work a slip stitch to close.

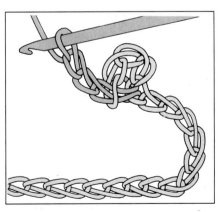

3. Continue working chain or required stitch.

Note: When working a picot closed with a slip stitch at the top of a chain arch, the picot will not appear central unless an extra chain is worked after the slip stitch.

Crossed Stitches

This method produces stitches that are not entangled with each other and so maintain a clear 'X' shape.

Crossed Treble

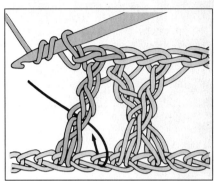

Skip two stitches and work the first treble into next stitch. Work one chain then work second treble into first of skipped stitches taking the hook behind the first treble before inserting.

See individual pattern instructions for variations on crossed stitch.

Placement of Stitches

All crochet stitches (except chains) require the hook to be inserted into existing work. It has already been shown how to work into a chain and into the top of a stitch, however stitches can also be worked into the following places.

Working into Chain Spaces

When a stitch, group, shell, cluster or bobble etc. is positioned over a chain or chains, the hook is often inserted into the space under the chain.

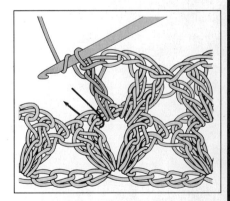

It is important to notice, however, if the pattern instructions stipulate working **into** a particular chain as this will change the appearance of the design.

If necessary information of this kind has been given as notes with the diagram.

Pattern Instructions

A bobble, popcorn or cluster that is worked into a chain space is shown in the diagram spread out more than one worked **into** a stitch, therefore on the diagrams they will not be closed at the base.

5dc bobble into a stitch or space

Working Around the Stem of a Stitch

Inserting the hook round the whole stem of a stitch creates raised or relief effects.

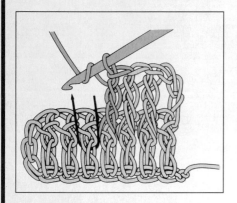

Working around the front of stem gives a stitch that lies on the front of the work.

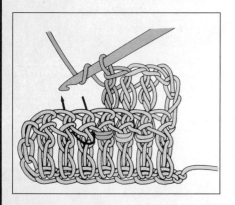

Working around the back of stem gives a stitch that lies on the back of the work.

Working Between Stitches

Inserting the hook between the stems of the stitches produces an open effect.

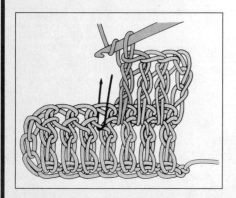

Ensure the number of stitches remains constant after each row.

Working Under the Front or Back Loop Only

Inserting the hook under one loop at the top of the stitch leaves the other loop as a horizontal bar.

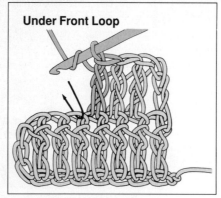

Under Front Loop

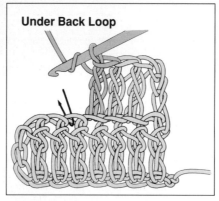

Under Back Loop

Working in Rows

If you work consistently into the front loop only you will make a series of ridges alternately on the back and front of the work. Working into the back loop only makes the ridges appear alternately on the front and back of the work.

If however you work alternately into the front loop only on one row and then the back loop only on the next row, the horizontal bars will all appear on the same side of the fabric.

Working in Rounds

Working always into the front loop only will form a bar on the back of the work, and vice versa.

Pattern Instructions

In order to follow crochet instructions you should know how to make the basic stitches and to be familiar with basic fabric-making procedures.

Any unusual stitches or combinations of stitches have been given as a Special Abbreviation with the particular pattern.

Any specific techniques - for example working with padding threads - are given at the start of the relevant section, in this case Irish Style Crochet.

All the patterns in this book have been given in the form of both written instructions and diagrams, so that you can choose to follow either method.

However, if you are more used to written instructions it is still a good idea to look at the diagram to get an overall picture of how the design has been put together.

Diagram followers may find it helpful to refer to the written instructions to confirm their interpretation of the diagram.

Working from a Diagram

Diagrams should be read exactly as the crochet is worked. For example, motifs are worked from the center outwards and all-over patterns from the bottom to the top. Where the direction of work, within a design, is not obvious an extra line drawing or arrows are given to show where the direction changes (for example I.3 on page 13). Each stitch is represented by a symbol that has been drawn to resemble its crocheted equivalent. The position of the symbol shows where the stitch should be worked.

Stitch symbols are drawn and laid out as realistically as possible but there are times when they have to be distorted for the sake of clarity. For example stitches may look extra long to show clearly where they are to be placed, but you should not try to make artificially long stitches. This distortion is particularly apparent on diagrams that represent fabrics not intended to lie flat (for example I.8 on page 15). Sometimes it has been necessary to use a colored arrow to indicate where particular stitches should be worked. This occurs most often in the Irish Style Crochet section, because many of the designs are three-dimensional.

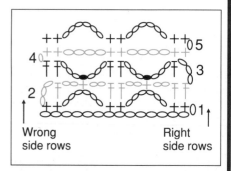

Wrong side rows   Right side rows

Right Side and Wrong Side Rows

Where the work is turned after each row only alternate rows are worked with the right side of the work facing. These 'right side rows' are printed in black on stitch diagrams and read from right to left. Wrong side rows are printed in blue and read from left to right. Row numbers are shown at the side of the diagrams at the **beginning** of the row.

Patterns worked in rounds have the right side rows facing on every round. To make them easier to follow we have printed alternate rounds in black and blue.

Starting Chains and Pattern Repeats

The number of starting chain required is given with each pattern. It may be given in the form of a multiple, for example:- **Starting chain: Multiple of 7 sts + 3.** This means you can make any length of chain that is a multiple of 7 + 3, such as 14 + 3ch, 21 + 3ch, 28 + 3ch etc.

In the written instructions the stitches that should be repeated are contained within brackets [ ] or follow an asterisk *. These stitches are repeated across the row or round the required number of times. On the diagrams the stitches that have to be repeated can be easily visualised. The extra stitches not included in the pattern repeat are there to balance the row or make it symmetrical and are only worked once. Obviously turning chains are only worked at the beginning of each row. Some diagrams consist of more than one pattern repeat so that you can see more clearly how the design is worked.

Working in Color

Capital letters A, B, C etc. are used to indicate different yarn colors in both written instructions and diagrams. They do not refer to any particular color. See page 7 for instructions on changing color within a pattern.

Tension (or Gauge)

This refers to the number of stitches and rows in a given area. When following a pattern for a garment or other article the instructions will include a specified tension. If you do not produce fabric with the same number of stitches and rows as indicated, your work will not come to the measurements given.

To ensure that you achieve the correct tension work a tension sample or swatch before starting the main part of the crochet. The hook size quoted in the pattern is a suggestion only. You must use whichever hook gives you the correct tension.

If you are going to use a stitch pattern from this book to design an article of your own, it is still important to work a tension sample in order to calculate the number of stitches you will require. It is worth experimenting with different hook sizes so that you find the best tension for your chosen

pattern and yarn. Some stitches look and feel better worked loosely and others need to be worked more firmly to be at their best.

Shaping

If you are working crochet to make something which requires shaping, such as decreasing for the neckline of a garment or increasing to add width for a sleeve, you need to know something about shaping.

Increasing is generally achieved by working two or more stitches in the pattern where there would normally be one stitch. Conversely, decreasing is achieved by working two or more stitches together, or

missing one or more stitches. However it can be difficult to know exactly where these adjustments are best made, and a visual guide would make the work easier!

On the diagrams below we show you some examples of shapings which cover a variety of possibilities. We recommend that you use this method yourself when planning a project. First pencil trace the diagram given with the stitch. If necessary repeat the tracing to match the repeat of the pattern until you have a large enough area to give you the shape you require. Once this is correct **ink it in** so that you can draw over it in pencil without destroying it. Now draw over this the shaping you require matching as near as possible the style of the particular pattern you are using.

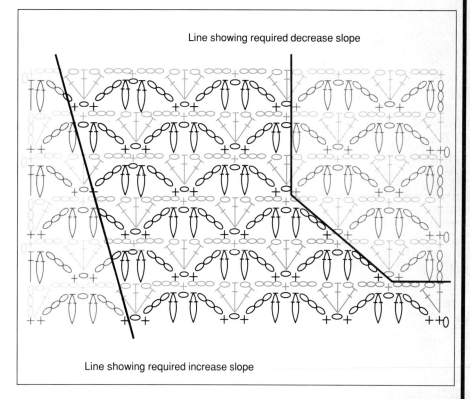

Line showing required decrease slope

Line showing required increase slope

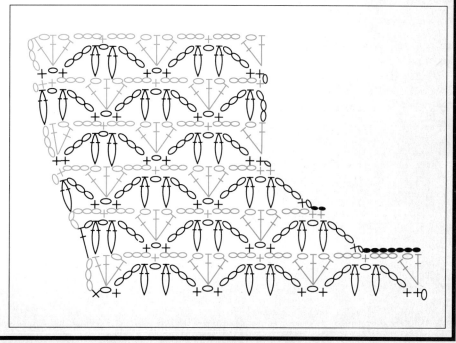

Abbreviations and Symbols

Joining Seams

Various methods can be used to join pieces of crochet. The use of the item will often dictate the method used, the seam could be invisible or decorative. Below are a few suggestions for joining pieces of crochet.

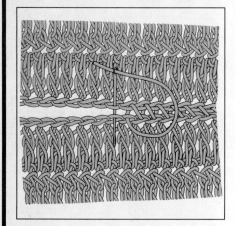

To join with an invisible sewn seam, place pieces edge to edge with the wrong sides uppermost and whip stitch together.

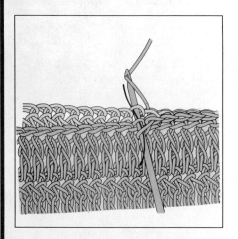

To join invisibly using a crochet hook, place right sides of pieces together and slip stitch through one loop of each piece as illustrated.

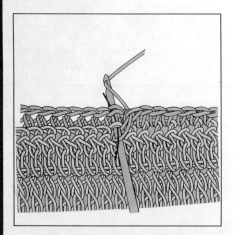

To create a decorative ridged seam on the right side of the work, place wrong sides together and join with single crochet working under two strands of each piece as illustrated.

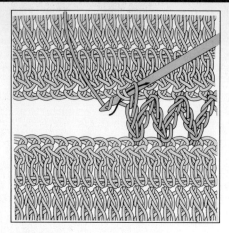

Alternatively with the right side of both pieces uppermost they can be joined with a row of fancy openwork chains.

Pressing and Finishing

The methods you use to finish your crochet depend largely on what you are using it for and what yarn you have used.

Cotton

Cotton yarns benefit from being wetted or thoroughly steamed. If you are using household starch (as opposed to spray starch) now is the time to apply it, either by immersing the crocheted piece or dabbing the wet starch on to the material. Pin out very near to the edge, at very close intervals, stretching or easing the material to ensure that it is even. Picots, bobbles or other intrinsic features should be carefully placed with a pin at this stage. Having satisfied yourself that the shape is correct, the work can now be pressed using a hot iron. Do not allow the full weight of the iron to rest on the work especially where interesting textures are involved. Remove the pins and if required make fine adjustments to the edges of the material to ensure that they are straight. Now leave until the work is **thoroughly** dry.

Motifs and Irish Style Pieces

Work as given above but leave the pins in position until the work is **thoroughly** dry. Ensure that all three-dimensional features show to their best advantage.

Other Yarns

In principal the methods given for working with cotton yarns apply, but you must read the finishing or pressing information usually included with your yarn. Not every yarn will be suitable for or require starching and some yarns cannot be pressed with a hot iron.

Abbreviations and Symbols

Listed below are the standard abbreviations and symbols that have been used for pages 13 to 84 of this book. Refer to pages 4 to 12 for more detailed instructions of these and other stitch variations. If a pattern contains an unusual combinations of stitches these are explained in the Special Abbreviation at the beginning of that pattern.

Separate abbreviations and symbols have been used for the Afghan (Tunisian) stitches in this book and these have been given at the beginning of that section on pages 85 to 89.

Abbreviations

Alt = alternate, **beg** = begin(ning), **ch(s)** = chain(s), **ch sp** = chain space, **cm** = centimetre(s), **dec** = decrease, **dc** = double crochet, **dtr** = double treble, **hdc** = half double crochet, **inc** = increase, **ins** = inches, **quadtr** = quadruple treble, **rep** = repeat, **sc** = single crochet, **sl st** = slip stitch, **sp(s)** = space(s), **st(s)** = stitch(es), **tog** = together, **tr** = treble, **ttr** = triple treble, **yo** = yarn over.

Basic Symbols used in Diagrams

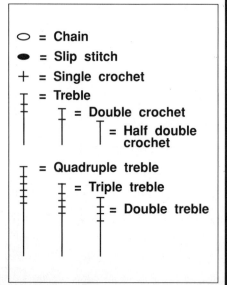

The number of strokes crossing the stems of stitches longer than a half double crochet represents the number of times the yarn is wrapped over the hook **before** the hook is inserted into the work.

I. All-over Patterns

I.1

Starting chain: Multiple of 16 sts + 2.

1st row (right side): Work 2sc into 2nd ch from hook, *1sc into each of next 7ch, skip 1ch, 1sc into each of next 7ch, 3sc into next ch; rep from * to end omitting 1sc at end of last rep, turn.

2nd row: 1ch, work 2sc into first sc, *1sc into each of next 7sc, skip 2sc, 1sc into each of next 7sc, 3sc into next sc; rep from * to end omitting 1sc at end of last rep, turn.

Rep 2nd row only.

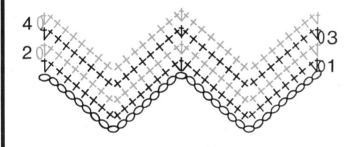

Diagram only: Rep 2nd and 3rd rows.

I.2

Work as given for I.1 **but** working 1 row each in colors A, B and C throughout.

I.3

Starting chain: Multiple of 6 sts + 3.

Special Abbreviations

Dc2tog = work 1dc into each of next 2 sts until 1 loop of each remains on hook, yo and through all 3 loops on hook.

Half Cluster = work 1dc into each of next 3 sts until 1 loop of each remains on hook, yo and through all 4 loops on hook.

Cluster = work 1dc into each of next 5 sts until 1 loop of each remains on hook, yo and through all 6 loops on hook.

1st row (right side): Work dc2tog working into 4th and 5th ch from hook, *3ch, 1sc into next ch, turn, 1ch, 1sc into last sc worked, 3sc into last 3ch sp formed, [turn, 1ch, 1sc into each of the 4sc] 3 times, work 1 cluster over next 5ch; rep from * to end but working half cluster at end of last rep, turn.

2nd row: 4ch (count as 1tr), work 2tr into top of first half cluster, skip 3sc, 1sc into next sc, *5tr into top of next cluster, skip 3sc, 1sc into next sc; rep from * to last dc2tog, 3tr into top of 3ch at beg of previous row, turn.

3rd row: 3ch (count as 1dc), skip first tr, work dc2tog over next 2tr, *3ch, 1sc into next sc, turn, 1ch, 1sc into last sc worked, 3sc into last 3ch sp formed, [turn, 1ch, 1sc into each of the 4sc] 3 times, work 1 cluster over next 5tr; rep from * to end but working half cluster at end of last rep placing last dc of half cluster into 4th of 4ch at beg of previous row, turn.

Rep 2nd and 3rd rows ending with a 2nd row.

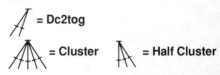

= Dc2tog   = Cluster   = Half Cluster

Line shows direction of work for first part of first row.

I.4

Starting chain: Multiple of 3 sts + 3.

Special Abbreviation

1dc/rf = work 1dc around stem of next st 2 rows below inserting hook round stem from right to left to draw up loops.

1st row (right side): Work 1sc into 2nd ch from hook, 1sc into each ch to end, turn.

2nd row: 1ch, work 1sc into each sc to end, turn.

3rd row: 1ch, work 1sc into each of first 2sc, *1dc/rf round next sc 2 rows below, 1sc into each of next 2sc; rep from * to end, turn.

4th row: 1ch, work 1sc into each st to end, turn.

5th row: 1ch, work 1sc into each of first 2sc, *1dc/rf round stem of next dc/rf 2 rows below, 1sc into each of next 2sc; rep from * to end, turn.

Rep 4th and 5th rows.

= 1dc/rf

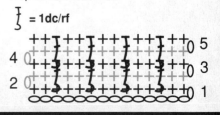

I. All-over Patterns

I.5

Starting chain: Multiple of 12 sts + 8.

Special Abbreviations

Puff st = *yo, insert hook into next st, yo and draw a loop through; rep from * 4 times more inserting hook into same st as before (11 loops on hook), yo and draw through 10 loops, yo and draw through 2 remaining loops.

1dc/rf = work 1dc around stem of next st 2 rows below inserting hook round stem from right to left to draw up loops.

1st row (right side): Work 1sc into 2nd ch from hook, 1sc into each ch to end, turn.

2nd and every alt row: 1ch, work 1sc into each st to end, turn.

3rd row: 1ch, work 1sc into each of first 2sc, 1dc/rf, 1sc into next sc, 1dc/rf, *1sc into each of next 4sc, 1 puff st into next sc, 1sc into each of next 4sc, 1dc/rf, 1sc into next sc, 1dc/rf; rep from * to last 2sc, 1sc into each of last 2sc, turn.

5th row: 1ch, work 1sc into each of first 2sc, 1dc/rf, 1sc into next sc, 1dc/rf, *1sc into each of next 2sc, 1 puff st into next sc, 1sc into each of next 3sc, 1 puff st into next sc, 1sc into each of next 2sc, 1dc/rf, 1sc into next sc, 1dc/rf; rep from * to last 2sc, 1sc into each of last 2sc, turn.

7th row: As 3rd row.

9th row: 1ch, 1sc into each of first 2sc, 1dc/rf, 1sc into next sc, 1dc/rf, *1sc into each of next 9sc, 1dc/rf, 1sc into next sc, 1dc/rf; rep from * to last 2sc, 1sc into each of last 2sc, turn.

Rep 2nd to 9th rows.

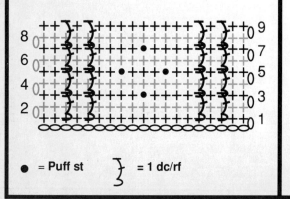

● = Puff st   } = 1 dc/rf

I.6

Starting chain: Multiple of 12 sts + 11.

1st row (right side): Using A, work 1sc into 2nd ch from hook, 1sc into each ch to end, turn.

2nd row: Using A, 1ch, work 1sc into each sc to end, turn.

3rd row: Using B, 3ch (count as 1dc), skip first sc, 1dc into next sc, 1hdc into next sc, 1sc into next sc, *2ch, skip 2sc, 1sc into next sc, 1hdc into next sc, 1dc into each of next 2sc, 1tr into each of next 2sc, 1dc into each of next 2sc, 1hdc into next sc, 1sc into next sc; rep from * to last 6sc, 2ch, skip 2sc, 1sc into next sc, 1hdc into next sc, 1dc into each of last 2sc, turn.

4th row: Using B, 3ch, skip first dc, work 1dc into next dc, 1hdc into next hdc, 1sc into next sc, *2ch, 1sc into next sc, 1hdc into next hdc, 1dc into each of next 2dc, 1tr into each of next 2tr, 1dc into each of next 2dc, 1hdc into next hdc, 1sc into next sc; rep from * to last 6 sts, 2ch, 1sc into next sc, 1hdc into next hdc, 1dc into next dc, 1dc into 3rd of 3ch at beg of previous row, turn.

5th row: Using A, 1ch, work 1sc into each of first 4 sts, [inserting hook from front of work, work 1sc into each of 2 free sc in A 3 rows below], *1sc into each of next 10 sts on previous row, work 2sc 3 rows below as before; rep from * to last 4 sts, 1sc into each of next 3 sts, 1sc into 3rd of

3ch at beg of previous row, turn.

6th row: Using A, 1ch, work 1sc into each sc to end, turn.

7th row: Using B, 1ch, *work 1sc into first sc, 1hdc into next sc, 1dc into each of next 2sc, 1tr into each of next 2sc, 1dc into each of next 2sc, 1hdc into next sc, 1sc into next sc, 2ch, skip 2sc; rep from * to end omitting 2ch at end of last rep, turn.

8th row: Using B, 1ch, *work 1sc into next sc, 1hdc into next hdc, 1dc into each of next 2dc, 1tr into each of next 2tr, 1dc into each of next 2dc, 1hdc into next hdc, 1sc into next sc, 2ch; rep from * to end omitting 2ch at end of last rep, turn.

9th row: Using A, 1ch, *1sc into each of next 10 sts, inserting hook from front of work, work 1sc into each of 2 free sc in A 3 rows below; rep from * to end omitting 2sc at end of last rep, turn.

Rep 2nd to 9th rows.

I.7

Work as given for I.6 **but** working 2 rows in A, 2 rows in B, 2 rows in A and 2 rows in C throughout.

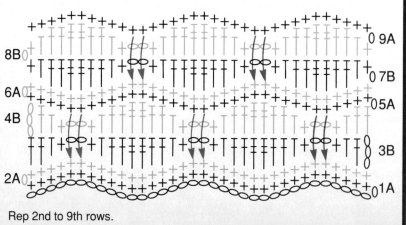

Rep 2nd to 9th rows.

Abbreviations and Symbols on page 12

I.8

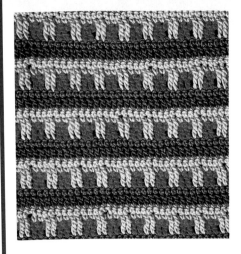

Starting chain: Multiple of 4 sts + 4.

1st row (right side): Using A, work 1dc into 4th ch from hook, 1dc into each ch to end, turn.

2nd row: Using A, 1ch, work 1sc into each dc to end working last sc into top of 3ch, turn.

3rd row: Using B, 3ch (count as 1dc), skip first sc, 1dc into next sc, *2ch, skip 2sc, 1dc into each of next 2sc; rep from * to end, turn.

4th row: Using B, 1ch, work 1sc into each of first 2dc, *2ch, 1sc into each of next 2dc; rep from * to end working last sc into 3rd of 3ch at beg of previous row, turn.

5th row: Using C, 1ch, 1sc into each of first 2sc, *1tr into each of the 2 skipped sc 3 rows below, 1sc into each of next 2sc; rep from * to end, turn.

6th row: Using C, 1ch, 1sc into each sc and each tr to end, turn.

7th row: Using A, 3ch, skip first sc, 1dc into each sc to end, turn.

8th row: Using A, 1ch, 1sc into each dc to end working last sc into 3rd of 3ch at beg of previous row, turn.

Rep 3rd to 8th rows.

= 1tr into skipped sc 3 rows below.

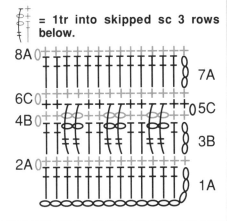

I.10

Starting chain: Multiple of 8 sts + 7.

Special Abbreviation

Bobble = work 3dc into next sc until last loop of each dc remains on hook, yo and through all 4 loops.

Note: Count each sc, ch sp and bobble as 1 st throughout.

1st row (wrong side): Using A, work 1dc into 4th ch from hook, 1dc into each of next 3ch, *3ch, skip 1ch, 1sc into next ch, 3ch, skip 1ch, 1dc into each of next 5ch; rep from * to end, turn.

2nd row: Using B, 1ch, work 1sc into each of first 5dc, *1ch, 1 bobble into next sc, 1ch, 1sc into each of next 5dc; rep from * to end placing last sc into top of 3ch, turn.

3rd row: Using B, 6ch (count as 1dc, 3ch), skip first 2sc, 1sc into next sc, 3ch, *skip 1sc, 1dc into each of next 5 sts (see note above), 3ch, skip 1sc, 1sc into next sc, 3ch; rep from * to last 2sc, skip 1sc, 1dc into last sc, turn.

4th row: Using A, 1ch, work 1sc into first dc, 1ch, 1 bobble into next sc, 1ch, *1sc into each of next 5dc, 1ch, 1 bobble into next sc, 1ch; rep from * to last dc, 1sc into 3rd of 6ch at beg of previous row, turn.

5th row: Using A, 3ch (count as 1dc), skip first sc, 1dc into each of next 4 sts, *3ch, skip 1sc, 1sc into next sc, 3ch, skip 1sc, 1dc into each of next 5 sts; rep from * to end, turn.

Rep 2nd to 5th rows.

= Bobble

I.9

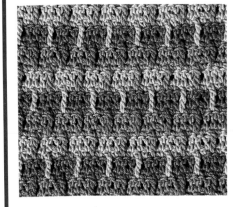

Starting chain: Multiple of 4 sts + 2.

1st row (right side): Using A, work 1sc into 2nd ch from hook, 1sc into next ch, *1ch, skip 1ch, 1sc into each of next 3ch; rep from * to end omitting 1sc at end of last rep, turn.

2nd row: Using A, 3ch (count as 1dc), skip first sc, work 1dc into next sc, *1ch, skip 1ch, 1dc into each of next 3sc; rep from * to end omitting 1dc at end of last rep, turn.

3rd row: Using B, 1ch, work 1sc into each of first 2dc, 1tr into first skipped starting ch, *1sc into next dc, 1ch, skip 1dc, 1sc into next dc, 1tr into next skipped starting ch; rep from * to last 2dc, 1sc into next dc, 1sc into 3rd of 3ch at beg of previous row, turn.

4th row: Using B, 3ch, skip first sc, work 1dc into each of next 3 sts, *1ch, skip 1ch, 1dc into each of next 3 sts; rep from * to last sc, 1dc into last sc, turn.

5th row: Using C, 1ch, work 1sc into each of first 2dc, *1ch, skip 1dc, 1sc into next dc, 1tr into next skipped dc 3 rows below, 1sc into next dc; rep from * to last 3dc, 1ch, skip 1dc, 1sc into next dc, 1sc into 3rd of 3ch at beg of previous row, turn.

6th row: Using C, 3ch, skip first sc, 1dc into next sc, *1ch, skip 1ch, 1dc into each of next 3 sts; rep from * to end omitting 1dc at end of last rep, turn.

7th row: Using A, 1ch, 1sc into each of first 2dc, 1tr into next skipped dc 3 rows below, *1sc into next dc, 1ch, skip 1dc, 1sc into next dc, 1tr into next skipped dc 3 rows below; rep from * to last 2dc, 1sc into each of last 2dc, turn.

8th row: As 4th row **but** using A instead of B.

Rep 5th to 8th rows continuing to work 2 rows each in colors B, C and A as set.

= Work tr into skipped st 3 rows below.

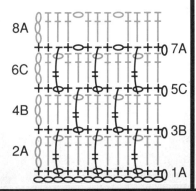

I. All-over Patterns

I.11

Starting chain: Multiple of 10 sts + 1.
Using A make required number of chain.

1st row (right side): Using A, work 1sc into 2nd ch from hook, 1sc into each ch to end, turn.

2nd row: Using A, 3ch (count as 1dc), skip first sc, work 1dc into each sc to end, turn.

3rd row: Using B, 1ch, work 1sc into each dc to end placing last sc into 3rd of 3ch at beg of previous row, turn.

4th row: Using B, 1ch, work 1sc into each sc to end, turn.

5th row: Using A, 1ch, work 1sc into each of first 3sc, *1ch, skip 1sc, 1sc into each of next 2sc, 1ch, skip 1sc, 1sc into each of next 6sc; rep from * to end omitting 3sc at end of last rep, turn.

On 6th row work dc into ch **not** ch space.
Rep 2nd to 9th rows.

 = 1dtr into skipped sc 3 rows **below.**

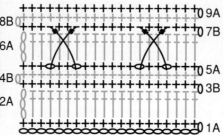

6th row: Using A, 3ch (count as 1dc), skip first sc, 1dc into each sc and into each ch to end, turn.

7th row: Using B, 1ch, 1sc into each of first 3dc, *work 1dtr into 2nd skipped sc 3 rows below, skip 1dc, 1sc into each of next 2dc, 1dtr into first skipped sc 3 rows below (thus crossing 2dtr), skip 1dc, 1sc into each of next 6dc; rep from * to end omitting 3sc at end of last rep and placing last sc into 3rd of 3ch at beg of previous row, turn.

8th row: Using B, 1ch, work 1sc into each st to end, turn.

9th row: Using A, 1ch, work 1sc into each sc to end, turn.

Rep 2nd to 9th rows.

I.12

Starting chain: Multiple of 10 sts + 12.

Special Abbreviation

1 Circle = rotating work as required work 6dc **down** and around stem of next dc 1 row below, then work 6dc **up** and around stem of previous dc 1 row below.

1st row (right side): Work 1dc into 4th ch from hook, 1dc into each ch to end, turn.

2nd row: 3ch (count as 1dc), skip first dc, work 1dc into each dc to end working last dc into 3rd of 3ch at beg of previous row, turn.

3rd row: 3ch, skip first dc, work 1dc into each of next 4dc, *work 1 circle, working behind circle work 1dc into each of next 10dc; rep from * to end omitting 5dc at end of last rep and working last dc into 3rd of 3ch at beg of previous row, turn.

4th, 5th and 6th rows: 3ch, skip first dc, work 1dc into each dc to end working last dc into 3rd of 3ch at beg of previous row, turn.

7th row: 3ch, skip first dc, work 1dc into each of next 9dc, *work 1 circle, 1dc into each of next 10dc; rep from * to end working last dc into 3rd of 3ch, turn.

8th and 9th rows: 3ch, skip first dc, work 1dc into each dc to end working last dc into 3rd of 3ch, turn.

Rep 2nd to 9th rows.

 = 1 Circle

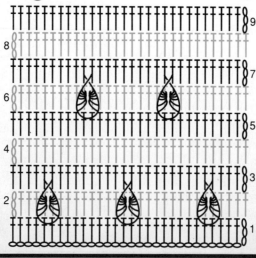

I.13

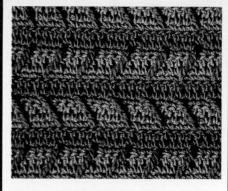

Starting chain: Multiple of 4 sts + 3.
Using A make the required number of chain.

1st row (right side): Using A, work 1sc into 2nd ch from hook, 1sc into each ch to end, turn.

2nd row: Using A, 3ch (count as 1dc), skip first sc, work 1dc into each sc to end, turn.

3rd row: Using B, 1ch, 1sc into each of first 4dc, 1ch, skip 1dc, *1sc into each of next 3dc, 1ch, skip 1dc; rep from * to last dc, 1sc into 3rd of 3ch at beg of previous row, turn.

4th row: Using B, 3ch, skip first sc, work 1dc into each ch and each sc to end, turn.

5th row: Using A, 1ch, 1sc into first dc, *1dtr into next skipped dc 3 rows below, skip 1dc on 4th row, 1sc into each of next 3dc; rep from * to last dc, 1sc into 3rd of 3ch at beg of previous row.

6th row: Using A, 3ch, skip first sc, work 1dc into each sc and each dtr to end, turn.

7th row: Using B, 1ch, work 1sc into first dc, *1ch, skip 1dc, 1sc into each of next 3dc; rep from * to last dc, 1sc into 3rd of 3ch, turn.

8th row: Using B, 3ch, skip first sc, work 1dc into each sc and each ch to end, turn.

9th row: Using A, 1ch, 1sc into each of first 4dc, work 1dtr into first skipped dc 3 rows below, skip next dc, *1sc into each of next 3dc, 1dtr into next skipped dc 3 rows below, skip next dc; rep from * to last dc, 1sc into 3rd of 3ch, turn.

10th row: Using A, 3ch, skip first sc, work 1dc into each dtr and each sc to end, turn.

Rep 3rd to 10th rows.

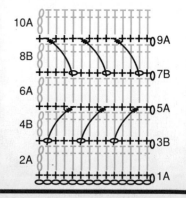 = 1dtr into skipped dc 3 rows below.

On 4th and 8th rows work dc into ch, **not** ch space.

Abbreviations and Symbols on page 12

I.14

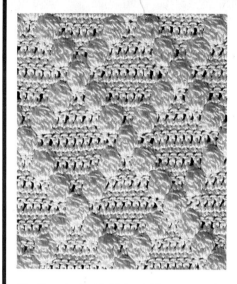

Starting chain: Multiple of 12 sts + 6.

Special Abbreviation

Bobble = working in front of work, work 5tr into ch sp 2 rows below until 1 loop of each tr remains on hook, yo and through all 6 loops.

1st row (right side): Work 1sc into 2nd ch from hook, 1sc into next ch, 1ch, skip 1ch, *1sc into each of next 11ch, 1ch, skip 1ch; rep from * to last 2ch, 1sc into each of last 2ch, turn.

2nd row: 3ch (count as 1dc), skip first sc, work 1dc into next sc, 1ch, skip 1ch sp, *1dc into each of next 11 sts, 1ch, skip 1ch sp; rep from * to last 2sc, 1dc into each of last 2sc, turn.

3rd row: 1ch, work 1sc into each of first 2dc, 1 bobble into ch sp 2 rows below, *1sc into next dc, 1ch, skip 1dc, 1sc into each of next 7dc, 1ch, skip 1dc, 1sc into next dc, 1 bobble into next ch sp 2 rows below; rep from * to last 2dc, 1sc into next dc, 1sc into 3rd of 3ch at beg of previous row, turn.

4th row: 3ch, skip first sc, 1dc into each of next 3 sts, *1ch, skip 1ch sp, 1dc into each of next 7 sts, 1ch, skip 1ch sp, 1dc into each of next 3 sts; rep from * to last sc, 1dc into last sc, turn.

5th row: 1ch, work 1sc into each of first 4dc, *1 bobble into ch sp 2 rows below, 1sc into next dc, 1ch, skip 1dc, 1sc into each of next 3dc, 1ch, skip 1dc, 1sc into next dc, 1 bobble into ch sp 2 rows below, 1sc into each of next 3dc; rep from * to last st, 1sc into 3rd of 3ch at beg of previous row, turn.

6th row: 3ch, skip first sc, work 1dc into each of next 5 sts, *1ch, skip 1ch sp, 1dc into each of next 3 sts, 1ch, skip 1ch sp, 1dc into each of next 7 sts; rep from * to end omitting 1dc at end of last rep, turn.

7th row: 1ch, work 1sc into each of first 6dc, *1 bobble into ch sp 2 rows below, 1sc into next dc, 1ch, skip 1dc, 1sc into next dc, 1 bobble into ch sp 2 rows below, 1sc into each of next 7dc; rep from * to end omitting 1sc at end of last rep, turn.

8th row: 3ch, skip first sc, work 1dc into each of next 7 sts, 1ch, skip 1ch sp, *1dc into each of next 11 sts, 1ch, skip 1ch sp; rep from * to last 8 sts, 1dc into each of last 8 sts, turn.

9th row: 1ch, work 1sc into each of first 6dc, *1ch, skip 1dc, 1sc into next dc, 1 bobble into ch sp 2 rows below, 1sc into next dc, 1ch, skip 1dc, 1sc into each of next 7dc; rep from * to end omitting 1sc at end of last rep, turn.

10th row: As 6th row.

11th row: 1ch, work 1sc into each of first 4dc, *1ch, skip 1dc, 1sc into next dc, 1 bobble into ch sp 2 rows below, 1sc into each of next 3dc, 1 bobble into ch sp 2 rows below, 1sc into next dc, 1ch, skip 1dc, 1sc into each of next 3dc; rep from * to last dc, 1sc into 3rd of 3ch, turn.

12th row: As 4th row.

13th row: 1ch, 1sc into each of first 2dc, 1ch, skip 1dc, 1sc into next dc, *1 bobble into ch sp 2 rows below, 1sc into each of next 7dc, 1 bobble into ch sp 2 rows below, 1sc into next dc, 1ch, skip 1dc, 1sc into next dc; rep from * to last dc, 1sc into 3rd of 3ch, turn.

Rep 2nd to 13th rows.

 = Bobble

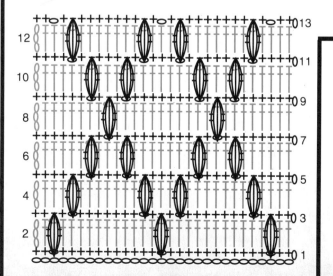

I.15

Starting chain: Multiple of 10 sts + 1.
Using A make required number of chain.

1st row (wrong side): Using A, work 1sc into 2nd ch from hook, 1sc into each ch to end, turn.

2nd row: Using B, 1ch, work 1sc into each of first 8sc, *1ch, skip 1sc, 1sc into each of next 2sc, 1ch, skip 1sc, 1sc into each of next 6sc; rep from * to last 2sc, 1 sc into each sc to end, turn.

3rd row: Using B, 3ch (count as 1dc), skip first sc, work 1dc into each sc and into each ch to end, turn.

4th row: Using A, 1ch, work 1sc into each of first 8dc *work 1dtr into 2nd skipped sc 3 rows below, skip 1dc, 1sc into each of next 2dc, 1dtr into first skipped sc 3 rows below (thus crossing 2dtr), skip 1dc, 1sc into each of next 6dc; rep from * to last 2dc, 1sc into next dc, 1sc into 3rd of 3ch at beg of previous row, turn.

5th row: Using A, 1ch, work 1sc into each st to end, turn.

6th row: Using B, 1ch, work 1sc into each of first 3sc, *1ch, skip 1sc, 1sc into each of next 2sc, 1ch, skip 1sc, 1sc into each of next 6sc; rep from * to end omitting 3sc at end of last rep, turn.

7th row: Using B, 3ch, skip first sc, 1dc into each sc and into each ch to end, turn.

8th row: Using A, 1ch, 1sc into each of first 3dc, *work 1dtr into 2nd skipped sc 3 rows below, skip 1dc, 1sc into each of next 2dc, 1dtr into first skipped sc 3 rows below (thus crossing 2dtr), skip 1dc, 1sc into each of next 6dc; rep from * to end omitting 3sc at end of last rep and placing last sc into 3rd of 3ch at beg of previous row, turn.

9th row: Using A, 1ch, work 1sc into each st to end, turn.

Rep 2nd to 9th rows.

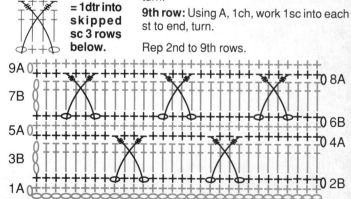

= 1dtr into skipped sc 3 rows below.

On 3rd and 7th rows work dc into ch **not** ch space.

17

I. All-over Patterns

I.16

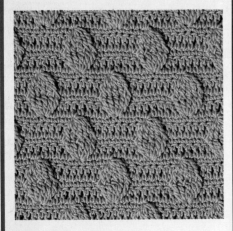

Starting chain: Multiple of 10 sts + 10.

Special Abbreviations

Lower Cluster = work 5tr into next skipped sc 2 rows below.

Upper Cluster = *[yo] twice then insert hook from right to left round stem of next tr 2 rows below, work 1tr in usual way until last loop of tr remains on hook; rep from * 4 times more, yo and through all 6 loops.

Note: Count each ch sp as 1 st throughout.

1st row (right side): Work 1sc into 2nd ch from hook, 1sc into each ch to end, turn.

2nd row: 3ch (count as 1dc), skip first sc, work 1dc into each of next 3sc, *1ch, skip 1sc, 1dc into each of next 9 sts; rep from * to end omitting 5dc at end of last rep, turn.

3rd row: 1ch, work 1sc into each of first 2dc, *work lower cluster, **skip 5 sts of previous row,** 1sc into each of next 5dc; rep from * to end omitting 3sc at end of last rep and placing last sc into 3rd of 3ch at beg of previous row, turn.

4th row: 3ch, skip first sc, work 1dc into each st to end, turn.

5th row: 1ch, work 1sc into each of first 4dc, *work upper cluster over next 5tr 2 rows below, skip next dc on previous row, 1sc into each of next 9dc; rep from * to end omitting 5sc at end of last rep and placing last sc into 3rd of 3ch at beg of previous row, turn.

6th row: 3ch, skip first sc, work 1dc into each of next 8 sts, *1ch, skip 1sc, 1dc into each of next 9 sts; rep from * to end.

I.17

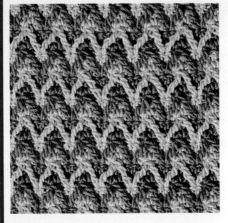

Starting chain: Multiple of 4 sts + 4.

Special Abbreviation

Tr2tog 3 rows below = work 1tr into same st as last tr until last loop of tr remains on hook, skip 3 sts, work 1tr into next skipped st 3 rows below until last loop of tr remains on hook, yo and through all 3 loops. **Note:** Sts either side of tr2tog must be worked behind tr2tog.

Using A make required number of chain.

7th row: 1ch, work 1sc into each of first 7dc, *work lower cluster, **skip 5 sts of previous row**, 1sc into each of next 5dc; rep from * to last 2dc,1sc into each of last 2dc, working last sc into 3rd of 3ch at beg of previous row, turn.

8th row: 3ch, skip first sc, work 1dc into each st to end, turn.

9th row: 1ch, work 1sc into each of first 9dc, *work upper cluster over next 5tr 2 rows below, skip next dc on previous row, 1sc into each of next 9dc; rep from * to end placing last sc into 3rd of 3ch at beg of previous row, turn.

Rep 2nd to 9th rows.

= **Lower cluster**

= **Upper cluster**

1st row (right side): Using A, work 1sc into 2nd ch from hook, 1sc into each of next 2ch, *1ch, skip 1ch, 1sc into each of next 3ch; rep from * to end, turn.

2nd row: Using A, 3ch (count as 1dc), skip first sc, work 1dc into each st to end (working into actual st of each ch, not into ch sp), turn.

3rd row: Using B, 1ch, 1sc into first dc, 1tr into first skipped starting ch, skip 1dc on 2nd row, 1sc into next dc, 1ch, skip 1dc, 1sc into next dc, *tr2tog 3 rows below (into skipped starting ch), skip 1dc on 2nd row, 1sc into next dc, 1ch, skip 1dc, 1sc into next dc; rep from * to last 2dc, 1tr into same ch as 2nd leg of last tr2tog, skip 1dc, 1sc into 3rd of 3ch at beg of previous row, turn.

4th row: Using B, 3ch, skip first sc, work 1dc into each st to end, turn.

5th row: Using A, 1ch, 1sc into first dc, 1tr into next skipped dc 3 rows below, skip 1dc on previous row, 1sc into next dc, 1ch, skip 1dc, 1sc into next dc, *tr2tog 3 rows below, skip 1dc on previous row, 1sc into next dc, 1ch, skip 1dc, 1sc into next dc; rep from * to last 2dc, 1tr into same dc as 2nd leg of last tr2tog, skip 1dc, 1sc into 3rd of 3ch at beg of previous row, turn.

6th row: As 4th row **but** using A instead of B.

7th row: As 5th row **but** using B instead of A.

Rep 4th to 7th rows.

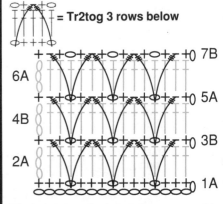
= **Tr2tog 3 rows below**

Work dc into actual st of ch on wrong side rows, not into ch sp.

I.18

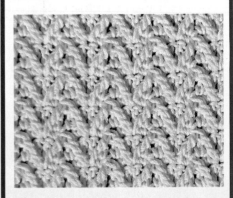

Work as given for I.17 **but** using one color throughout.

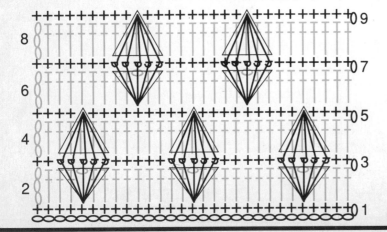

Abbreviations and Symbols on page 12

I.19

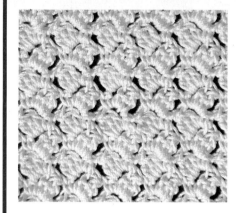

Starting chain: Multiple of 4 sts + 6.

Special Abbreviation

Cluster = work 3dc into next st until 1 loop of each remains on hook, yo and through all 4 loops on hook.

1st row (right side): Work 1 cluster into 5th ch from hook (1dc, 1ch formed at beg of row), 1ch, skip 2ch, 1sc into next ch, *3ch, 1 cluster into next ch, 1ch, skip 2ch, 1sc into next ch; rep from * to last 2ch, 2ch, 1dc into last ch, turn.

2nd row: 4ch (count as 1dc, 1ch), 1 cluster into first 2ch sp, 1ch, *1sc into next 3ch sp, 3ch, 1 cluster into same sp as last sc, 1ch; rep from * to last ch sp, 1sc into last ch sp, 2ch, 1dc into 3rd of 4ch at beg of previous row, turn.

Rep 2nd row.

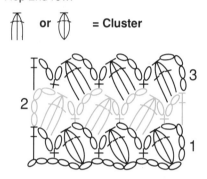

Diagram only: Rep 2nd and 3rd rows.

I.20

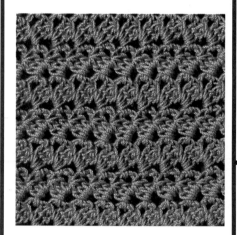

Starting chain: Multiple of 3 sts + 5.

Special Abbreviation

Cluster4 = work 3dc over stem of dc just worked but leaving last loop of each dc on hook, then work 4th dc as indicated leaving last loop as before (5 loops on hook), yo and through all 5 loops.

1st row (right side): Work 1dc into 6th ch from hook, *3ch, skip 2ch, work cluster4 placing 4th dc into next ch; rep from * to last 2ch, 3ch, work cluster4 placing 4th dc in last ch, turn.

2nd row: 3ch (count as 1dc), 1dc into next 3ch sp, *3ch, work cluster4 placing 4th dc into next 3ch sp; rep from * to end placing final dc into top of ch at beg of previous row, turn.

Rep 2nd row.

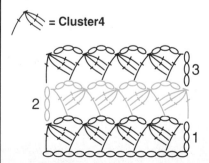

Diagram only: Rep 2nd and 3rd rows.

I.21

Starting chain: Multiple of 8 sts + 2.

Special Abbreviation

Popcorn = work 4dc into next st, drop loop from hook, insert hook from the front into top of first of these dc, pick up dropped loop and draw through dc, 1ch to secure popcorn.

1st row (right side): Work 1sc into 2nd ch from hook, *1ch, skip 3ch, 1dc into next ch, 1ch, into same ch as last dc work [1dc, 1ch, 1dc], 1ch, skip 3ch, 1sc into next ch; rep from * to end, turn.

2nd row: 6ch (count as 1dc, 3ch), skip 1dc, 1sc into next dc, *3ch, 1 popcorn into next sc, 3ch, skip 1dc, 1sc into next dc; rep from * to last sc, 3ch, 1dc into last sc, turn.

I.22

Starting chain: Multiple of 8 sts + 2.

Special Abbreviations

Cr3R (Cross 3 Right) = skip 2sc, work 1tr into next sc, working behind last tr work 1dc into each of 2 skipped sc.

Cr3L (Cross 3 Left) = skip 1sc, work 1dc into each of next 2sc, working in front of last 2dc work 1tr into skipped sc.

1st row (wrong side): Work 1sc into 2nd ch from hook, 1sc into each ch to end, turn.

2nd row: 3ch (count as 1dc), skip first sc, *Cr3R, 1dc into next sc, Cr3L, 1dc into next sc; rep from * to end, turn.

3rd row: 1ch, work 1sc into each st to end placing last sc into 3rd of 3ch at beg of previous row, turn.

Rep 2nd and 3rd rows.

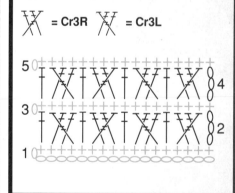

3rd row: 1ch, 1sc into first dc, *1ch, 1dc into next sc, 1ch, into same st as last dc work [1dc, 1ch, 1dc], 1ch, 1sc into top of next popcorn; rep from * to end, placing last sc into 3rd of 6ch at beg of previous row, turn.

Rep 2nd and 3rd rows.

 = Popcorn

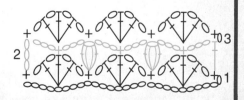

I. All-over Patterns

I.23

Starting chain: Multiple of 20 sts + 25.

Special Abbreviations

Dc2tog = work 2dc into next st until 1 loop of each remains on hook, yo and through all 3 loops on hook.

Bobble = work 3dc into next st until 1 loop of each remains on hook, yo and through all 4 loops on hook.

1st row (right side): Work 1sc into 7th ch from hook, 5ch, skip 3ch, 1sc into next ch, 1ch, skip 3ch, into next ch work [1 bobble, 1ch] 3 times, *skip 3ch, 1sc into next ch, [5ch, skip 3ch, 1sc into next ch] 3 times, 1ch, skip 3ch, into next ch work [1 bobble, 1ch] 3 times; rep from * to last 10ch, skip 3ch, 1sc into next ch, 5ch, skip 3ch, 1sc into next ch, 2ch, 1dc into last ch, turn.

2nd row: 1ch, 1sc into first dc, 5ch, 1sc into first 5ch arch, 1ch, [1 bobble into next ch sp, 1ch] 4 times, *1sc into next 5ch arch, [5ch, 1sc into next 5ch arch] twice, 1ch, [1 bobble into next ch sp, 1ch] 4 times; rep from * to last 2 arches, 1sc into next 5ch arch, 5ch, skip 2ch, 1sc into next ch, turn.

3rd row: 5ch (count as 1dc, 2ch), 1sc into first 5ch arch, 1ch, [1 bobble into next ch sp, 1ch] 5 times, *1sc into next 5ch arch, 5ch, 1sc into next 5ch arch, 1ch, [1 bobble into next ch sp, 1ch] 5 times; rep from * to last arch, 1sc into last arch, 2ch, 1dc into last sc, turn.

4th row: 1ch, 1sc into first dc, skip 2ch sp, *2ch, [1 bobble into next ch sp, 2ch] 6 times, 1sc into next 5ch arch; rep from * to end placing last sc into 3rd of 5ch at beg of previous row, turn.

5th row: 5ch (count as 1dc, 2ch), skip first 2ch sp, 1sc into next 2ch sp, [5ch, 1sc into next 2ch sp] 4 times, *1ch, into next sc work [1dc, 1ch] twice, skip next 2ch sp, 1sc into next 2ch sp, [5ch, 1sc into next 2ch sp] 4 times; rep from * to last 2ch sp, 2ch, 1dc into last sc, turn.

6th row: 3ch (count as 1dc), into first dc work [1dc, 1ch, 1 bobble], 1ch, 1sc into next 5ch arch, [5ch, 1sc into next 5ch arch] 3 times, *1ch, skip 1ch sp, into next ch sp work [1 bobble, 1ch] 3 times, 1sc into next 5ch arch, [5ch, 1sc into next 5ch arch] 3 times; rep from * to last sp, 1ch, into 3rd of 5ch at beg of previous row work [1 bobble, 1ch, dc2tog], turn.

7th row: 3ch (count as 1dc), [1 bobble into next ch sp, 1ch] twice, 1sc into first 5ch arch, [5ch, 1sc into next 5ch arch] twice, *1ch, [1 bobble into next ch sp, 1ch] 4 times, 1sc into next 5ch arch, [5ch, 1sc into next 5ch arch] twice; rep from * to last bobble, [1ch, 1 bobble into next ch sp] twice, 1dc into 3rd of 3ch at beg of previous row, turn.

8th row: 3ch, 1dc into first dc, 1ch, [1 bobble into next ch sp, 1ch] twice, 1sc into next 5ch arch, 5ch, 1sc into next 5ch arch, *1ch, [1 bobble into next ch sp, 1ch] 5 times, 1sc into next 5ch arch, 5ch, 1sc into next 5ch arch; rep from * to last 2 bobbles, 1ch, [1 bobble into next ch sp, 1ch] twice, dc2tog into 3rd of 3ch at beg of previous row, turn.

9th row: 4ch (count as 1dc, 1ch), [1 bobble into next ch sp, 2ch] 3 times, 1sc into next 5ch arch, *2ch, [1 bobble into next ch sp, 2ch] 6 times, 1sc into next 5ch arch; rep from * to last 2 bobbles, [2ch, 1 bobble into next ch sp] 3 times, 1ch, 1dc into 3rd of 3ch at beg of previous row, turn.

10th row: 1ch, 1sc into first dc, 5ch, skip first ch sp, 1sc into next 2ch sp, 5ch, 1sc into next 2ch sp, 1ch, into next sc work [1dc, 1ch] twice, *skip next 2ch sp, 1sc into next 2ch sp, [5ch, 1sc into next 2ch sp] 4 times, 1ch, into next sc work [1dc, 1ch] twice; rep from * to last 3 bobbles, skip next 2ch sp, [1sc into next 2ch sp, 5ch] twice, 1sc into 3rd of 4ch at beg of previous row, turn.

11th row: 5ch (count as 1dc, 2ch), 1sc into first 5ch arch, 5ch, 1sc into next 5ch arch, 1ch, skip 1ch sp, into next ch sp work [1 bobble, 1ch] 3 times, *1sc into next 5ch arch, [5ch, 1sc into next 5ch arch] 3 times, 1ch, skip 1ch sp, into next ch sp work [1 bobble, 1ch] 3 times; rep from * to last 2 arches, 1sc into next 5ch arch, 5ch, 1sc into next 5ch arch, 2ch, 1dc into last sc, turn.

Rep 2nd to 11th rows.

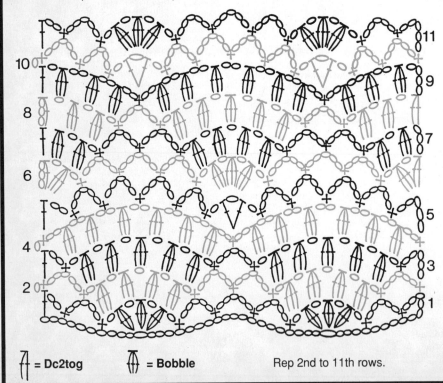

⫮ = Dc2tog   ⫲ = Bobble   Rep 2nd to 11th rows.

I.24

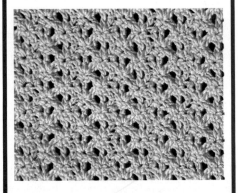

Starting chain: Multiple of 6 sts + 2.

1st row (right side): Work 1sc into 2nd ch from hook, *skip 2ch, 1dc into next ch, 2ch, into same ch as last dc work [1dc, 2ch, 1dc], skip 2ch, 1sc into next ch; rep from * to end, turn.

2nd row: 5ch (count as 1dc, 2ch), 1dc into first sc, skip 1dc, 1sc into next dc, *1dc into next sc, 2ch, into same st as last dc work [1dc, 2ch, 1dc], skip 1dc, 1sc into next dc; rep from * to last sc, into last sc work [1dc, 2ch, 1dc], turn.

3rd row: 1ch, 1sc into first dc, *1dc into next sc, 2ch, into same st as last dc work [1dc, 2ch, 1dc], skip 1dc, 1sc into next dc; rep from * to end placing last sc into 3rd of 5ch at beg of previous row, turn.

Rep 2nd and 3rd rows.

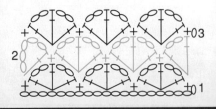

Abbreviations and Symbols on page 12

I.25

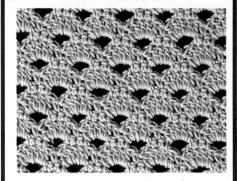

Starting chain: Multiple of 5 sts + 2.

1st row (wrong side): Work 1sc into 2nd ch from hook, 1sc into next ch, *3ch, skip 2ch, 1sc into each of next 3ch; rep from * to end omitting 1sc at end of last rep, turn.

2nd row: 1ch, 1sc into first sc, *5dc into next 3ch arch, skip 1sc, 1sc into next sc; rep from * to end, turn.

3rd row: 3ch (count as 1hdc, 1ch), skip first 2 sts, 1sc into each of next 3dc, *3ch, skip next 3 sts, 1sc into each of next 3dc; rep from * to last 2 sts, 1ch, 1hdc into last sc, turn.

4th row: 3ch (count as 1dc), 2dc into first ch sp, skip 1sc, 1sc into next sc, *5dc into next 3ch arch, skip 1sc, 1sc into next sc; rep from * to last sp, 2dc into last sp, 1dc into 2nd of 3ch at beg of previous row, turn.

5th row: 1ch, 1sc into each of first 2dc, *3ch, skip 3 sts, 1sc into each of next 3dc; rep from * to end omitting 1sc at end of last rep and placing last sc into 3rd of 3ch at beg of previous row, turn.

Rep 2nd to 5th rows.

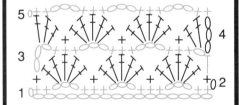

I.26

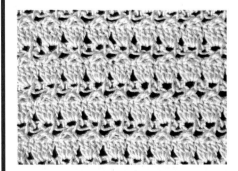

Starting chain: Multiple of 4 sts + 7.

Special Abbreviation

Cross2dc = skip 3dc, work 1dc into next dc, 2ch, working behind last dc work 1dc into the first of the skipped dc.

I.27

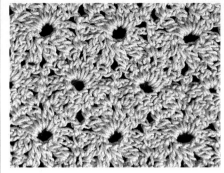

Starting chain: Multiple of 11 sts + 3.

Special Abbreviation

Dc2tog = work 2dc into next st until 1 loop of each remains on hook, yo and through all 3 loops on hook.

1st row (right side): Work 1sc into 2nd ch from hook, 1ch, skip 1ch, 1sc into next ch, [3ch, skip 3ch, 1sc into next ch] twice, *2ch, skip 2ch, 1sc into next ch, [3ch, skip 3ch, 1sc into next ch] twice; rep from * to last 2ch, 1ch, skip 1ch, 1sc into last ch, turn.

2nd row: 3ch (count as 1dc), into first ch sp work [dc2tog, 2ch, dc2tog], 1ch, skip 1sc, 1sc into next sc, *1ch, skip 3ch sp, dc2tog into next 2ch sp, into same sp as last dc2tog work [2ch, dc2tog] 3 times, 1ch, skip 3ch sp, 1sc into next sc; rep from * to last 2 sps, 1ch, skip 3ch sp, into last ch sp work [dc2tog, 2ch, dc2tog], 1dc into last sc, turn.

3rd row: 1ch, 1sc into first dc, *3ch, work 1dc2tog into top of each of next 4dc2tog, 3ch, 1sc into next 2ch sp; rep from * to end placing last sc into 3rd of 3ch at beg of previous row, turn.

4th row: 1ch, 1sc into first sc, *3ch, 1sc into top of next dc2tog, 2ch, skip 2dc2tog, 1sc into top of next dc2tog, 3ch, 1sc into next sc; rep from * to end, turn.

5th row: 1ch, work 1sc into first sc, *1ch, skip 3ch sp, dc2tog into next 2ch sp, into same sp as last dc2tog work [2ch, dc2tog]

1st row (right side): Work 4dc into 5th ch from hook, *skip 3ch, 4dc into next ch; rep from * to last 2ch, 1dc into last ch, turn.

2nd row: 3ch (count as 1dc), skip first dc, *cross2dc; rep from * to end, 1dc into top of 3ch at beg of previous row, turn.

3rd row: 3ch, work 4dc into each 2ch sp to end, 1dc into 3rd of 3ch at beg of previous row, turn.

Rep 2nd and 3rd rows.

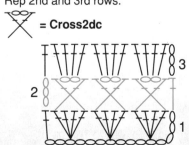

= Cross2dc

3 times, 1ch, skip 3ch sp, 1sc into next sc; rep from * to end, turn.

6th row: 3ch, work 1dc2tog into top of each of next 2dc2tog, 3ch, 1sc into next 2ch sp, 3ch, *dc2tog into top of each 4dc2tog, 3ch, 1sc into next 2ch sp, 3ch; rep from * to last 2dc2tog, work 1dc2tog into each of last 2dc2tog, 1dc into last sc, turn.

7th row: 1ch, 1sc into first dc, 1ch, skip 1dc2tog, 1sc into next dc2tog, 3ch, 1sc into next sc, 3ch, *1sc into top of next dc2tog, 2ch, skip 2dc2tog, 1sc into top of next dc2tog, 3ch, 1sc into next sc, 3ch; rep from * to last 2dc2tog, 1sc into next dc2tog, 1ch, skip 1dc2tog, 1sc into 3rd of 3ch at beg of previous row, turn.

Rep 2nd to 7th rows.

 = Dc2tog

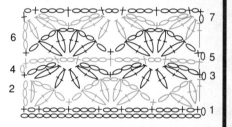

I.28

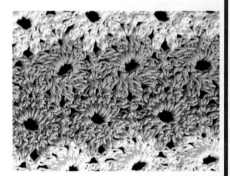

Work as I.27 **but** working 1st and 2nd rows in A, then work 3 rows each in B, C and A throughout.

I.29

Work as I.27 **but** working 1st and 2nd rows in A then 3 rows each in B and A throughout. **Note:** Cut yarn after each color change.

I. All-over Patterns

I.30

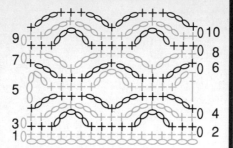

Starting chain: Multiple of 8 sts + 2.

1st row (wrong side): Work 1sc into 2nd ch from hook, 1sc into each ch to end, turn.

2nd row: 1ch, 1sc into each of first 3sc, *5ch, skip 3sc, 1sc into each of next 5sc; rep from * to end omitting 2sc at end of last rep, turn,

3rd row: 1ch, 1sc into each of first 2sc, *3ch, 1sc into next 5ch arch, 3ch, skip 1sc, 1sc into each of next 3sc; rep from * to end omitting 1sc at end of last rep, turn.

4th row: 1ch, 1sc into first sc, *3ch, 1sc into next 3ch arch, 1sc into next sc, 1sc into next 3ch arch, 3ch, skip 1sc, 1sc into next sc; rep from * to end, turn.

5th row: 5ch (count as 1dc, 2ch), 1sc into next 3ch arch, 1sc into each of next 3sc, 1sc into next 3ch arch, *5ch, 1sc into next 3ch arch, 1sc into each of next 3sc, 1sc into next 3ch arch; rep from * to last sc, 2ch, 1dc into last sc, turn.

6th row: 1ch, 1sc into first dc, 3ch, skip 1sc, 1sc into each of next 3sc, *3ch, 1sc into next 5ch arch, 3ch, skip 1sc, 1sc into each of next 3sc; rep from * to last 2ch arch, 3ch, 1sc into 3rd of 5ch at beg of previous row, turn.

7th row: 1ch, 1sc into first sc, 1sc into first 3ch arch, 3ch, skip 1sc, 1sc into next sc, *3ch, 1sc into next 3ch arch, 1sc into next sc, 1sc into next 3ch arch, 3ch, skip 1sc, 1sc into next sc; rep from * to last 3ch arch, 3ch, 1sc into 3ch arch, 1sc into last sc, turn.

8th row: 1ch, 1sc into each of first 2sc, *1sc into next 3ch arch, 5ch, 1sc into next 3ch arch, 1sc into each of next 3sc; rep from * to end omitting 1sc at end of last rep, turn.

Rep 3rd to 8th rows.

I.31

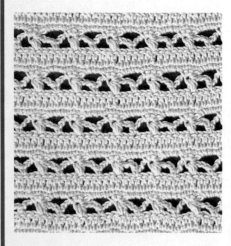

Starting chain: Multiple of 6 sts + 4.

Special Abbreviation

Puff st = [yo, insert hook into next st, yo and draw a loop through] 3 times into same st, yo and draw through 7 loops on hook, work 1 firm ch to close puff st.

1st row (right side): Work 1sc into 2nd ch from hook, 1sc into each ch to end, turn.

2nd row: 3ch (count as 1dc), skip first sc, 1dc into each sc to end, turn.

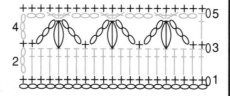

3rd row: 1ch, 1sc into each of first 2dc, *3ch, skip 2dc, 1 puff st into next dc, 3ch, skip 2dc, 1sc into next dc; rep from * to last dc, 1sc into 3rd of 3ch at beg of previous row, turn.

4th row: 5ch (count as 1dc, 2ch), work 3sc into closing ch of next puff st, *3ch, 3sc into closing ch of next puff st; rep from * to last 2sc, 2ch, 1dc into last sc, turn.

5th row: 1ch, 1sc into first dc, 2sc into first 2ch sp, *1sc into each of next 3sc, 3sc into next 3ch sp; rep from * to end working last sc into 3rd of 5ch at beg of previous row, turn.

Rep 2nd to 5th rows.

I.32

Starting chain: Multiple of 10 sts + 2.

Special Abbreviations

Bobble = work 4dc into next st until 1 loop of each remains on hook, yo and through all 5 loops on hook.

Dc2tog = work 2dc into next st until 1 loop of each remains on hook, yo and through all 3 loops on hook.

1st row (right side): Work 1sc into 2nd ch from hook, 1sc into each of next 2ch, *3ch, skip 2ch, 1 bobble into next ch, 3ch, skip 2ch, 1sc into each of next 5ch; rep from * to end omitting 2sc at end of last rep; turn.

2nd row: 1ch, 1sc into each of first 2sc, *3ch, 1sc into next 3ch sp, 1sc into top of next bobble, 1sc into next 3ch sp, 3ch, skip 1sc, 1sc into each of next 3sc; rep from * to end omitting 1sc at end of last rep, turn.

3rd row: 3ch (count as 1dc), 1dc into first sc (half bobble made at beg of row), *3ch, 1sc into next 3ch sp, 1sc into each of next 3sc, 1sc into next 3ch sp, 3ch, skip 1sc, 1 bobble into next sc; rep from * to end but working half bobble of dc2tog at end of last rep, turn.

4th row: 1ch, 1sc into top of half bobble, 1sc into first 3ch sp, 3ch, skip 1sc, 1sc into each of next 3sc, *3ch, 1sc into next 3ch sp, 1sc into top of next bobble, 1sc into next 3ch sp, 3ch, skip 1sc, 1sc into each of next 3sc; rep from * to last 3ch sp, 3ch, 1sc into last 3ch sp, 1sc into 3rd of 3ch at beg of previous row, turn.

5th row: 1ch, 1sc into each of first 2sc, *1sc into next 3ch sp, 3ch, skip 1sc, 1 bobble into next sc, 3ch, 1sc into next 3ch sp, 1sc into each of next 3sc; rep from * to end omitting 1sc at end of last rep, turn.

Rep 2nd to 5th rows.

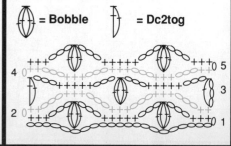

Abbreviations and Symbols on page 12

I.33

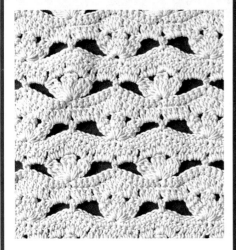

Starting chain: Multiple of 16 sts + 3.

Special Abbreviations

Cluster = work 1dc into same arch as last 3dc until 2 loops remain on hook, skip 1sc, work 1dc into next arch until 3 loops remain on hook, yo and through all 3 loops on hook.

Bobble = work 3tr into next sc until 1 loop of each remains on hook, yo and through all 4 loops on hook.

1st row (right side): Work 1dc into 4th ch from hook, 1dc into each of 6ch, work 3dc into next ch, 1dc into each of next 6ch, *work 1dc into next ch until 2 loops remain on hook, skip 1ch, 1dc into next ch until 3 loops remain on hook, yo and through all 3 loops on hook, work 1dc into each of next 6ch, 3dc into next ch, 1dc into each of next 6ch; rep from * to last 2 ch, work 1dc into next ch until 2 loops remain on hook, 1dc into last ch until 3 loops remain on hook, yo and through all 3 loops (cluster made at end of row), turn.

2nd row: 1ch, work 1sc into each st to last dc, skip last dc, 1sc into top of 3ch, turn.

3rd row: 4ch, work 1tr into first sc (half bobble made at beg of row), 2ch, 1 bobble into same sc as half bobble, 4ch, skip 7sc, 1sc into next sc, *4ch, skip 7sc, work 1 bobble into next sc, into same sc as last bobble work [2ch, 1 bobble] twice, 4ch, skip 7sc, 1sc into next sc; rep from * to last 8sc, 4ch, work 1 bobble into last sc, 2ch, work 2tr into same sc as last bobble until 1 loop of each remains on hook, yo and through all 3 loops on hook (half bobble made at end of row), turn.

I.34

4th row: 3ch (count as 1dc), 1dc into top of first half bobble, work 2dc into 2ch sp, 1dc into next bobble, 3dc into next 4ch arch, 1 cluster, 3dc into same arch as 2nd leg of last cluster, *1dc into top of next bobble, 2dc into 2ch sp, 3dc into top of next bobble, 2dc into next 2ch sp, 1dc into top of next bobble, 3dc into next 4ch arch, 1 cluster, 3dc into same arch as 2nd leg of last cluster; rep from * to last bobble, 1dc into last bobble, 2dc into next 2ch sp, 2dc into top of half bobble, turn.

5th row: 1ch, 1sc into each st to end, placing last sc into 3rd of 3ch at beg of previous row, turn.

6th row: 1ch, 1sc into first sc, *4ch, skip 7sc, 1 bobble into next sc, into same sc as last bobble work [2ch, 1 bobble] twice, 4ch, skip 7 sc, 1sc into next sc; rep from * to end, turn.

7th row: 3ch, 4dc into first 4ch arch, 1dc into next bobble, 2dc into next 2ch sp, 3dc into next bobble, 2dc into next 2ch sp, 1dc into next bobble, *3dc into next 4ch arch, 1 cluster, 3dc into same arch as 2nd leg of last cluster, 1dc into next bobble, 2dc into next 2ch sp, 3dc into next bobble, 2dc into next 2ch sp, 1dc into next bobble; rep from * to last 4ch arch, 3dc into last arch, 1 cluster working into last arch and last sc, turn.

Rep 2nd to 7th rows.

Starting chain: Multiple of 8 sts + 2.

Special Abbreviation

Bobble = work 4dc into next st until 1 loop of each remains on hook, yo and through all 5 loops on hook.

1st row (wrong side): Work 1sc into 2nd ch from hook, 1sc into each ch to end, turn.

2nd row: 4ch (count as 1dc, 1ch), skip first 2sc, 1 bobble into next sc, 1ch, skip 1sc, 1dc into next sc, *1ch, skip 1sc, 1 bobble into next sc, 1ch, skip 1sc, 1dc into next sc; rep from * to end, turn.

3rd row: 1ch, work 1sc into each dc, ch sp and bobble to end, working last 2sc into 4th and 3rd of 4ch at beg of previous row, turn.

4th row: 1ch, 1sc into each of first 3sc, *5ch, skip 3sc, 1sc into each of next 5sc; rep from * to end omitting 2sc at end of last rep, turn.

5th row: 1ch, 1sc into each of first 2sc, *3ch, 1sc into 5ch arch, 3ch, skip 1sc, 1sc into each of next 3sc; rep from * to end omitting 1sc at end of last rep, turn.

6th row: 1ch, 1sc into first sc, *3ch, 1sc into next 3ch arch, 1sc into next sc, 1sc into next 3ch arch, 3ch, skip 1sc, 1sc into next sc; rep from * to end, turn.

7th row: 5ch (count as 1dc, 2ch), 1sc into next 3ch arch, 1sc into each of next 3sc, 1sc into next 3ch arch, *5ch, 1sc into next 3ch arch, 1sc into each of next 3sc, 1sc into next 3ch arch; rep from * to last sc, 2ch, 1dc into last sc, turn.

8th row: 1ch, 1sc into first dc, *3ch, skip 1sc, 1sc into each of next 3sc, 3ch, 1sc into next 5ch arch; rep from * to end placing last sc into 3rd of 5ch at beg of previous row, turn.

9th row: 1ch, 1sc into first sc, *1sc into next 3ch arch, 3ch, skip 1sc, 1sc into next sc, 3ch, 1sc into next 3ch arch, 1sc into next sc; rep from * to end, turn.

10th row: 1ch, 1sc into each of first 2sc, *1sc into next 3ch arch, 3ch, 1sc into next 3ch arch, 1sc into each of next 3sc; rep from * to end omitting 1sc at end of last rep, turn.

11th row: 1ch, 1sc into each of first 3sc, *3sc into next 3ch arch, 1sc into each of next 5sc; rep from * to end omitting 2sc at end of last rep, turn.

Rep 2nd to 11th rows.

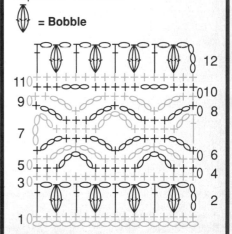

= Bobble

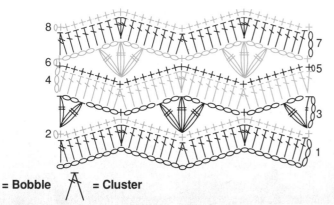

= Bobble ⟋⟍ = Cluster

I. All-over Patterns

I.35

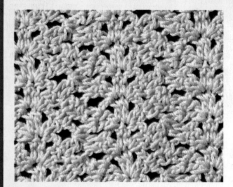

Starting chain: Multiple of 10 sts + 2.

Special Abbreviations

2dc Cluster = work 1dc into each of next 2dc until 1 loop of each remains on hook, yo and through all 3 loops on hook.

4dc Cluster = work 1dc into each of next 4dc until 1 loop of each remains on hook, yo and through all 5 loops on hook.

1st row (right side): Work 1sc into 2nd ch from hook, *2ch, skip 4ch, 2dc into next ch, into same ch as last 2dc work [2ch, 2dc] twice, 2ch, skip 4ch, 1sc into next ch; rep from * to end, turn.

Diagram only: Rep 2nd and 3rd row.

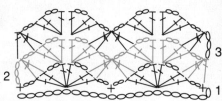

2nd row: 3ch (count as 1dc), work a 2dc cluster over next 2dc, 2ch, into next dc work [2dc, 2ch, 1dc], into next dc work [1dc, 2ch, 2dc], 2ch, *work a 4dc cluster over next 4dc, 2ch, into next dc work [2dc, 2ch, 1dc], into next dc work [1dc, 2ch, 2dc], 2ch; rep from * to last 2dc, work a 2dc cluster over last 2dc, 1dc into last sc, turn.

3rd row: 3ch (count as 1dc), skip first dc and cluster, work a 2dc cluster over next 2dc, 2ch, into next dc work [2dc, 2ch, 1dc], into next dc work [1dc, 2ch, 2dc], 2ch, *work a 4dc cluster over next 4dc (excluding 4dc cluster of previous row), 2ch, into next dc work [2dc, 2ch, 1dc], into next dc work [1dc, 2ch, 2dc], 2ch; rep from * to last 4 sts (excluding 2ch sp), work a 2dc cluster over next 2dc, 1dc into 3rd of 3ch at beg of previous row, turn.

Rep 3rd row only.

I.36

Starting chain: Multiple of 10 sts + 2.

Special Abbreviation

Dc2tog = work 2dc into next 3ch arch until 1 loop of each remains on hook, yo and through all 3 loops on hook.

1st row (wrong side): Work 1sc into 2nd ch from hook, *3ch, skip 3ch, 1sc into next ch, 3ch, skip 1ch, 1sc into next ch, 3ch, skip 3ch, 1sc into next ch; rep from * to end, turn.

2nd row: 1ch, 1sc into first sc, *1ch, skip next 3ch sp, dc2tog into next 3ch arch, into same arch as last dc2tog work [3ch, dc2tog] 4 times, 1ch, skip next 3ch sp, 1sc into next sc; rep from * to end, turn.

3rd row: 7ch (count as 1tr, 3ch), skip next 3ch arch, 1sc into next 3ch arch, 3ch, 1sc into next 3ch arch, 3ch, 1tr into next sc, *3ch, skip next 3ch arch, 1sc into next 3ch arch, 3ch, 1sc into next 3ch arch, 3ch, 1tr into next sc; rep from * to end, turn.

4th row: 1ch, 1sc into first tr, *1ch, skip next 3ch sp, dc2tog into next 3ch arch, into same arch as last dc2tog work [3ch, dc2tog] 4 times, 1ch, 1sc into next tr; rep from * to end, working last sc into 4th of 7ch at beg of previous row, turn.

Rep 3rd and 4th rows.

= Dc2tog

I.37

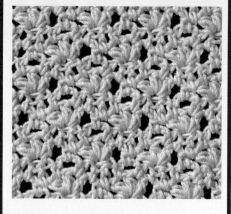

Starting chain: Multiple of 6 sts + 2.

Special Abbreviations

Hdc2tog = *yo, insert hook into st, yo and draw a loop through (3 loops on hook); rep from * once more into same st, yo and through all 5 loops on hook.

Dc2tog = work 1dc into next ch sp until 2 loops remain on hook, work a 2nd dc into next ch sp until 3 loops remain on hook, yo and through all 3 loops on hook.

1st row (right side): Work 1sc into 2nd ch from hook, *1ch, skip 2ch, into next ch work [hdc2tog, 1ch] 3 times, skip 2ch, 1sc into next ch; rep from * to end, turn.

2nd row: 4ch (count as 1dc, 1ch), skip first ch sp, 1sc into next ch sp, 3ch, 1sc into next ch sp, *1ch, dc2tog over next 2 ch sps, 1ch, 1sc into next ch sp, 3ch, 1sc into next ch sp; rep from * to last sc, 1ch, 1dc into last sc, turn.

3rd row: 3ch (count as 1hdc, 1ch), hdc2tog into first dc, 1ch, 1sc into next 3ch sp, 1ch, *into top of next dc2tog work [hdc2tog, 1ch] 3 times, 1sc into next 3ch sp, 1ch; rep from * to last ch sp, into 3rd of 4ch at beg of previous row work [hdc2tog, 1ch, 1hdc], turn.

4th row: 1ch, 1sc into first hdc, 1sc into first ch sp, 1ch, dc2tog over next 2 ch sps, 1ch, *1sc into next ch sp, 3ch, 1sc into next ch sp, 1ch, dc2tog over next 2 ch sps, 1ch; rep from * to last ch sp, 1sc into last ch sp, 1sc into 2nd of 3ch at beg of previous row, turn.

5th row: 1ch, 1sc into first sc, *1ch, into top of next dc2tog work [hdc2tog, 1ch] 3 times, 1sc into next 3ch sp; rep from * to end placing last sc into last sc, turn.

Rep 2nd to 5th rows.

= Hdc2tog   = Dc2tog

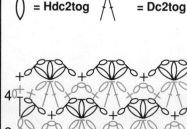

Abbreviations and Symbols on page 12

I.38

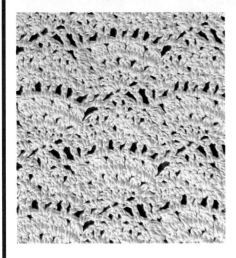

Starting chain: Multiple of 24 sts + 5.

Special Abbreviations

Dc2tog = work 2dc into next st until 1 loop of each remains on hook, yo and through all 3 loops on hook.

Bobble = work 4dc into next st until 1 loop of each remains on hook, yo and through all 5 loops on hook.

Group = work 1dc into next st, into same st as last dc work [1ch, 1dc] twice.

1st row (right side): Work 1dc into 5th ch from hook, skip 2ch, 1sc into next ch, skip 2ch, 1 group into next ch, skip 2ch, 1sc into next ch, skip 2ch, 5dc into next ch, *skip 2ch, 1sc into next ch, [skip 2ch, 1 group into next ch, skip 2ch, 1sc into next ch] 3 times, skip 2ch, 5dc into next ch; rep from * to last 12ch, skip 2ch, 1sc into next ch, skip 2ch, 1 group into next ch, skip 2ch, 1sc into next ch, skip 2ch, into last ch work [1dc, 1ch, 1dc], turn.

2nd row: 1ch, 1sc into first dc, 1 group into next sc, 1sc into center dc of next group, skip 1dc, 2dc into each of next 5dc, *1sc into center dc of next group, [1 group into next sc, 1sc into center dc of next group] twice, skip 1dc, 2dc into each of next 5dc; rep from * to last group, 1sc into center dc of next group, 1 group into next sc, skip [1dc, 1ch], 1 sc into next ch, turn.

3rd row: 4ch (count as 1dc, 1ch), 1dc into first sc, 1sc into center dc of first group, 2ch, [1 bobble between next pair of dc, 2ch] 5 times, *1sc into center dc of next group, 1 group into next sc, 1sc into center dc of next group, 2ch, [1 bobble between next pair of dc, 2ch] 5 times; rep from * to last group, 1sc into center dc of last group, into last sc work [1dc, 1ch, 1dc], turn.

4th row: 1ch, 1sc into first dc, *1ch, 1dc into next 2ch sp, [1ch, 1dc into top of next bobble, 1ch, 1dc into next 2ch sp] 5 times, 1ch, 1sc into center dc of next group; rep from * to end placing last sc into 3rd of 4ch at beg of previous row, turn.

5th row: 3ch (count as 1dc), 2dc into first sc, *skip 1ch sp, 1sc into next ch sp, [skip 1ch sp, 1 group into next dc, skip 1ch sp, 1sc into next ch sp] 3 times, 5dc into next sc; rep from * to end omitting 2dc at end of last rep, turn.

6th row: 3ch (count as 1dc), 1dc into first dc, 2dc into each of next 2dc, 1sc into center dc of next group, [1 group into next sc, 1sc into center dc of next group] twice, *skip 1dc, 2dc into each of next 5dc, 1sc into center dc of next group, [1 group into next sc, 1sc into center dc of next group] twice; rep from * to last 5 sts, skip next dc and sc, 2dc into each of next 2dc, 2dc into 3rd of 3ch at beg of previous row, turn.

7th row: 3ch (count as 1dc), dc2tog between first pair of dc, 2ch, [1 bobble between next pair of dc, 2ch] twice, 1sc into center dc of next group, 1 group into next sc, 1sc into center dc of next group, *2ch, skip [1dc, 1sc], [1 bobble between next pair of dc, 2ch] 5 times, 1sc into center dc of next group, 1 group into next sc, 1sc into center dc of next group; rep from * to last 3 pairs of dc, [2ch, 1 bobble between next pair of dc] twice, 2ch, dc2tog between last pair of dc, 1dc into 3rd of 3ch at beg of previous row, turn.

8th row: 4ch (count as 1dc, 1ch), 1dc into first 2ch sp, 1ch, [1dc into top of next bobble, 1ch, 1dc into next 2ch sp, 1ch] twice, 1sc into center dc of next group, *1ch, 1dc into next 2ch sp, 1ch, [1dc into top of next bobble, 1ch, 1dc into next 2ch sp, 1ch] 5 times, 1sc into center dc of next group; rep from * to last 3 2ch sps, 1ch, 1dc into next 2ch sp, [1ch, 1dc into top of next bobble, 1ch, 1dc into next 2ch sp] twice, 1ch, 1dc into 3rd of 3ch at beg of previous row, turn.

9th row: 4ch (count as 1dc, 1ch), 1dc into first dc, skip 1ch sp, 1sc into next ch sp, skip 1ch sp, 1 group into next dc, skip 1ch sp, 1sc into next ch sp, 5dc into next sc, *skip 1ch sp, 1sc into next ch sp, [skip 1ch sp, 1 group into next dc, skip 1ch sp, 1sc into next ch sp] 3 times, 5dc into next sc; rep from * to last 6 ch sps, skip 1ch sp, 1sc into next ch sp, skip 1ch sp, 1 group into next dc, skip 1ch sp, 1sc into next ch sp, into 3rd of 4ch at beg of previous row work [1dc, 1ch, 1dc], turn.

Rep 2nd to 9th rows.

I.39

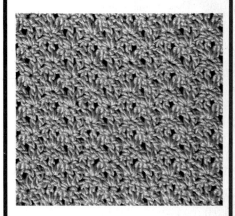

Starting chain: Multiple of 6 sts + 2.

1st row (right side): Work 1sc into 2nd ch from hook, *skip 2ch, 1dc into next ch, 1ch, into same ch as last dc work [1dc, 1ch, 1dc], skip 2ch, 1sc into next ch; rep from * to end, turn.

2nd row: 4ch (count as 1dc, 1ch), 1dc into first sc, skip 1dc, 1sc into next dc, *1dc into next sc, 1ch, into same st as last dc work [1dc, 1ch, 1dc], skip 1dc, 1sc into next dc; rep from * to last sc, into last sc work [1dc, 1ch, 1dc], turn.

3rd row: 1ch, 1sc into first dc, *1dc into next sc, 1ch, into same st as last dc work [1dc, 1ch, 1dc], skip 1dc, 1sc into next dc; rep from * to end placing last sc into 3rd of 4ch at beg of previous row, turn.

Rep 2nd and 3rd rows.

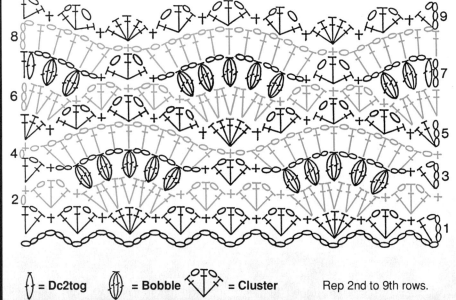

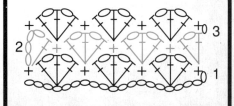

= Dc2tog   = Bobble   = Cluster   Rep 2nd to 9th rows.

I. All-over Patterns

I.40

Diagram only: Rep 2nd to 7th rows.

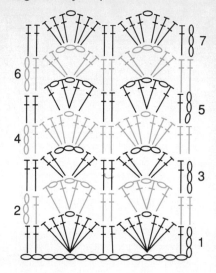

Starting chain: Multiple of 7 sts + 4.

1st row (right side): Work 1dc into 4th ch from hook, *skip 2ch, into next ch work [3dc, 1ch, 3dc], skip 2ch, 1dc into each of next 2ch; rep from * to end, turn.

2nd row: 3ch (count as 1dc), skip first dc, 1dc into next dc, *skip 2dc, 1dc into next dc, 1ch, into next ch sp work [1dc, 1ch, 1dc], 1ch, 1dc into next dc, skip 2dc, 1dc into each of next 2dc; rep from * to end placing last dc into 3rd of 3ch at beg of previous row, turn.

3rd row: 3ch, skip first dc, 1dc into next dc, *skip next ch sp, into next ch sp work [2dc, 3ch, 2dc], skip 2dc, 1dc into each of next 2dc; rep from * to end placing last dc into 3rd of 3ch at beg of previous row, turn.

4th row: 3ch, skip first dc, 1dc into next dc, *into next 3ch sp work [3dc, 1ch, 3dc], skip 2dc, 1dc into each of next 2dc; rep from * to end placing last dc into 3rd of 3ch at beg of previous row, turn.

Rep 2nd to 4th rows.

I.41

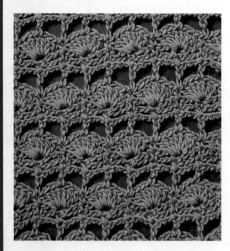

Starting chain: Multiple of 8 sts + 4.

1st row (right side): Work 3dc into 4th ch from hook, skip 3ch, 1sc into next ch, *skip 3ch, 7dc into next ch, skip 3ch, 1sc into next ch; rep from * to last 4ch, skip 3ch, 4dc into last ch, turn.

2nd row: 6ch (count as 1dc, 3ch), 1dc into next sc, *3ch, skip 3dc, 1dc into next dc, 3ch, 1dc into next sc; rep from * to last 4 sts, 3ch, 1dc into top of 3ch at beg of previous row, turn.

3rd row: 1ch, *1sc into next dc, 3ch; rep from * to last st, 1sc into 3rd of 6ch at beg of previous row, turn.

4th row: 1ch, 1sc into first sc, *3ch, 1sc into next sc; rep from * to end, turn.

5th row: 1ch, 1sc into first sc, *7dc into next sc, 1sc into next sc; rep from * to end, turn.

6th row: 6ch, skip 3dc, 1dc into next dc, 3ch, 1dc into next sc, *3ch, skip 3dc, 1dc into next dc, 3ch, 1dc into next sc; rep from * to end, turn.

7th and 8th rows: As 3rd and 4th rows.

9th row: 3ch (count as 1dc), 3dc into first sc, 1sc into next sc, *7dc into next sc, 1sc into next sc; rep from * to last sc, 4dc into last sc, turn.

Rep 2nd to 9th rows.

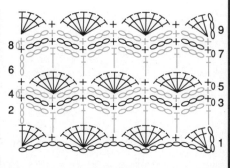

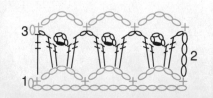

I.42

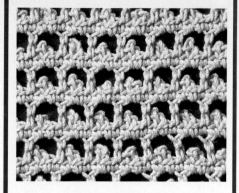

Starting chain: Multiple of 3 sts + 2.

1st row (right side): Work 1sc into 2nd ch from hook, 1sc into next ch, *4ch, sl st into 4th ch from hook (1 picot made), 1sc into each of next 3sc; rep from * to end omitting 1sc at end of last rep, turn.

2nd row: 5ch (count as 1dc, 2ch), skip 2sc, 1dc into next sc, *2ch, skip 2sc, 1dc into next sc; rep from * to end, turn.

3rd row: 1ch, 1sc into first dc, *into next 2ch sp work [1sc, 1 picot, 1sc], 1sc into next dc; rep from * to end placing last sc into 3rd of 5ch at beg of previous row, turn.

Rep 2nd and 3rd rows.

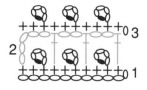

I.43

Starting chain: Multiple of 5 sts + 2.

1st row (wrong side): Work 1sc into 2nd ch from hook, *5ch, skip 4ch, 1sc into next ch; rep from * to end, turn.

2nd row: 5ch (count as 1tr, 1ch), *into next 5ch arch work [1tr, 1dc, 4ch, sl st into 4th ch from hook, 1dc, 1tr], 2ch; rep from * to end omitting 1ch at end of last rep, 1tr into last sc, turn.

3rd row: 1ch, 1sc into first tr, *5ch, 1sc into next 2ch sp; rep from * to end placing last sc into 4th of 5ch at beg of previous row, turn.

Rep 2nd and 3rd rows.

Abbreviations and Symbols on page 12

I.44

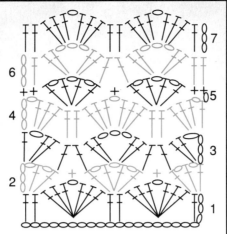

Rep 2nd to 7th rows.

I.44

Starting chain: Multiple of 9 sts + 4.

Special Abbreviations

Shell = work 1dc into next dc, 1ch, between last dc and next dc work [1dc, 1ch, 1dc], 1ch, 1dc into next dc.

Half shell at beg of row = 4ch (count as 1dc, 1ch), 1dc between first 2dc, 1ch, 1dc into next dc.

Half shell at end of row = 1dc into next dc, 1ch, 1dc between last dc worked into and last dc (the 3ch at beg of previous row), 1ch, 1dc into 3rd of 3ch at beg of previous row.

1st row (right side): Work 1dc into 4th ch from hook, *skip 3ch, into next ch work [3dc, 1ch, 3dc], skip 3ch, 1dc into each of next 2ch; rep from * to end, turn.

2nd row: Work half shell over first 2dc, 1sc into next ch sp, *skip 3dc, 1 shell over next 2dc, 1sc into next ch sp; rep from * to last 5 sts, skip 3dc, half shell over last 2dc, turn.

3rd row: 4ch (count as 1dc, 1ch), 2dc into first ch sp, skip 1dc, 1dc into each of next 2dc, *skip 1ch sp, into next ch sp work [2dc, 3ch, 2dc], skip 1dc, 1dc into each of next 2dc; rep from * to last 2dc, 2dc into last ch sp, 1ch, 1dc into 3rd of 4ch at beg of previous row, turn.

= Shell   = Half shell at end

= Half shell at beg

4th row: 4ch (count as 1dc, 1ch), 3dc into first ch sp, skip 2dc, 1dc into each of next 2dc, *into next 3ch sp work [3dc, 1ch, 3dc], skip 2dc, 1dc into each of next 2dc; rep from * to last 3dc, work 3dc into last ch sp, 1ch, 1dc into 3rd of 4ch at beg of previous row, turn.

5th row: 1ch, 1sc into first dc, 1sc into first ch sp, *skip 3dc, 1 shell over next 2dc, 1sc into next ch sp; rep from * to end, 1sc into 3rd of 4ch at beg of previous row, turn.

6th row: 3ch (count as 1dc), skip first sc, 1dc into next sc, skip 1ch sp, into next ch sp work [2dc, 3ch, 2dc], *skip 1dc, work 1dc into each of next 2dc, skip 1ch sp, into next ch sp work [2dc, 3ch, 2dc]; rep from * to last 2dc, 1dc into each of last 2sc, turn.

7th row: 3ch (count as 1dc), skip first dc, 1dc into next dc, *into next 3ch sp work [3dc, 1ch, 3dc], skip 2dc, 1dc into each of next 2dc; rep from * to end placing last dc into 3rd of 3ch at beg of previous row, turn.

Rep 2nd to 7th rows.

I.45

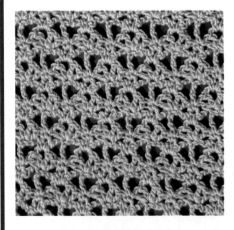

Starting chain: Multiple of 8 sts + 2.

1st row (right side): Work 1sc into 2nd ch from hook, *skip 3ch, into next ch work [1dc, 1ch, 1dc, 3ch, 1dc, 1ch, 1dc], skip 3ch, 1sc into next ch; rep from * to end, turn.

2nd row: 7ch (count as 1tr, 3ch), *skip 1ch sp, into next 3ch sp work [1sc, 3ch, 1sc], 3ch, 1tr into next sc, 3ch; rep from * to end omitting 3ch at end of last rep, turn.

3rd row: 4ch (count as 1dc, 1ch), into first tr work [1dc, 1ch, 1dc], skip 3ch sp, 1sc into next 3ch sp, *into next tr work [1dc, 1ch, 1dc, 3ch, 1dc, 1ch, 1dc], skip 3ch sp, 1sc into next 3ch sp; rep from * to last sp, skip 3ch, 1dc into next ch, work [1ch, 1dc] twice into same ch as last dc, turn.

4th row: 1ch, 1sc into first dc, 1sc into first ch sp, 3ch, 1tr into next sc, *3ch, skip 1ch sp, into next 3ch sp work [1sc, 3ch, 1sc], 3ch, 1tr into next sc; rep from * to last 3dc, 3ch, skip 1ch sp, 1sc into each of next 2ch, turn.

5th row: 1ch, 1sc into first sc, *into next tr work [1dc, 1ch, 1dc, 3ch, 1dc, 1ch, 1dc], skip 3ch sp, 1sc into next 3ch sp; rep from * to end placing last sc into last sc, turn.

Rep 2nd to 5th rows.

I.46

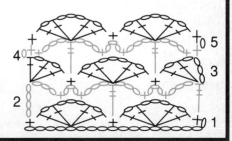

Starting chain: Multiple of 12 sts + 6.

1st row (right side): Work [1tr, 1ch] 3 times into 6th ch from hook, skip 5ch, 1sc into next ch, *1ch, skip 5ch, into next ch work [1tr, 1ch] 7 times, skip 5ch, 1sc into next ch; rep from * to last 6ch, 1ch, into last ch work [1tr, 1ch] 3 times, 1tr into same ch as last 3tr, turn.

2nd row: 1ch, 1sc into first tr, *6ch, 1sc into next sc, 6ch, skip 3tr, 1sc into next tr; rep from * to end placing last tr into 4th of 5ch at beg of previous row, turn.

3rd row: 1ch, 1sc into first sc, *6ch, 1sc into next sc; rep from * to end, turn.

4th row: 1ch, 1sc into first sc, *1ch, into next sc work [1tr, 1ch] 7 times, 1sc into next sc; rep from * to end, turn.

5th row: 1ch, 1sc into first sc, *6ch, skip 3tr, 1sc into next tr, 6ch, 1sc into next sc; rep from * to end, turn.

6th row: 1ch, 1sc into first sc, *6ch, 1sc into next sc; rep from * to end, turn.

7th row: 5ch (count as 1tr, 1ch), into first sc work [1tr, 1ch] 3 times, 1sc into next sc, *1ch, into next sc work [1tr, 1ch] 7 times, 1sc into next sc; rep from * to last sc, into last sc work [1ch, 1tr] 4 times, turn.

Rep 2nd to 7th rows.

I. All-over Patterns

I.47

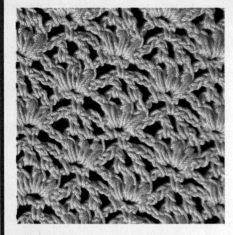

⬚ = Puff st

Starting chain: Multiple of 10 sts + 14.

Special Abbreviation

Puff st = [yo, insert hook into sp, yo and draw a loop through] 3 times into same space, yo and through all 7 loops on hook, work 1 firm ch to close puff st.

1st row (wrong side): Work 1sc into 9th ch from hook, (first 3ch sp made), 1ch, skip 1ch, 1sc into next ch, *3ch, skip 2ch, 1dc into next ch, 1ch, skip 1ch, 1dc into next ch, 3ch, skip 2ch, 1sc into next ch, 1ch, skip 1ch, 1sc into next ch; rep from * to last 3ch, 3ch, skip 2ch, 1dc into last ch, turn.

2nd row: 1ch, 1sc into first dc, *3ch, skip 3ch sp, 1 puff st into next ch sp, 2ch, into same ch sp as last puff st work [1 puff st, 2ch, 1 puff st], 3ch, skip 3ch sp, 1sc into next ch sp; rep from * to end working last sc into 4th ch, turn.

3rd row: 1ch, 1sc into first sc, 3ch, skip first 3ch arch, 1dc into next 2ch arch, 1ch, 1dc into next 2ch arch, 3ch, 1sc into next 3ch arch, *1ch, 1sc into next 3ch arch, 3ch, 1dc into next 2ch arch, 1ch, 1dc into next 2ch arch, 3ch, 1sc into next 3ch arch; rep from * to end placing last sc into last sc, turn.

4th row: 6ch (count as 1dc, 3ch), skip 3ch arch, 1sc into next ch sp, *3ch, skip 3ch arch, 1 puff st into next ch sp, 2ch, into same ch sp as last puff st work [1 puff st, 2ch, 1 puff st], 3ch, skip 3ch arch, 1sc into next ch sp; rep from * to last 3ch arch, 3ch, 1dc into last sc, turn.

5th row: 6ch (count as 1dc, 3ch), 1sc into first 3ch arch, 1ch, 1sc into next 3ch arch, *3ch, 1dc into next 2ch arch, 1ch, 1dc into next 2ch arch, 3ch, 1sc into next 3ch arch, 1ch, 1sc into next 3ch arch; rep from * to end, 3ch, 1dc into 3rd of 6ch at beg of previous row, turn.

Rep 2nd to 5th rows.

I.48

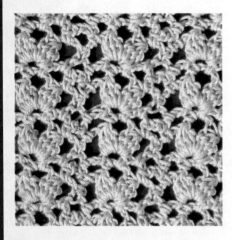

Starting chain: Multiple of 9 sts + 14.

Special Abbreviations

Cluster = work 4dc into next 3ch arch until 1 loop of each remains on hook, yo and through all 5 loops on hook.

Dc2tog over next 3 3ch arches = work 1dc into next 3ch arch until 2 loops remain on hook, skip next 3ch arch, 1dc into next 3ch arch until 3 loops remain on hook, yo and through all 3 loops on hook.

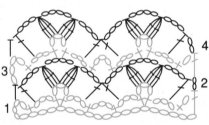

⬚ = Cluster   **⤬ = Dc2tog over next 3 3ch arches**

1st row (wrong side): Work 1sc into 6th ch from hook, 3ch, skip 2ch, into next ch work [1sc, 3ch, 1sc], *[3ch, skip 2ch, 1sc into next ch] twice, 3ch, skip 2ch, into next ch work [1sc, 3ch, 1sc]; rep from * to last 5ch, 3ch, skip 2ch, 1sc into next sc, 1ch, skip 1ch, 1dc into last ch, turn.

2nd row: 2ch (count as 1hdc), 1dc into first 3ch arch, 3ch, into next 3ch arch work [1 cluster, 4ch, 1 cluster], 3ch, *dc2tog over next 3 3ch arches, 3ch, into next 3ch arch work [1 cluster, 4ch, 1 cluster], 3ch; rep from * to last 2 arches, work 1dc into next 3ch arch, skip 1ch, 1hdc into next ch, turn.

3rd row: 4ch (count as 1dc, 1ch), 1sc into next 3ch arch, 3ch, into next 4ch arch work [1sc, 3ch, 1sc], *3ch, [1sc into next 3ch arch, 3ch] twice, into next 4ch arch work [1sc, 3ch, 1sc]; rep from * to last 3ch arch, 3ch, 1sc into last 3ch arch, 1ch, 1dc into 2nd of 2ch at beg of previous row, turn.

Rep 2nd and 3rd rows.

I.49

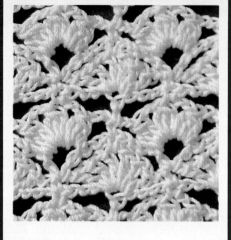

Starting chain: Multiple of 10 sts + 5.

Special Abbreviation

Cluster = work 3dc into next space until 1 loop of each remains on hook, yo and through all 4 loops on hook.

1st row (right side): Work [1dc, 1ch, 1dc] into 5th ch from hook (1dc and 1ch sp formed at beg of row), 1ch, skip 4ch, 1sc into next ch, *1ch, skip 4ch, into next ch work [1dc, 1ch] 6 times, skip 4ch, 1sc into next ch; rep from * to last 5ch, 1ch, 1dc into last ch, [1ch, 1dc] twice into same ch as last dc, turn.

2nd row: 1ch, 1sc into first dc, 3ch, into next sc work [1dc, 3ch, 1dc], *3ch, skip 3dc, 1sc into next ch sp, 3ch, into next sc work [1dc, 3ch, 1dc]; rep from * to last 3dc, 3ch, 1sc into 3rd of 4ch at beg of previous row, turn.

3rd row: 1ch, 1sc into first sc, *2ch, skip 3ch sp, 1 cluster into next 3ch sp, 2ch, into same sp as last cluster work [1 cluster, 2ch] twice, 1sc into next sc; rep from * to end, turn.

4th row: 7ch (count as 1dc, 4ch), *skip 1 cluster, 1sc into next cluster, 4ch, 1dc into next sc, 4ch; rep from * to end omitting 4ch at end of last rep, turn.

5th row: 4ch (count as 1dc, 1ch), into first dc work [1dc, 1ch] twice, 1sc into next sc, *1ch, into next dc work [1dc, 1ch] 6 times, 1sc into next sc; rep from * to last dc, 1ch, work 1dc into 3rd of 7ch at beg of previous row, [1ch, 1dc] twice into same ch as last dc, turn.

Rep 2nd to 5th rows.

⬚ = Cluster

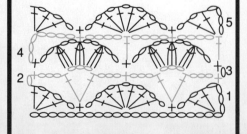

Abbreviations and Symbols on page 12

I.50

Starting chain: Multiple of 30 sts + 32.

1st row (right side): Work 1sc into 2nd ch from hook, [skip 2ch, 5dc into next ch, skip 2ch, 1sc into next ch] twice, skip 2ch, 1dc into next ch, 1ch, into same ch as last dc work [1dc, 1ch, 1dc], *skip 2ch, 1sc into next ch, [skip 2ch, 5dc into next ch, skip 2ch, 1sc into next ch] 4 times, skip 2ch, 1dc into next ch, 1ch, into same ch as last dc work [1dc, 1ch, 1dc]; rep from * to last 15ch, skip 2ch, 1sc into next ch, [skip 2ch, 5dc into next ch, skip 2ch, 1sc into next ch] twice, turn.

2nd row: 3ch (count as 1dc), 2dc into first sc, skip 2dc, 1sc into next dc, 5dc into next sc, skip 2dc, 1sc into next dc, 1ch, skip 2dc, 1dc into next dc, 1ch, [1dc into next ch sp, 1ch, 1dc into next dc, 1ch] twice, *skip 2dc, 1sc into next dc, [5dc into next sc, skip 2dc, 1sc into next dc] 3 times, 1ch, skip 2dc, 1dc into next dc, 1ch, [1dc into next ch sp, 1ch, 1dc into next dc, 1ch] twice; rep from * to last 2 groups of 5dc, skip 2dc, 1sc into next dc, 5dc into next sc, skip 2dc, 1sc into next dc; 3dc into last sc, turn.

3rd row: 1ch, 1sc into first dc, 5dc into first sc, skip 2dc, 1sc into next dc, 2ch, skip 2dc, [1dc into next dc, 2ch] 5 times, *skip 2dc, 1sc into next dc, [5dc into next sc, skip 2dc, 1sc into next dc] twice, 2ch, skip 2dc, [1dc into next dc, 2ch] 5 times; rep from * to last group of 5dc, skip 2dc, 1sc into next dc, 5dc into next sc, 1sc into 3rd of 3ch at beg of previous row, turn.

4th row: 3ch (count as 1dc), 2dc into first sc, skip 2dc, 1sc into next dc, 1ch, 1dc into next 2ch sp, [1ch, 1dc into next dc, 1ch, 1dc into next 2ch sp] 5 times, *1ch, skip 2dc, 1sc into next dc, 5dc into next sc, skip 2dc, 1sc into next dc, 1ch, 1dc into next 2ch sp, [1ch, 1dc into next dc, 1ch, 1dc into next 2ch sp] 5 times; rep from * to last group of 5dc, 1ch, skip 2dc, 1sc into next dc, 3dc into last sc, turn.

5th row: 1ch, 1sc into first dc, *5dc into next sc, skip 1ch sp, 1sc into next ch sp, [skip 1ch sp, 5dc into next dc, skip 1ch sp, 1sc into next ch sp] 3 times, 5dc into next sc, 1sc into center dc of next group of 5; rep from * to end placing last sc into 3rd of 3ch at beg of previous row, turn.

6th row: 4ch (count as 1dc), 1dc into first sc, 1sc into center dc of first group of 5, [5dc into next sc, 1sc into center dc of next group of 5] 4 times, *1dc into next sc, 1ch, into same st as last dc work [1dc, 1ch, 1dc], 1sc into center dc of next group of 5, [5dc into next sc, 1sc into center dc of next group of 5] 4 times; rep from * to last sc, into last sc work [1dc, 1ch, 1dc], turn.

7th row: 4ch (count as 1dc), 1dc into first ch sp, 1ch, 1dc into next dc, 1ch, 1sc into center dc of first group of 5, [5dc into next sc, 1sc into center dc of next group of 5] 3 times, *1ch, skip 2dc, 1dc into next dc, 1ch, [1dc into next ch sp, 1ch, 1dc into next dc, 1ch] twice, 1sc into center dc of next group of 5, [5dc into next sc, 1sc into center dc of next group of 5] 3 times; rep from * to last 4dc, 1ch, skip 2dc, 1dc into next dc, 1ch, 1dc into last ch sp, 1ch, 1dc into 3rd of 4ch at beg of previous row, turn.

8th row: 5ch (count as 1dc, 2ch), skip first dc, [1dc into next dc, 2ch] twice, 1sc into center dc of group of 5, [5dc into next sc, 1sc into center dc of next group of 5] twice, *2ch, skip 2dc, [1dc into next dc, 2ch] 5 times, 1sc into center dc of next group of 5, [5dc into next sc, 1sc into center dc of next group of 5] twice; rep from * to last 5dc, 2ch, skip 2dc, [1dc into next dc, 2ch] twice, 1dc into 3rd of 4ch at beg of previous row, turn.

9th row: 4ch (count as 1dc, 1ch), 1dc into first 2ch sp, 1ch, [1dc into next dc, 1ch, 1dc into next 2ch sp, 1ch] twice, 1sc into center dc of first group of 5, 5dc into next sc, 1sc into center dc of next group of 5, *1ch, 1dc into next 2ch sp, 1ch, [1dc into next dc, 1ch, 1dc into next 2ch sp, 1ch] 5 times, 1sc into center dc of next group of 5, 5dc into next sc, 1sc into center dc of next group of 5; rep from * to last 5dc, 1ch, 1dc into next 2ch sp, 1ch, [1dc into next dc, 1ch, 1dc into next 2ch sp, 1ch] twice, 1dc into 3rd of 5ch at beg of previous row, turn.

10th row: 3ch (count as 1dc), 2dc into first dc, skip 1ch sp, 1sc into next ch sp, skip 1ch sp, 5dc into next dc, skip 1ch sp, 1sc into next ch sp, 5dc into next sc, 1sc into center dc of next group of 5, 5dc into next sc, *skip 1ch sp, 1sc into next ch sp, [skip 1ch sp, 5dc into next dc, skip 1ch sp, 1sc into next ch sp] 3 times, 5dc into next sc, 1sc into center dc of next group of 5, 5dc into next sc; rep from * to last 6dc, skip 1ch sp, 1sc into next ch sp, skip 1ch sp, 5dc into next dc, skip 1ch sp, 1sc into next ch sp, 3dc into 3rd of 4ch at beg of previous row, turn.

11th row: 1ch, 1sc into first dc, [5dc into next sc, 1sc into center dc of next group of 5] twice, 1dc into next sc, 1ch, into same st as last dc work [1dc, 1ch, 1dc], *1sc into center dc of next group of 5, [5dc into next sc, 1sc into center dc of next group of 5] 4 times, 1dc into next sc, 1ch, into same st as last dc work [1dc, 1ch, 1dc]; rep from * to last 2 groups of 5dc, [1sc into center dc of next group of 5, 5dc into next sc] twice, 1sc into 3rd of 3ch at beg of previous row, turn.

Rep 2nd to 11th rows.

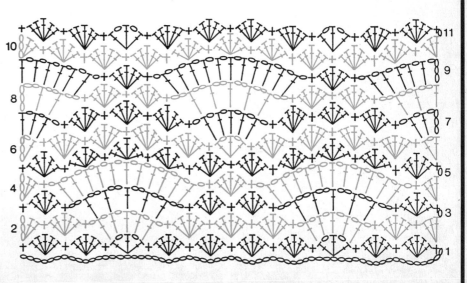

I. All-over Patterns

I.51

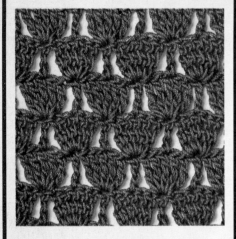

Starting chain: Multiple of 8 sts + 12.

1st row (right side): Work 5tr into 8th ch from hook, skip 3ch, 1tr into next ch, *skip 3ch, 5tr into next ch, skip 3ch, 1tr into next ch; rep from * to end, turn.

2nd row: 4ch (count as 1tr), 2tr into first tr, skip 2tr, 1tr into next tr, *skip 2tr, 5tr into next tr, skip 2tr, 1tr into next tr; rep from * to last 3 sts, skip 2tr, 3tr into next ch, turn.

3rd row: 4ch, *skip 2tr, 5tr into next tr, skip 2tr, 1tr into next tr; rep from * to end placing last tr into 4th of 4ch at beg of previous row, turn.

Rep 2nd and 3rd rows.

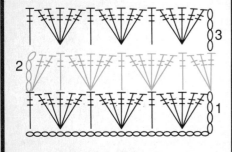

I.52

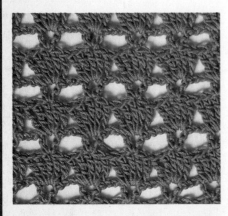

Starting chain: Multiple of 5 sts + 6.

1st row (wrong side): Work [1dc, 2ch, 1dc] into 8th ch from hook, *3ch, skip 4ch, work [1dc, 2ch, 1dc] into next ch; rep from * to last 3ch, 2ch, 1dc into last ch, turn.

I.53

Starting chain: Multiple of 8 sts + 3.

1st row (wrong side): Work 1dc into 4th ch from hook, *1ch, skip 2ch, into next ch work [1dc, 3ch, 1dc], 1ch, skip 2ch, 1dc into each of next 3ch; rep from * to end omitting 1dc at end of last rep, turn.

2nd row: 4ch (count as 1dc, 1ch), work 7dc into next 3ch arch, *1ch, skip 2dc, 1dc into next dc, 1ch, 7dc into next 3ch arch; rep from * to last 3dc, 1ch, skip 2dc, 1dc into top of 3ch, turn.

3rd row: 4ch, 1dc into first dc, 1ch, skip 2dc, 1dc into each of next 3dc, *1ch, skip 2dc, into next dc work [1dc, 3ch, 1dc], 1ch, skip 2dc, 1dc into each of next 3dc; rep from * to last 3dc, skip 2dc, into 3rd of 4ch at beg of previous row work [1dc, 1ch, 1dc], turn.

4th row: 3ch (count as 1dc), 3dc into first ch sp, 1ch, skip 2dc, 1dc into next dc, *1ch, 7dc into next 3ch arch, 1ch, skip 2dc, 1dc into next dc; rep from * to last 3dc, 1ch, skip 2dc, 3dc into last ch sp, 1dc into 3rd of 4ch at beg of previous row, turn.

5th row: 3ch, skip first dc, 1dc into next dc, *1ch, skip 2dc, into next dc work [1dc, 3ch, 1dc], 1ch, skip 2dc, 1dc into each of next 3dc; rep from * to end omitting 1dc at end of last rep and placing last dc into 3rd of 3ch at beg of previous row, turn.

Rep 2nd to 5th rows.

2nd row: 4ch (count as 1tr), skip first 2ch sp, work 5tr into next 2ch sp, *skip 3ch sp, work 5tr into next 2ch sp; rep from * to last sp, skip 2ch, 1tr into next ch, turn.

3rd row: 5ch (count as 1dc, 2ch), skip first 3tr, into next tr work [1dc, 2ch, 1dc], *3ch, skip 4tr, into next tr work [1dc, 2ch, 1dc]; rep from * to last 3tr, 2ch, 1dc into 4th of 4ch at beg of previous row, turn.

Rep 2nd and 3rd rows.

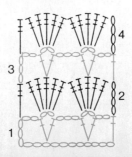

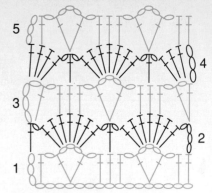

Rep 2nd to 5th rows.

I.54

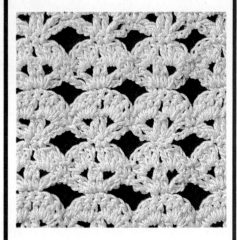

Starting chain: Multiple of 9 sts + 2.

1st row (right side): Work 1sc into 2nd ch from hook, *skip 3ch, into each of next 2ch work [1dc, 2ch, 1dc], skip 3ch, 1sc into next ch; rep from * to end, turn.

2nd row: 1ch, 1sc into first sc, *into next 2ch sp work [1hdc, 3dc], into next 2ch sp work [3dc, 1hdc], 1sc into next sc; rep from * to end, turn.

3rd row: 7ch (count as 1tr, 3ch), skip first 4 sts, 1sc into each of next 2dc, *7ch, skip 7 sts, 1sc into each of next 2dc; rep from * to last 4 sts, 3ch, 1tr into last sc, turn.

4th row: 1ch, 1sc into first tr, *into each of next 2sc work [1dc, 2ch, 1dc], 1sc into 7ch arch; rep from * to end placing last sc into 4th of 7ch at beg of previous row, turn.

Rep 2nd to 4th rows.

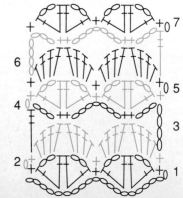

Diagram only: Rep 2nd to 7th rows.

I.55

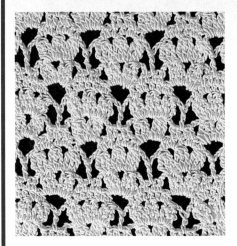

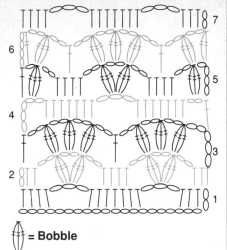

= Bobble

Starting chain: Multiple of 10 sts + 2.

Special Abbreviation

Bobble = work 3tr into next st until 1 loop of each remains on hook, yo and through all 4 loops on hook.

1st row (right side): Work 1hdc into 3rd ch from hook, 1hdc into each of next 2ch, *3ch, skip 3ch, 1hdc into each of next 7ch; rep from * to end omitting 3hdc at end of last rep, turn.

2nd row: 2ch (count as 1hdc), working between sts work 1hdc between first and 2nd hdc then between 2nd and 3rd hdc, 2ch, into next 3ch sp work [1 bobble, 2ch] twice, *skip 1hdc, [1hdc between next 2hdc] 4 times, 2ch, into next 3ch sp work [1 bobble, 2ch] twice; rep from * to last 4 sts, skip 1hdc, 1hdc between next 2hdc, 1hdc between last hdc and 2ch, 1hdc into top of 2ch, turn.

3rd row: 5ch (count as 1dc, 2ch), *1 bobble into next bobble, 2ch, 1 bobble into next 2ch sp, 2ch, 1 bobble into next bobble, 2ch, 1dc between 2nd and 3rd hdc, 2ch; rep from * to end omitting 2ch at end of last rep and placing last dc into 2nd of 2ch at beg of previous row, turn.

4th row: 5ch, *1hdc into next bobble, [2hdc into next 2ch sp, 1hdc into next bobble] twice, 3ch; rep from * to end omitting 1ch at end of last rep, work 1dc into 3rd of 5ch at beg of previous row, turn.

5th row: 4ch (count as 1dc, 1ch), 1 bobble into first 2ch sp, 2ch, skip 1hdc, [1hdc between next 2hdc] 4 times, *2ch, into next 3ch sp work [1 bobble, 2ch] twice, skip 1hdc, [1hdc between next 2hdc] 4 times; rep from * to last 2ch sp, 2ch, work 1 bobble into last 2ch sp, 1ch, 1dc into 3rd of 5ch at beg of previous row, turn.

6th row: 4ch (count as 1tr), 1tr into first ch sp, 2ch, 1 bobble into next bobble, 2ch, skip 1hdc, 1dc between next 2hdc, 2ch, *1 bobble into next bobble, 2ch, 1 bobble into next 2ch sp, 2ch, 1 bobble into next bobble, 2ch, skip 1hdc, 1dc between next 2hdc; rep from * to last bobble, 2ch, 1 bobble into next bobble, 2ch, work 1tr into last ch sp until last loop of tr remains on hook, 1tr into 3rd of 4ch until 3 loops remain on hook, yo and through all 3 loops on hook, turn.

7th row: 2ch, 2hdc into first 2ch sp, 1hdc into next bobble, 3ch, *1hdc into next bobble, [2hdc into next 2ch sp, 1hdc into next bobble] twice, 3ch; rep from * to last bobble, 1hdc into last bobble, 2hdc into next 2ch sp, 1hdc into 4th of 4ch at beg of previous row, turn.

Rep 2nd to 7th rows.

I.56

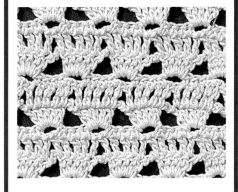

Starting chain: Multiple of 7 sts + 3.

1st row (right side): Work 1sc into 2nd ch from hook, 1sc into each of next 2ch, *3ch, skip 3ch, 1sc into each of next 4ch; rep from * to end omitting 1sc at end of last rep, turn.

2nd row: 4ch (count as 1dc, 1ch), work 5dc into first 3ch sp, *3ch, 5dc into next 3ch sp; rep from * to last 3sc, 1ch, 1dc into last sc, turn.

3rd row: 3ch (count as 1dc), skip first dc, *1dc into next dc, [1ch, 1dc into next dc] 4 times; rep from * to last dc, 1dc into 3rd of 4ch at beg of previous row, turn.

4th row: 1ch, 1sc into first dc, 1ch, [1sc

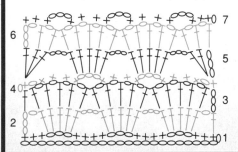

I.57

Starting chain: Multiple of 4 sts + 3.

Special Abbreviation

Bobble = work 3dc into next st until 1 loop of each remains on hook, yo and through all 4 loops on hook.

1st row (wrong side): Work 1dc into 4th ch from hook, 1dc into each of next 2ch, *2ch, skip 1ch, 1dc into each of next 3ch; rep from * to last ch, 1dc into last ch, turn.

2nd row: 3ch (count as 1dc), skip first 2dc, into next dc work [1 bobble, 3ch, 1 bobble], *skip 2dc, into next dc work [1 bobble, 3ch, 1 bobble]; rep from * to last 2dc, 1dc into 3rd of 3ch at beg of previous row, turn.

3rd row: 3ch, work 3dc into first 3ch arch, *2ch, 3dc into next 3ch arch; rep from * to last 2 sts, 1dc into 3rd of 3ch at beg of previous row, turn.

Rep 2nd and 3rd rows.

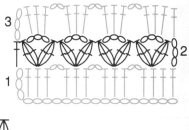

 = Bobble

into next ch sp, skip 1dc] 4 times, *3ch, [1sc into next ch sp, skip 1dc] 4 times; rep from * to last 2dc, 1ch, 1sc into 3rd of 3ch at beg of previous row, turn.

5th row: 3ch, 2dc into first sc, 3ch, *5dc into next 3ch sp, 3ch; rep from * to last sc, 3dc into last sc, turn.

6th row: 4ch, skip first dc, 1dc into next dc, 1ch, 1dc into next dc, *1dc into next dc, [1ch, 1dc into next dc] 4 times; rep from * to last 3dc, [1dc into next dc, 1ch] twice, 1dc into 3rd of 3ch at beg of previous row, turn.

7th row: 1ch, 1sc into first dc, [1sc into next ch sp, skip 1dc] twice, 3ch, *[1sc into next ch sp, skip 1dc] 4 times, 3ch; rep from * to last 3dc, 1sc into next ch sp, skip 1dc, 1sc into next ch sp, 1sc into 3rd of 4ch at beg of previous row, turn.

Rep 2nd to 7th rows.

I. All-over Patterns

I.58

Starting chain: Multiple of 6 sts + 5.

Special Abbreviations

Dc2tog = work 2dc into next st until 1 loop of each remains on hook, yo and through all 3 loops on hook.

Shell = work [dc2tog, 1dc, dc2tog] all into next st.

Group = into first dc2tog of shell work 2dc until 1 loop of each remains on hook, 1dc into dc of same shell until 4 loops remain on hook, into 2nd dc2tog of shell work 2dc until 1 loop of each remains on hook, yo and through all 6 loops.

1st row (right side): Work 1dc into 8th ch from hook (1dc and 2ch sp at beg of row), *1ch, skip 2ch, work 1 shell into next ch, 1ch, skip 2ch, 1dc into next ch; rep from * to last 3ch, 2ch, skip 2ch, 1dc into last ch, turn.

2nd row: 5ch (count as 1dc, 2ch), skip first dc, 1dc into next dc, 2ch, *work 1 group over next shell, 2ch, 1dc into next dc, 2ch; rep from * to last dc, skip 2ch, 1dc into next ch, turn.

3rd row: 4ch (count as 1dc, 1ch), skip first dc, *work 1 shell into next dc, 1ch, 1dc into top of next group, 1ch; rep from * to end omitting 1ch at end of last rep and placing last dc into 3rd of 5ch at beg of previous row, turn.

4th row: 5ch, *work 1 group over next shell, 2ch, 1dc into next dc, 2ch; rep from * to end omitting 2ch at end of last rep and placing last dc into 3rd of 4ch at beg of previous row, turn.

5th row: 5ch, 1dc into top of next group, *1ch, work 1 shell into next dc, 1ch, 1dc into top of next group; rep from * to last dc, 2ch, 1dc into 3rd of 5ch at beg of previous row, turn.

Rep 2nd to 5th rows.

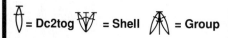

= Dc2tog   = Shell   = Group

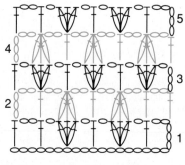

I.59

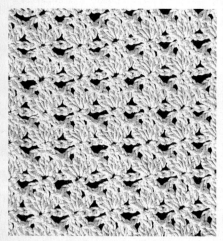

Starting chain: Multiple 5 sts + 6.

Special Abbreviation

Dc2tog = work 2dc into next st until 1 loop of each remains on hook, yo and through all 3 loops on hook.

1st row (right side): Work dc2tog into 6th ch from hook, (1dc and 2ch sp at beg of row), *skip 4ch, dc2tog into next ch, 2ch, into same ch as last dc2tog work [dc2tog, 2ch, dc2tog]; rep from * to last 5ch, skip 4ch, into last ch work [dc2tog, 2ch, 1dc], turn.

2nd row: 1ch, 1sc into first dc, *4ch, skip 2 dc2tog, 1sc into top of next dc2tog; rep from * to end placing last sc into 3rd ch, turn.

3rd row: 5ch (count as 1dc, 2ch), work dc2tog into first sc, *work dc2tog into next sc, 2ch, into same st as last dc2tog work [dc2tog, 2ch, dc2tog]; rep from * to last sc, into last sc work [dc2tog, 2ch, 1dc], turn.

Rep 2nd and 3rd rows.

= Dc2tog

I.60

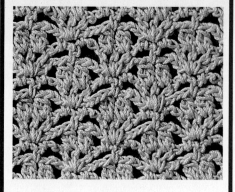

Starting chain: Multiple of 10 sts + 2.

Special Abbreviation

Dc2tog = work 2dc into next st until 1 loop of each remains on hook, yo and through all 3 loops on hook.

1st row (right side): Work 1sc into 2nd ch from hook, 1sc into next ch, 3ch, skip 2ch, dc2tog into next ch, 1ch, skip 1ch, dc2tog into next ch, *3ch, skip 2ch, 1sc into next ch, 1ch, skip 1ch, 1sc into next ch, 3ch, skip 2ch, dc2tog into next ch, 1ch, skip 1ch, dc2tog into next ch; rep from * to last 4ch, 3ch, skip 2ch, 1sc into each of last 2ch, turn.

2nd row: 4ch (count as 1dc, 1ch), 1dc into first sc, 3ch, skip next 3ch sp, 1sc into next ch sp, *3ch, skip next 3ch sp, 1dc into next ch sp, 1ch, into same ch sp as last dc work [1dc, 1ch, 1dc], 3ch, skip next 3ch sp, 1sc into next ch sp; rep from * to last 3ch sp, 3ch, into last sc work [1dc, 1ch, 1dc], turn.

3rd row: 3ch (count as 1dc), dc2tog into first ch sp, 3ch, 1sc into next 3ch sp, 1ch, 1sc into next 3ch sp, *3ch, dc2tog into next ch sp, 1ch, dc2tog into next ch sp, 3ch, 1sc into next 3ch sp, 1ch, 1sc into next 3ch sp; rep from * to last ch sp, 3ch, dc2tog into last ch sp, 1dc into 3rd of 4ch at beg of previous row, turn.

4th row: 1ch, 1sc into first dc, *skip next 3ch sp, 3ch, 1dc into next ch sp, 1ch, into same ch sp as last dc work [1dc, 1ch, 1dc], 3ch, skip next 3ch sp, 1sc into next ch sp; rep from * to end placing last sc into 3rd of 3ch at beg of previous row, turn.

5th row: 1ch, 1sc into first sc, 1sc into first 3ch sp, 3ch, dc2tog into next ch sp, 1ch, dc2tog into next ch sp, *3ch, 1sc into next 3ch sp, 1ch, 1sc into next 3ch sp, 3ch, dc2tog into next ch sp, 1ch, dc2tog into next ch sp; rep from * to last 3ch sp, 3ch, 1sc into last 3ch sp, 1sc into last sc, turn.

Rep 2nd to 5th rows.

= Dc2tog

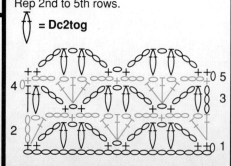

Abbreviations and Symbols on page 12

I.61

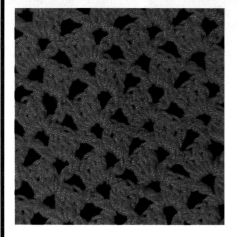

Starting chain: Multiple of 6 sts + 5.

1st row (right side): Work 1dc into 6th ch from hook, 1dc into each of next 2ch, 3ch, 1dc into next ch, *skip 2ch, 1dc into each of next 3ch, 3ch, 1dc into next ch; rep from * to last 2ch, skip 1ch, 1dc into last ch, turn.

I.62

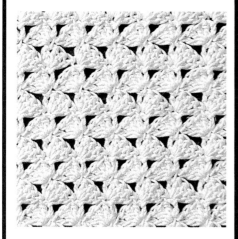

Starting chain: Multiple of 4 sts + 4.

1st row (right side): Work 4dc into 4th ch from hook, skip 3ch, 1sc into next ch, *2ch, 4dc into same ch as last sc, skip 3ch, 1sc into next ch; rep from * to end, turn.

2nd row: 5ch, work 4dc into 4th ch from hook, *skip 4dc, 1sc between last dc skipped and next 2ch, 2ch, 4dc into side of last sc worked; rep from * to last 4dc, skip 4dc, 1sc into next ch, turn.

Rep 2nd row.

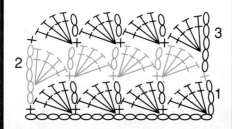

Diagram only: Rep 2nd and 3rd rows.

Diagram only: Rep 2nd and 3rd rows.

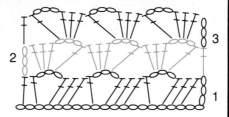

2nd row: 3ch (count as 1dc), *into next 3ch arch work [3dc, 3ch, 1dc]; rep from * to last 3dc, skip 3dc, 1dc into next ch, turn.

3rd row: 3ch, *into next 3ch arch work [3dc, 3ch, 1dc]; rep from * to last 4dc, skip 3dc, 1dc into 3rd of 3ch at beg of previous row, turn.

Rep 3rd row.

I.63

Starting chain: Multiple of 13 sts + 9.

1st row (right side): Work 3dc into 4th ch from hook, skip 4ch, 4dc into next ch, *3ch, skip 3ch, 1sc into next ch, 3ch, skip 3ch, 4dc into next ch, skip 4ch, 4dc into next ch; rep from * to end, turn.

2nd row: 3ch (count as 1dc), 3dc into first dc, skip 6dc, work 4dc into next dc, *3ch, 1sc into next sc, 3ch, 4dc into next dc, skip 6dc, 4dc into next dc; rep from * to end placing last group of 4dc into top of 3ch, turn.

3rd row: 6ch (count as 1dc, 3ch), work 1sc between next 2 groups of 4dc, *3ch, skip 3dc, 4dc into each of next 2dc, 3ch, 1sc between next 2 groups of 4dc; rep from * to last group, 3ch, 1dc into 3rd of 3ch at beg of previous row, turn.

4th row: 6ch, work 1sc into first sc, 3ch, *4dc into next dc, skip 6dc, 4dc into next dc, 3ch, 1sc into next sc, 3ch; rep from * to last arch, 1dc into 3rd of 6ch at beg of previous row, turn.

5th row: 3ch, 3dc into first dc, work 4dc into next dc, *3ch, 1sc between next 2 groups of 4dc, 3ch, skip 3dc, 4dc into each of next 2dc; rep from * to end placing last group of 4dc into 3rd of 6ch at beg of previous row, turn.

Rep 2nd to 5th rows.

I.64

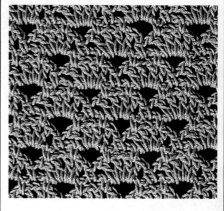

Starting chain: Multiple of 7 sts + 4.

1st row (wrong side): Work 1sc into 5th ch from hook, 3ch, skip 3ch, 1sc into next ch, *3ch, skip 2ch, 1sc into next ch, 3ch, skip 3ch, 1sc into next ch; rep from * to last 2ch, 1ch, 1hdc into last ch, turn.

2nd row: 1ch, 1sc into first hdc, *1ch, into next 3ch arch work [1dc, 1ch] 4 times, 1sc into next 3ch arch; rep from * to end placing last sc into 2nd ch, turn.

3rd row: 4ch (count as 1dc, 1ch), skip first ch sp, 1sc into next ch sp, 3ch, skip 1ch sp, 1sc into next ch sp, *3ch, skip 2ch sps, 1sc into next ch sp, 3ch, skip 1ch sp, 1sc into next ch sp; rep from * to last ch sp, 1ch, 1dc into last sc, turn.

4th row: 3ch (count as 1dc), work [1dc, 1ch] twice into first ch sp, 1sc into next 3ch arch, *1ch, work [1dc, 1ch] 4 times into next 3ch arch, 1sc into next 3ch arch; rep from * to last sp, 1ch, work [1dc, 1ch, 1dc] into last ch sp, 1dc into 3rd of 4ch at beg of previous row, turn.

5th row: 3ch (count as 1hdc, 1ch), 1sc into first ch sp, 3ch, skip 2ch sps, 1sc into next ch sp, *3ch, skip 1ch sp, 1sc into next ch sp, 3ch, skip 2ch sps, 1sc into next ch sp; rep from * to last 2dc, 1ch, 1hdc into 3rd of 3ch at beg of previous row, turn.

Rep 2nd to 5th rows.

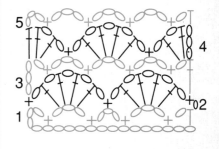

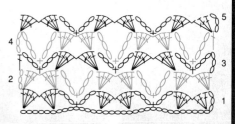

I. All-over Patterns

I.65

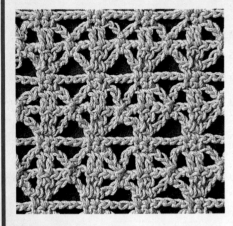

Starting chain: Multiple of 6 sts + 3.

1st row (right side): Work 1sc into 2nd ch from hook, 1sc into next ch, *6ch, skip 4ch, 1sc into each of next 2ch; rep from * to end, turn.

2nd row: 3ch (count as 1dc), skip first sc, 1dc into next sc, *2ch, 1sc into 6ch arch, 2ch, 1dc into each of next 2sc; rep from * to end, turn.

3rd row: 3ch, skip first dc, 1dc into next dc, *3ch, 1 sl st into next sc, 3ch, 1dc into each of next 2dc; rep from * to end placing last dc into 3rd of 3ch at beg of previous row, turn.

4th row: 1ch, 1sc into each of first 2dc, *4ch, 1sc into each of next 2dc; rep from * to end placing last sc into 3rd of 3ch at beg of previous row, turn.

5th row: 1ch, 1sc into each of first 2sc, *6ch, 1sc into each of next 2sc; rep from * to end, turn.

Rep 2nd to 5th rows.

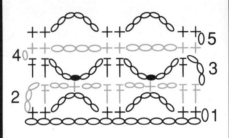

I.66

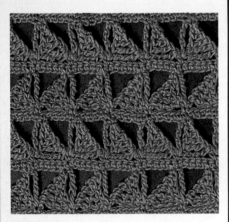

Starting chain: Multiple of 6 sts + 2.

1st row (right side): Work 1sc into 2nd ch from hook, 1sc into each ch to end, turn.

2nd row: 1ch, 1sc into first sc, *6ch, work 1sc into 2nd ch from hook, then working 1 st into each of next 4ch work 1hdc, 1dc, 1tr and 1dtr, skip 5sc on previous row, 1sc into next sc; rep from * to end, turn.

3rd row: 5ch (count as 1dtr), *1sc into ch at top of next triangle, 4ch, 1dtr into next sc; rep from * to end, turn.

4th row: 1ch, work 1sc into each [dtr, ch and sc] to end, placing last sc into top of 5ch at beg of previous row, turn.

Rep 2nd to 4th rows.

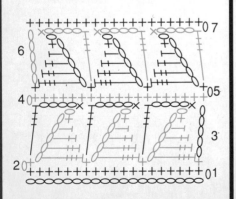

Diagram only: Rep 2nd to 7th rows.

I.67

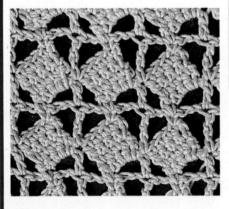

Starting chain: Multiple of 6 sts + 6.

1st row (right side): Work 1sc into 9th ch from hook (1dc and 3ch sp formed at beg of row), turn, 1ch, 1sc into sc, 3sc into 3ch sp, [turn, 1ch, 1sc into each of the 4sc] 3 times, skip next 2ch on starting chain, 1dc into next ch, *3ch, skip next 2ch on starting ch, 1sc into next ch, turn, 1ch, 1sc into sc, 3sc into 3ch sp, [turn, 1ch, 1sc into each of the 4sc] 3 times, skip next 2ch on starting chain, 1dc into next ch; rep from * to end, turn.

2nd row: 6ch (count as 1tr, 2ch), skip 1dc and 3sc, 1sc into next sc, 2ch, 1tr into next dc, *2ch, skip 3sc, 1sc into next sc, 2ch, 1tr into next dc; rep from * to end placing last tr into top of ch at beg of previous row, turn.

I.68

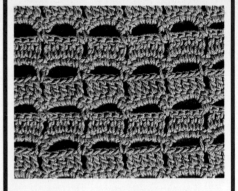

Starting chain: Multiple of 5 sts + 2.

1st row (right side): Work 1sc into 2nd ch from hook, *5ch, skip 4ch, 1sc into next ch; rep from * to end, turn.

2nd row: 1ch, work 1sc into first sc, *5sc into 5ch sp, 1sc into next sc; rep from * to end, turn.

3rd row: 3ch (count as 1dc), skip first sc, work 1dc into each of next 5sc, *1ch, skip 1sc, 1dc into each of next 5sc; rep from * to last sc, 1dc into last sc, turn.

4th row: 1ch, 1sc into first dc, *5ch, 1sc into next ch sp; rep from * to end placing last sc into 3rd of 3ch at beg of previous row, turn.

Rep 2nd to 4th rows.

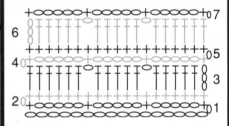

Diagram only: Rep 2nd to 7th rows.

3rd row: 6ch (count as 1dc, 3ch), 1sc into first sc, turn, 1ch, 1sc into sc, 3sc into 3ch sp, [turn, 1ch, 1sc into each of the 4sc] 3 times, 1dc into next tr, *3ch, 1sc into next sc, turn, 1ch, 1sc into sc, 3sc into 3ch sp, [turn, 1ch, 1sc into each of the 4sc] 3 times, 1dc into next tr; rep from * to end placing last dc into 4th of 6ch at beg of previous row, turn.

Rep 2nd and 3rd rows ending with a 2nd row.

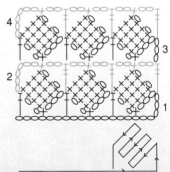

Line shows direction of work for first part of first row.

Abbreviations and Symbols on page 12

I.69

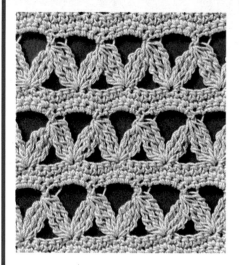

1st row (right side): Work 1sc into 2nd ch from hook, 1sc into each ch to end, turn.

2nd row: 1ch, work 1sc into each sc to end, turn.

3rd row: 5ch (count as 1dtr), skip first 3sc, work 1dtr group into next sc, 5ch, *1 double dtr group, 5ch; rep from * to last 3sc, into same sc as last group work 3dtr until 1 loop of each remains on hook (4 loops on hook), 1dtr into last sc until 5 loops remain on hook, yo and through all 5 loops, turn.

4th row: 1ch, 1sc into top of first group, 5sc into 5ch arch, *1sc into top of next group, 5sc into next 5ch arch; rep from * to last group, 1sc into 5th of 5ch at beg of previous row, turn.

5th row: 1ch, work 1sc into each sc to end, turn.

Rep 2nd to 5th rows.

Starting chain: Multiple of 6 sts + 2.

Special Abbreviations

Dtr group = work 3dtr into next sc until 1 loop of each remains on hook, yo and through all 4 loops on hook.

Double dtr group = work 3dtr into same sc as last group until 1 loop of each remains on hook (4 loops on hook), skip 5sc, into next sc work 3dtr until 1 loop of each remains on hook, yo and through all 7 loops on hook.

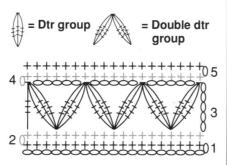

= Dtr group   = Double dtr group

I.70

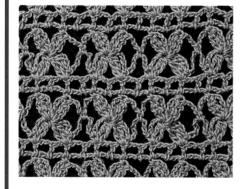

Starting chain: Multiple of 12 sts + 11.

Special Abbreviation

Tr2tog = work 2tr into next st until 1 loop of each remains on hook, yo and through all 3 loops on hook.

1st row (right side): Work 1dc into 8th ch from hook, *2ch, skip 2ch, 1dc into next ch; rep from * to end, turn.

2nd row: 1ch, 1sc into first dc, *9ch, skip 1dc, into next dc work [1sc, 4ch, tr2tog], skip 1dc, into next dc work [tr2tog, 4ch, 1sc]; rep from * to last 2 sps, 9ch, skip 1dc, 1sc into 3rd ch, turn.

3rd row: 10ch (count as ttr, 4ch), 1sc into first 9ch arch, *4ch, into top of next tr2tog work [tr2tog, 4ch, 1 sl st, 4ch, tr2tog], 4ch, 1sc into next 9ch arch; rep from * to end, 4ch, 1ttr into last sc, turn.

4th row: 1ch, 1sc into first ttr, *5ch, 1sc into top of next tr2tog; rep from * to end placing last sc into 6th of 10ch at beg of previous row, turn.

5th row: 5ch (count as 1dc, 2ch), 1dc into next 5ch arch, 2ch, 1dc into next sc, *2ch, 1dc into next 5ch arch, 2ch, 1dc into next sc; rep from * to end, turn.

Rep 2nd to 5th rows.

= Tr2tog

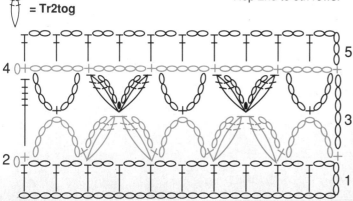

I.71

Starting chain: Multiple of 16 sts + 7.

Special Abbreviation

Bobble = work 4dc into next st until 1 loop of each remains on hook, yo and through all 5 loops on hook.

1st row (right side): Work 1dc into 4th ch from hook, 1dc into each of next 3ch, *4ch, skip 4ch, 1sc into next ch, 3ch, skip 1ch, 1sc into next ch, 4ch, skip 4ch, 1dc into each of next 5ch; rep from * to end, turn.

2nd row: 3ch (count as 1dc), skip first dc, 1dc into each of next 4dc, *2ch, 1sc into next 4ch arch, 1ch, work 7dc into next 3ch arch, 1ch, 1sc into next 4ch arch, 2ch, 1dc into each of next 5dc; rep from * to end placing last dc into top of 3ch at beg of previous row, turn.

3rd row: 3ch, skip first dc, 1dc into each of next 4dc, *1ch, 1 bobble into next dc, [3ch, skip 1dc, 1 bobble into next dc] 3 times, 1ch, 1dc into each of next 5dc; rep from * to end placing last dc into 3rd of 3ch at beg of previous row, turn.

4th row: 3ch, skip first dc, 1dc into each of next 4dc, *2ch, 1sc into next 3ch arch, [3ch, 1sc into next 3ch arch] twice, 2ch, 1dc into each of next 5dc; rep from * to end placing last dc into 3rd of 3ch at beg of previous row, turn.

5th row: 3ch, skip first dc, 1dc into each of next 4dc, *4ch, skip 2ch sp, 1sc into next 3ch arch, 3ch, 1sc into next 3ch arch, 4ch, 1dc into each of next 5dc; rep from * to end placing last dc into 3rd of 3ch at beg of previous row.

Rep 2nd to 5th rows.

= Bobble

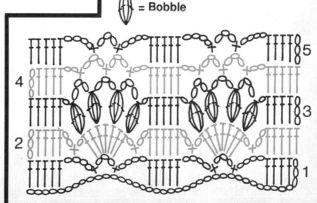

I. All-over Patterns

I.72

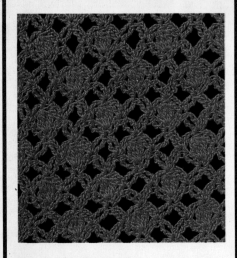

Starting chain: Multiple of 12 sts + 8.

Special Abbreviations

Cluster = 3ch, 1tr worked until 2 loops remain on hook (first leg), 1tr worked until 3 loops remain, yo and through all 3 loops, 3ch, 1sc into same st as last tr (2nd leg).

Bobble on cluster = work first leg of cluster then work 4tr into next sc until 1 loop of each remains on hook (6 loops on hook), work 2nd leg of cluster but bringing yarn through all 7 loops on hook to finish tr, complete 2nd leg as for cluster.

1st row (right side): Work 1sc into 2nd ch from hook, *work first leg of cluster into same ch as last sc, skip 5ch, work 2nd leg of cluster into next ch; rep from * to end, turn.

2nd row: 4ch (count as 1tr), into top of first cluster work [1tr, 3ch, 1sc], *work next cluster placing 2nd leg into top of next cluster; rep from * finishing with 2nd leg worked into top of last cluster, work first leg of cluster, 1tr into last sc until 3 loops remain, yo and through all 3 loops, turn.

3rd row: 1ch, 1sc into first st, *work cluster placing 2nd leg into top of next cluster; rep from * to end **but** working bobble on next and every alt cluster, turn.

4th row: As 2nd row.

5th row: As 3rd row **but** working bobble on first then every alt cluster, turn.

Rep 2nd to 5th rows.

= Cluster

= Bobble on cluster

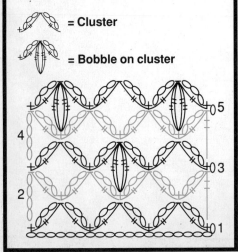

I.73

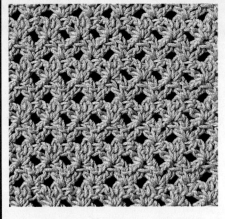

Starting chain: Multiple of 4 sts + 2.

1st row (right side): Work 1sc into 2nd ch from hook, *2ch, into same ch as last sc work 1dc until 2 loops remain on hook, skip 3ch, work 1dc into next ch until 3 loops remain on hook, yo and through all 3 loops, 2ch, 1sc into same ch as last dc, (1 cluster made); rep from * to end, turn.

2nd row: 3ch (count as 1dc), work 1dc into top of first cluster, *2ch, into same cluster as last dc work [1sc, 2ch, 1dc until 2 loops remain on hook], 1dc into top of next cluster until 3 loops remain on hook, yo and through all 3 loops; rep from * to end placing last dc into last sc, turn.

3rd row: 1ch, into first cluster work [1sc, 2ch, 1dc until 2 loops remain on hook], 1dc into top of next cluster until 3 loops remain on hook, yo and through all 3 loops, *2ch, into same cluster as last dc work [1sc, 2ch, 1dc until 2 loops remain on hook], 1dc into next cluster until 3 loops remain on hook, yo and through all 3 loops; rep from * to end, 2ch, 1sc into 3rd of 3ch at beg of previous row, turn.

Rep 2nd and 3rd rows.

I.74

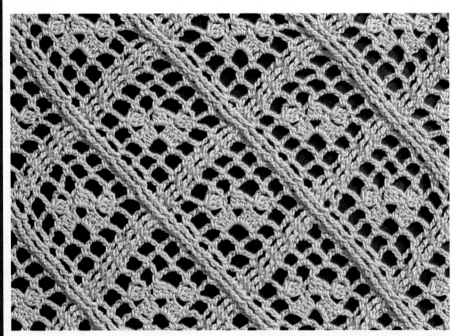

Starting chain: Multiple of 24 sts + 6.

Special Abbreviations

Bobble = work 3dc into next st until 1 loop of each dc remains on hook, yo and through all 4 loops on hook.

Tr/rf (Treble round front) = on a right side row: **working from front of work**, work 1tr inserting hook from right to left under stem of next dc or tr in previous row.

Tr/rb (Treble round back) = on a wrong side row: **working at back** (right side of work), work 1tr inserting hook from right to left under stem of next dc or tr in previous row. (See page 10).

Cross 4tr/rf (Cross 4 treble round front) = skip next 2tr, work 1tr/rf round each of next 2tr, 1ch, work 1tr/rf around each of the 2 skipped tr.

1st row (right side): Work 1sc into 2nd ch from hook, 3ch, skip 1ch, 2dc into next ch, skip 1ch, 1sc into next ch, 5ch, skip 3ch, 1sc into next ch, 4ch, 1 bobble into side of last sc worked, skip 3ch, 1sc into next ch, 2ch, skip 1ch, 1 bobble into next ch, 2ch, skip 1ch, 1sc into next ch, 4ch, 1 bobble into side of last sc worked, skip 3ch, 1sc into next ch, 5ch, skip 3ch, 1sc into next ch, skip 1ch, *into next ch work [2dc, 1ch, 2dc], skip 1ch, 1sc into next ch, 5ch, skip 3ch, 1sc into next ch, 4ch, 1 bobble into side of last sc worked, skip 3ch, 1sc into next ch, 2ch, skip 1ch, 1 bobble into next ch, 2ch, skip 1ch, 1sc into next ch, 4ch, 1 bobble into side of last sc worked, skip 3ch, 1sc into next ch, 5ch, skip 3ch, 1sc into next ch, skip 1ch; rep from * to last 3ch, 2dc into next ch, 3ch, skip 1ch, 1sc into last ch, turn.

2nd row: 6ch (count as 1tr, 2ch), 1sc into next 3ch arch, *3ch, 1tr/rb around each of next 2dc, 1sc into next 5ch arch, 5ch, 1sc into next 4ch arch, 5ch, 1sc into top of next bobble, 5ch, 1sc into next 4ch arch, 5ch, 1sc into next 5ch arch, 1tr/rb around each of next 2dc, 3ch, 1sc into next ch sp; rep from * to last sc placing last sc into last 3ch arch, 2ch, 1tr into last sc, turn.

3rd row: 1ch, 1sc into first tr, 5ch, skip 2ch arch, *1sc into next 3ch arch, 3ch, 1tr/rf around each of next 2tr, 1sc into next 5ch arch, [5ch, 1sc into next 5ch arch] 3 times, 1tr/rf around each of next 2tr, 3ch, 1sc into next 3ch arch, 5ch; rep from * to last 2ch sp, 1sc into 4th of 6ch at beg of previous row, turn.

4th row: 6ch, 1sc into next 5ch arch, *5ch, 1sc into next 3ch arch, 3ch, 1tr/rb around each of next 2tr, 1sc into next 5ch arch, [5ch, 1sc into next 5ch arch] twice, 1tr/rb around each of next 2tr, 3ch, 1sc into next 3ch arch, 5ch, 1sc into next 5ch arch; rep from * to last sc, 2ch, 1tr into last sc, turn.

5th row: 1ch, 1sc into first tr, 5ch, 1sc into next 5ch arch, 5ch, 1sc into next 3ch arch, 3ch, 1tr/rf around each of next 2tr, 1sc into next 5ch arch, 5ch, 1sc into next 5ch arch, 1tr/rf around each of next 2tr, *3ch, 1sc into next 3ch arch, 5ch, [1sc into next 5ch arch, 5ch] twice, 1sc into next 3ch arch, 3ch, 1tr/rf around each of next 2tr, 1sc into next 5ch arch, 5ch, 1sc into next 5ch arch, 1tr/rf around each of next 2tr; rep from * to last 3 arches, 3ch, 1sc into next 3ch arch, 5ch, 1sc into next 5ch arch, 5ch, 1sc into 4th of 6ch at beg of previous row, turn.

6th row: 4ch (count as 1tr), work [1dc, 2ch, 3dc] into first 5ch arch, 1sc into next 5ch arch, 5ch, 1sc into next 3ch arch, 3ch, 1tr/rb around each of next 2tr, 1sc into next 5ch arch, 1tr/rb around each of next 2tr, *3ch, 1sc into next 3ch arch, 5ch, 1sc into next 5ch arch, into next 5ch arch work [3dc, 3ch, 3dc], 1sc into next 5ch arch, 5ch, 1sc into next 3ch arch, 3ch, 1tr/rb around each of next 2tr, 1sc into next 5ch arch, 1tr/rb around each of next 2tr; rep from * to last 3 arches, 3ch, 1sc into next 3ch arch, 5ch, 1sc into next 5ch arch, work [3dc, 2ch, 1dc] into last 5ch arch, 1tr into last sc, turn.

7th row: 1ch, 1sc into first tr, 2ch, 1 bobble into first 2ch sp, 2ch, 1sc into next dc, *4ch, 1 bobble into side of last sc worked, 1sc into next 5ch arch, 5ch, 1sc into next 3ch arch, cross 4tr/rf, 1sc into next 3ch arch, 5ch, 1sc into next 5ch arch, 4ch, 1 bobble into side of last sc worked, skip 2dc, 1sc into next dc, 2ch, 1 bobble into next 3ch arch, 2ch, 1sc into next dc; rep from * to end placing last bobble into last 2ch sp and last sc into 4th of 4ch at beg of previous row, turn.

8th row: 6ch, work 1sc into top of first bobble, *5ch, 1sc into next 4ch arch, 5ch, 1sc into next 5ch arch, 1tr/rb around each of next 2tr, 3ch, 1sc into ch sp, 3ch, 1tr/rb around each of next 2tr, 1sc into next 5ch arch, 5ch, 1sc into next 4ch arch, 5ch, 1sc into top of next bobble; rep from * to last sc, 2ch, 1tr into last sc, turn.

9th row: 1ch, 1sc into first tr, [5ch, 1sc into next 5ch arch] twice, 1tr/rf around each of next 2tr, 3ch, 1sc into next 3ch arch, 5ch, 1sc into next 3ch arch, 3ch, 1tr/rf around each of next 2tr, *1sc into next 5ch arch, [5ch, 1sc into next 5ch arch] 3 times, 1tr/rf around each of next 2tr, 3ch, 1sc into next 3ch arch, 5ch, 1sc into next 3ch arch, 3ch, 1tr/rf around each of next 2tr; rep from * to last 3 arches, [1sc into next 5ch arch, 5ch] twice, 1sc into 4th of 6ch, turn.

10th row: 6ch, 1sc into first 5ch arch, 5ch, 1sc into next 5ch arch, 1tr/rb around each of next 2tr, 3ch, 1sc into next 3ch arch, 5ch, 1sc into next 5ch arch, 5ch, 1sc into next 3ch arch, 3ch, 1tr/rb around each of next 2tr, *1sc into next 5ch arch, [5ch, 1sc into next 5ch arch] twice, 1tr/rb around each of next 2tr, 3ch, 1sc into next 3ch arch, 5ch, 1sc into next 5ch arch, 5ch, 1sc into next 3ch arch, 3ch, 1tr/rb around each of next 2tr; rep from * to last 2 arches, 1sc into next 5ch arch, 5ch, 1sc into last 5ch arch, 2ch, 1tr into last sc, turn.

11th row: 1ch, 1sc into first tr, 5ch, 1sc into next 5ch arch, *1tr/rf around each of next 2tr, 3ch, 1sc into next 3ch arch, 5ch, [1sc into next 5ch arch, 5ch] twice, 1sc into next 3ch arch, 3ch, 1tr/rf around each of next 2tr, 1sc into next 5ch arch, 5ch, 1sc into next 5ch arch; rep from * to end placing last sc into 4th of 6ch, turn.

12th row: 6ch, 1sc into first 5ch arch, *1tr/rb around each of next 2tr, 3ch, 1sc into next 3ch arch, 5ch, 1sc into next 5ch arch, into next 5ch arch work [3dc, 3ch, 3dc], 1sc into next 5ch arch, 5ch, 1sc into next 3ch arch, 3ch, 1tr/rb around each of next 2tr, 1sc into next 5ch arch; rep from * to last sc, 2ch, 1tr into last sc, turn.

13th row: 1ch, 1sc into first tr, 1tr/rf around each of next 2tr, 3ch, 1sc into next 3ch arch, 5ch, 1sc into next 5ch arch, 4ch, 1 bobble into side of last sc worked, skip 2dc, 1sc into next dc, 2ch, 1 bobble into next 3ch arch, 2ch, 1sc into next dc, 4ch, 1 bobble into side of last sc worked, 1sc into next 5ch arch, 5ch, 1sc into next 3ch arch, *cross 4tr/rf, 1sc into next 3ch arch, 5ch, 1sc into next 5ch arch, 4ch, 1 bobble into side of last sc worked, skip 2dc, 1sc into next dc, 2ch, 1 bobble into next 3ch arch, 2ch, 1sc into next dc, 4ch, 1 bobble into side of last sc worked, 1sc into next 5ch arch, 5ch, 1sc into next 3ch arch; rep from * to last 2tr, 3ch, 1tr/rf around each of next 2tr, 1sc into 4th of 6ch, turn.

14th row: 6ch, 1sc into first 3ch arch, 3ch, 2tr into same 3ch arch as last sc, 1sc into next 5ch arch, 5ch, 1sc into next 4ch arch, 5ch, 1sc into top of next bobble, 5ch, 1sc into next 4ch arch, 5ch, 1sc into next 5ch arch, *1tr/rb around each of next 2tr, 3ch, 1sc into next ch sp, 3ch, 1tr/rb around each of next 2tr, 1sc into next 5ch arch, 5ch, 1sc into next 4ch arch, 5ch, 1sc into top of next bobble, 5ch, 1sc into next 4ch arch, 5ch, 1sc into next 5ch arch; rep from * to last 3ch arch, into last 3ch arch work [2tr, 3ch, 1sc], 2ch, 1tr into last sc, turn.

Rep 3rd to 14th rows.

= Tr/rf	= Tr/rb	= Bobble	=Cross 4 tr/rf

= 1sc, 4ch, work 1 bobble into side of sc just worked

I. All-over Patterns

I.75

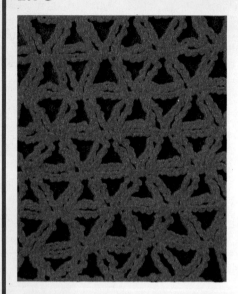

Starting chain: Multiple of 8 sts + 4.

1st row (right side): Work 1sc into 2nd ch from hook, 1sc into next ch, 9ch, 1sc into next ch, 5ch, skip 5ch, 1sc into next ch, *[9ch, 1sc into next ch] twice, 5ch, skip 5ch, 1sc into next ch; rep from * to last 2ch, 9ch, 1sc into each of last 2ch, turn.

2nd row: 7ch (count as 1tr, 3ch), *1sc into next 9ch loop, 1ch, 1sc into next 9ch loop, 5ch; rep from * to end omitting 2ch at end of last rep, 1tr into last sc, turn.

3rd row: 1ch, 1sc into first tr, 3ch, *1sc into next sc, 9ch, 1sc into next ch sp, 9ch, 1sc into next sc, 5ch; rep from * to end omitting 2ch at end of last rep, 1sc into 4th of 7ch at beg of previous row, turn.

4th row: 5ch (count as 1tr, 1ch), *1sc into next 9ch loop, 5ch, 1sc into next 9ch loop, 1ch; rep from * to end, 1tr into last sc, turn.

5th row: 1ch, 1sc into first tr, 1sc into next ch sp, 9ch, 1sc into next sc, 5ch, *1sc into next sc, 9ch, 1sc into next ch sp, 9ch, 1sc into next sc, 5ch; rep from * to last sc, 1sc into last sc, 9ch, 1sc into ch sp, 1sc into 4th of 5ch at beg of previous row, turn.

Rep 2nd to 5th rows ending with a 2nd or 4th row.

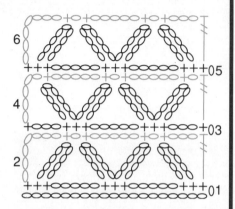

I.76

Starting chain: Multiple of 18 sts + 8.

1st row (right side): Work 1dc into 8th ch from hook, *2ch, skip 2ch, 1dc into next ch; rep from * to end, turn.

2nd row: 5ch (count as 1dc, 2ch), skip first dc, 1dc into next dc, *4ch, 1tr into each of next 4dc, 4ch, 1dc into next dc, 2ch, 1dc into next dc; rep from * to end placing last dc into 3rd turning ch at beg of previous row, turn.

3rd row: 5ch, skip first dc, 1dc into next dc, *4ch, 1sc into each of next 4tr, 4ch, 1dc into next dc, 2ch, 1dc into next dc; rep from * to end placing last dc into 3rd of 5ch at beg of previous row, turn.

4th row: 5ch, skip first dc, 1dc into next dc, *4ch, 1sc into each of next 4sc, 4ch, 1dc into next dc, 2ch, 1dc into next dc; rep from * to end placing last dc into 3rd of 5ch at beg of previous row, turn.

5th row: As 4th row.

6th row: 5ch, skip first dc, 1dc into next dc, *2ch, [1tr into next sc, 2ch] 4 times, 1dc into next dc, 2ch, 1dc into next dc; rep from * to end placing last dc into 3rd of 5ch at beg of previous row, turn.

7th row: 5ch, skip first dc, 1dc into next dc, *2ch, [1dc into next tr, 2ch] 4 times, 1dc into next dc, 2ch, 1dc into next dc; rep from * to end placing last dc into 3rd of 5ch at beg of previous row, turn.

Rep 2nd to 7th rows.

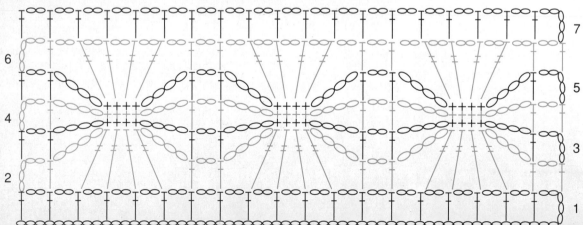

Abbreviations and Symbols on page 12

Filet Charts

Filet crochet is based on a simple network or 'ground' made of double crochet and chain stitches. Patterns are therefore usually presented in the form of squared charts. Designs of all kinds - flowers, geometric patterns, lettering and even whole scenes - can be created by 'filling in' some of the squares or spaces with dc instead of chain.

Like stitch diagrams, charts are read from the bottom to the top, right side rows from right to left and wrong side rows from left to right. Each open square represents an open space whilst a filled-in square represents a 'block' of stitches. Every row starts with three chain (count as 1dc), bringing you to the correct height and balancing the pattern.

The basis of filet crochet is rectangular. Ideally each space or block should be square, but this is hard to achieve because of variations in tension. Small variations to the ratio between height and width can be made by changing the way you hold the yarn or hook. To test your tension first work a swatch based on sample 'b' below. This is worked so that each open square on the chart represents a space formed by two chain and a double crochet. The other edge of the space is formed by the last stitch of the preceeding space or block or by the three chain at the beginning of the row. When a square is filled the two chain space is replaced by two double crochet making a single block of three double crochet. Each additional block therefore adds three double crochet, so two blocks together (with a space either side), appear as seven double crochet, and three blocks, as ten double crochet.

If you cannot adjust the ratio between height and width sufficiently by changing the way you hold the work it may be necessary to change the size of the blocks and spaces. A space could be reduced to 1ch and 1dc, with a 2dc block (sample 'a'), or enlarged to a 3ch and 1dc space with a 4dc block (sample 'c'). The photographs of the samples show the differences between the three variations.

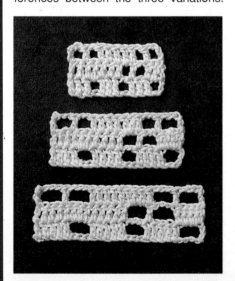

The worked samples in this section have been made following the style of sample

'b', but whatever your tension look at the other methods as there may be times you would wish to use these purely for their decorative effect.

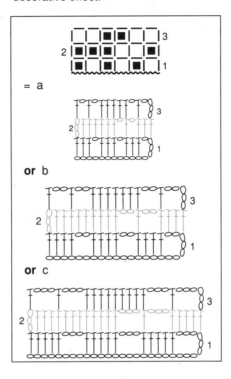

= a

or b

or c

Starting Chain

When working as sample 'b', the number of chain required to start filet crochet is calculated by multiplying the number of squares required by three. Add five chain if the first square to be worked is a space or three chain if the first square to be worked is a block (see diagram b above).

To work samples 'a' or 'c', multiply the number of squares by two or four, adding four or six chain for a space and three chain for a block (see diagrams 'a' and 'c').

Lacets and Bars

Variations on blocks and spaces include 'V' shapes known as lacets, and longer chains known as bars.

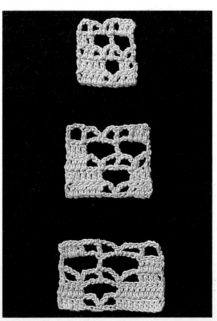

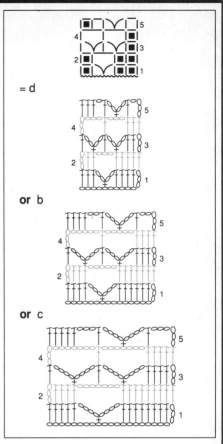

= d

or b

or c

The diagrams above show the stitches and their positioning for each variation.

Increasing and Decreasing

In filet crochet increases are usually made in whole squares rather than stitches. If increases are made at the beginning of rows and decreases at the ends of rows no special techniques are required as the following stitch diagram shows.

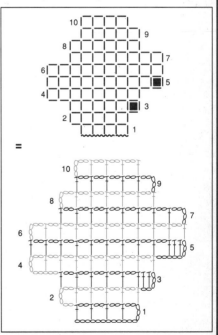

=

When increases are needed at the end of a row or decreases at the beginning of a row, the following techniques should be used.

II. Filet Crochet

To increase a space at the end of a row

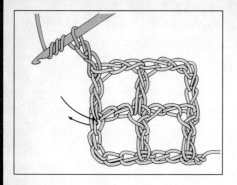

1. Work two chain, then work a double treble into same place as previous double crochet.

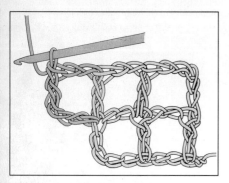

2. The double treble makes the outer edges of the increased space.

To increase a block at the end of a row

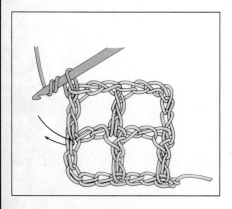

1. Work a treble into same place as previous double crochet.

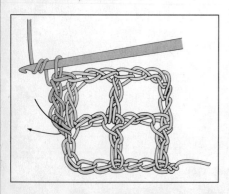

2. Then work [a treble into bottom segment of previous treble] twice.

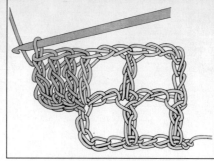

3. Thus making an increased block.

To decrease at the beginning of a row

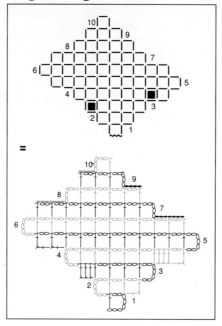

=

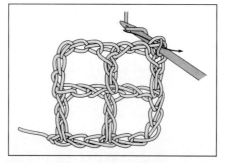

1. Turn work. Slip stitch into top of last double crochet worked, then into each of next two chain (or top of double crochet if last square in previous row is a block) and into top of next double crochet.

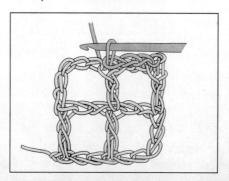

2. Hook is in position to commence row.

Using Filet Patterns

The patterns in this book can be used exactly as they are to produce fabrics with all-over patterns, borders, insertions and motifs. Different effects can be achieved by working the charts downwards or sideways or by repeating or combining designs. Graph paper should be used to plot out any changes.

Key

☐ = Block

▣ = Space

▭ = Bar

⊻ = Lacet

Pressing and Finishing Filet

The feature of Filet which distinguishes it from other styles of crochet is its rectangular appearance. For information on how to press and finish your filet crochet see the general instructions on page 12 but remember, at every stage, to check that all the vertical and horizontal lines of the work are laying at right-angles. After removing the pins and while the work is still quite damp, use your fingertips to gently ease the edges into perfectly straight lines.

Filet crochet is often used for borders, edgings and insertions on items like tablecloths and tray mats. The crochet piece is sewn on to a piece of fabric. Firstly turn under the raw edges to form a hem, and slip-stitch in place. Then whip stitch the crochet piece to the outer fold of the fabric, (see II.26 on page 47).

TIP

Larger items, such as curtains and bedspreads, can easily be made in Filet. Work a small piece of alternate blocks and spaces to ascertain the number of blocks and rows to 10cms or 4 inches. From that you can calculate the number of squares you will need in Filet to cover the area you require and this can then be drawn on to graph paper. Any of the designs given in this section can then be added, either singly or in repeats, or you can even design your own exclusive pattern!

II.1

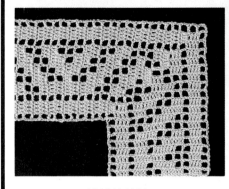

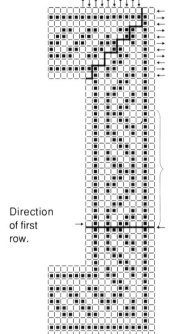

↑↓↑↓↑↓↑↓↑↓↑↓

Rep these 18 rows to adjust length.

Direction of first row. →

Start and finish here.

Turning corners

Following chart, work short rows to corner, then turn piece and work into the side of completed stitches.

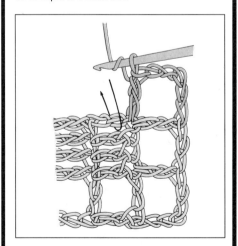

It is important to remember when working a mitered corner that the final row, before changing direction, should be worked towards the the inner edge so that the yarn is in the correct position to turn and work at right angles to the edge.

Join the start and finish together with a neat seam (see page 12).

II.2

Rep these 2 squares

Rep these 2 rows.

II.3

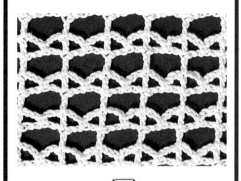

Rep these 2 squares

Rep these 2 rows.

II.4

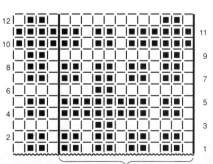

Rep these 12 squares

Rep these 12 rows.

II.5

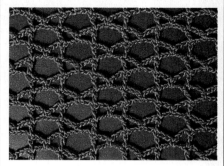

Rep these 4 squares

Rep these 2 rows.

II.6

Rep these 4 squares

Rep these 4 rows.

II.7

Rep these 10 squares

Rep these 10 rows.

41

II. Filet Crochet

II.8

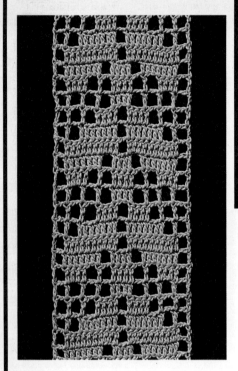

II.11

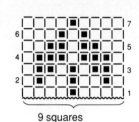

9 squares

Rep 2nd to 7th rows.

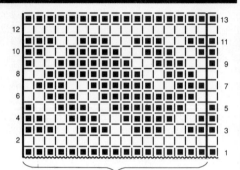

Rep these 17 squares

II.9

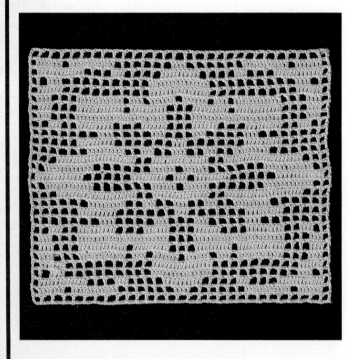

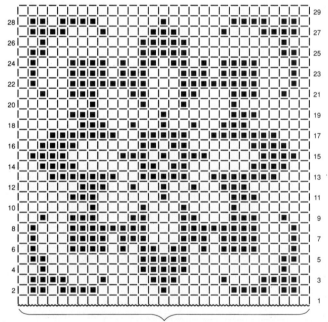

29 squares

II.10

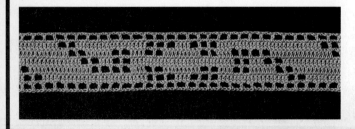

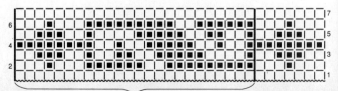

Rep these 24 squares

Key to Filet symbols on page 41. For more information see pages 39-40.

II.12

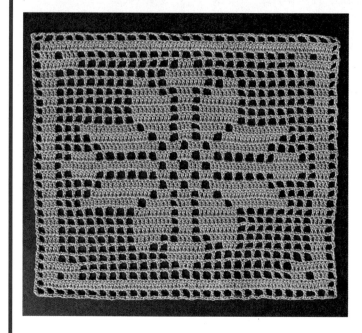

29 squares

II.13

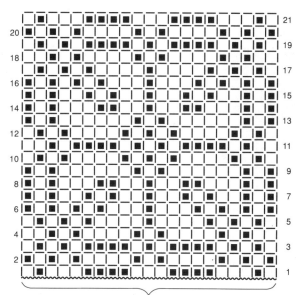

21 squares

II.14

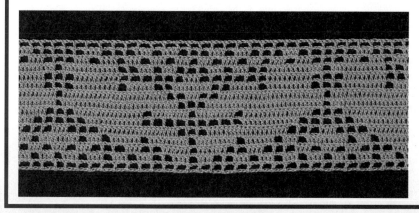

Rep these 22 squares

II. Filet Crochet

II.15

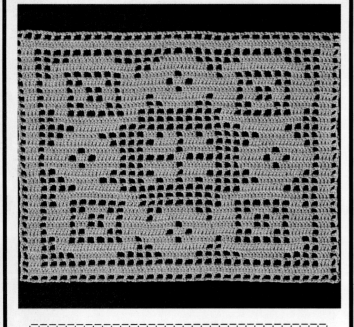

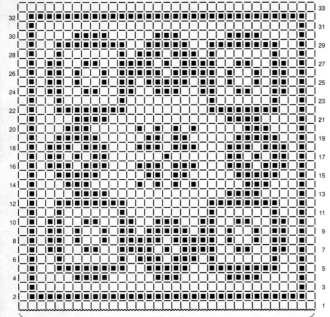

33 squares

II.17

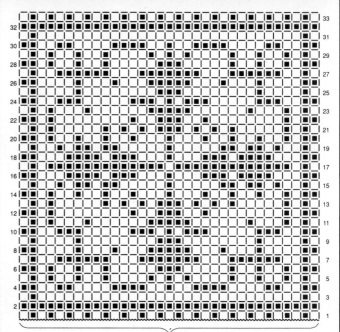

33 squares

II.16

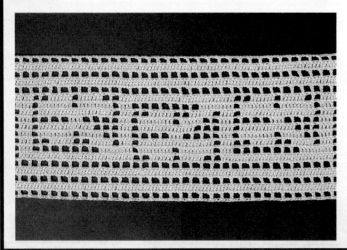

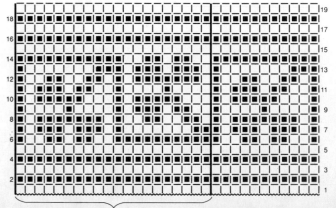

Rep these 20 squares

Key to Filet symbols on page 41. For more information see pages 39-40.

II.18

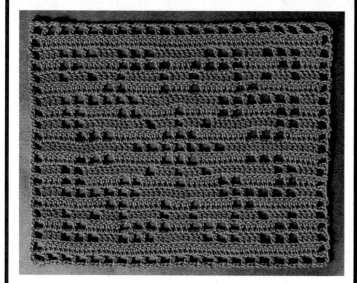

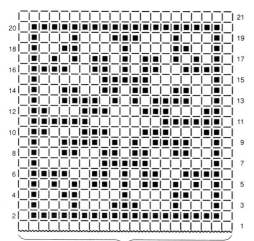

21 squares

II.19

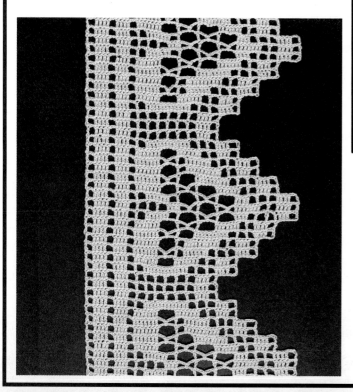

II.20

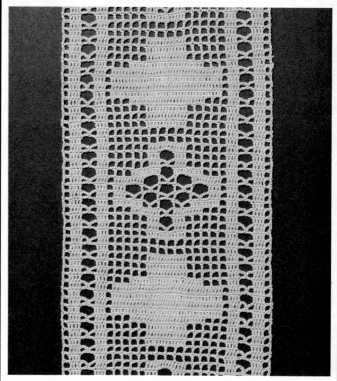

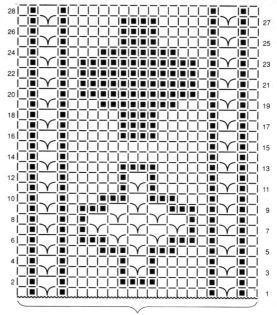

24 squares

Rep these 28 rows.

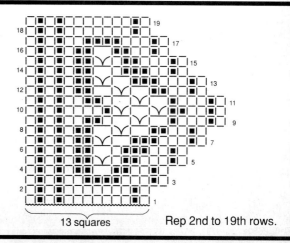

13 squares

Rep 2nd to 19th rows.

II. Filet Crochet

II.21

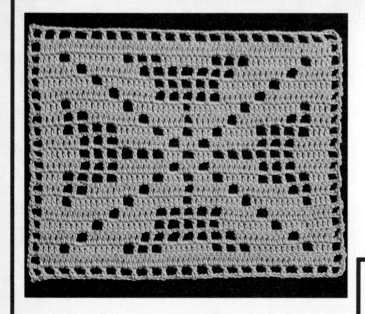

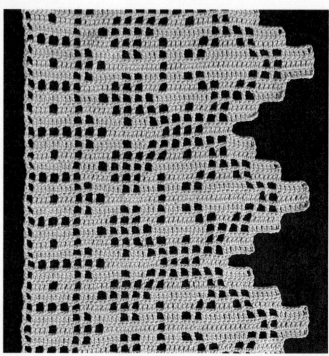

21 squares

II.22

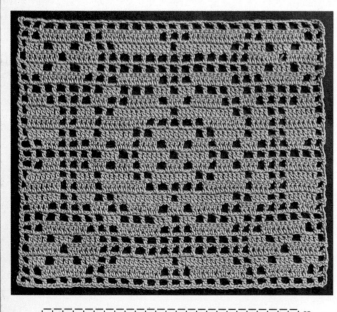

II.23

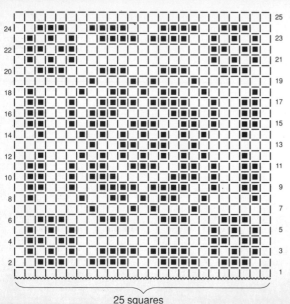

Rep
these
12
rows

25 squares

17 squares

Key to Filet symbols on page 41. For more information see pages 39-40.

II.24

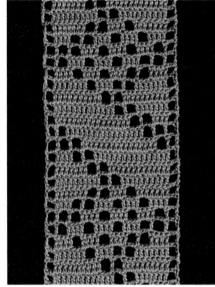

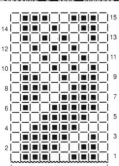

10 squares

Rep 2nd to 15th rows.

II.25

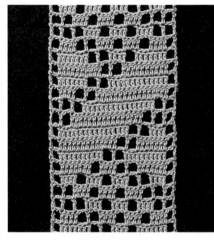

10 squares

Rep 2nd to 15th rows.

II.26

Work first 10 rows of whole diagram, then work the 10 squares of right hand side of 11th row. Continue on right hand side only, finishing with a row as 35th row. Do not turn but make a chain for base of center top (a multiple of 14 + 11 squares). Break yarn, rejoin at X and work left side to match right but finishing on a row as 36th row. Do not turn but continue in pattern across chain already made (taking care that the chain is not twisted), then work 36th row across right side to end. Complete remaining 9 rows.

If preferred, edging may be worked starting and ending at line A with 10 squares, working first row in direction of arrow and making mitered corner at line B (see page 40).

See page 41 for attaching to fabric.

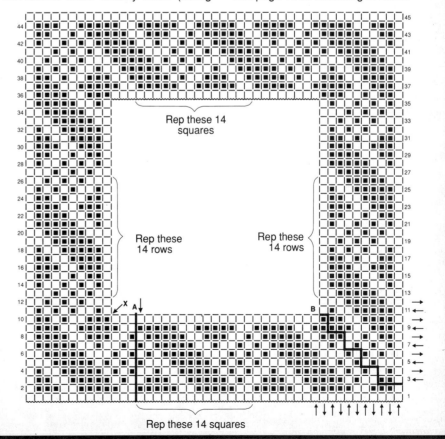

Rep these 14 squares

Rep these 14 rows

Rep these 14 rows

Rep these 14 squares

III. Motifs

Working in Rounds

Most motifs are not worked in rows but are worked from the center outwards in rounds. Unless otherwise indicated do not turn the work between rounds but continue with the same side facing and treat this as the right side of the fabric. The center ring is usually formed by a number of chains joined together with a slip stitch.

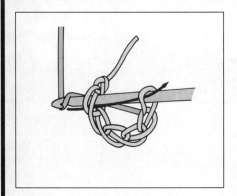

1. Insert the hook back into the first chain made.

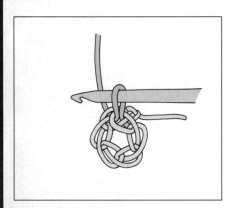

2. Make a slip stitch to join into a ring.

At the beginning of each round one or more chain can be worked to match the height of the following stitches. (This is equivalent to a turning chain).

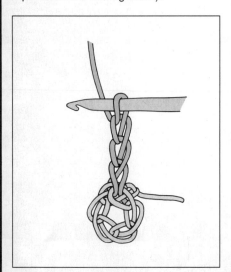

3. When working double crochet three starting chain are required.

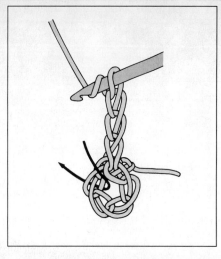

4. The stitches of the first round are worked by inserting the hook into the space at the center of the chain ring. Occasionally the first round is worked into the first chain (see III.9).

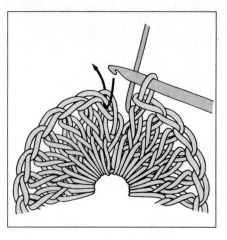

5. When each round is complete insert the hook into the top of the chain or stitch at the beginning of the round and slip stitch together.

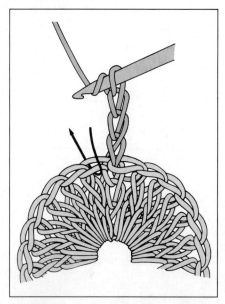

6. When working second and subsequent rounds, unless otherwise stated, insert the hook under the two top loops of the stitches in the previous round.

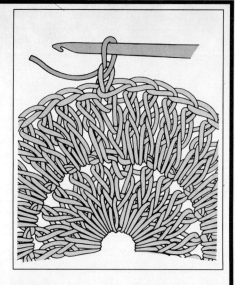

7. After joining final round with a slip stitch, fasten off by making a chain, then cutting the yarn and drawing the end through.

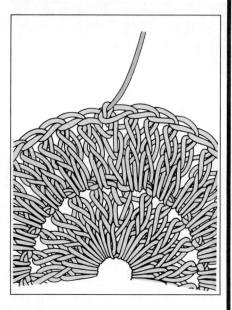

8. Tighten gently to form a knot.

Joining Motifs
Motif Layout

Some motifs such as triangles, squares and hexagons fit together exactly while others leave interesting spaces when joined. These spaces can themselves be a decorative part of an openwork fabric or can be filled in a variety of ways. Smaller spaces can be filled with suitable combinations of chains and stitches and larger ones with small motifs. Most motifs can be joined in more than one way so that any individual motif can form the basis of several different fabric designs. If motifs are worked in different colors they can be laid out to produce patchwork effects. Solid motifs are particularly suitable for working colored patchwork.

Opposite are just a few examples of how motifs of various shapes can be positioned to create interesting patterns.

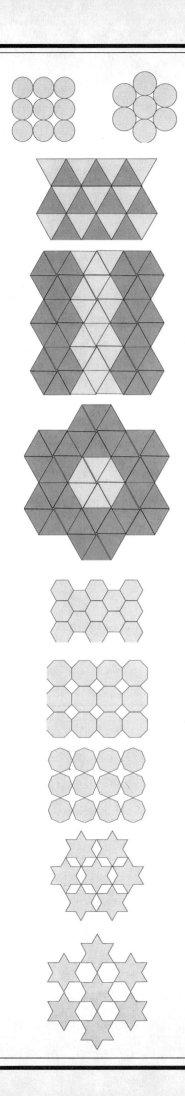

Methods of Joining

Layouts that involve motifs fitting together along straight edges can be joined with a flat seam or by working a row of slip stitch or single crochet through both edges (see page 12). The crochet joins should be done with the right sides of the motifs together so they will be invisible on the right side of the fabric. Alternatively a crochet join can be used as a decorative feature when worked on the right side.

Some designs, particularly those with chain arches or picots round their edges, can be joined to previous motifs during the course of their final rounds. This is done by interrupting the picots or arches at half

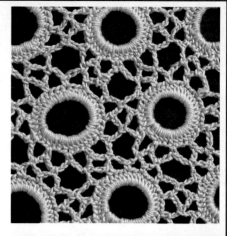

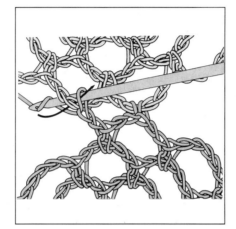

way and slip stitching to the corresponding places on the adjacent motifs.

Spaces between motifs are sometimes filled with small motifs, made and joined in at the same time as they are worked.

Joined Motifs

We show here a few motifs joined in various ways. The possibilities are infinite and only depend on the shape of the motif and your ingenuity!

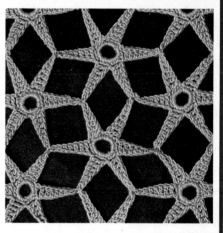

III. Motifs

III.1

Special Abbreviation

Popcorn = work 5dc into next st, drop loop off hook, insert hook into first of these dc, pick up dropped loop and draw through.

Make 5ch, sl st into first ch to form a ring.

1st round: 4ch (count as 1dc, 1ch), work [1dc, 1ch] 11 times into ring, sl st into 3rd of 4ch at beg of round.

2nd round: 6ch (count as 1dc, 3ch), 1 popcorn into next dc, 3ch, [1dc into next dc, 3ch, 1 popcorn into next dc, 3ch] 5 times, sl st into 3rd of 6ch at beg of round.

3rd round: 1ch, 1sc into same st as last sl st, 4ch, 1sc into top of next popcorn, 4ch, [1sc into next dc, 4ch, 1sc into top of next popcorn, 4ch] 5 times, sl st into first sc.

4th round: Sl st into first 4ch arch, 2ch (count as 1hdc), into same arch work [1dc, 1tr, 1dtr, 1tr, 1dc, 1hdc], into each of next 11 4ch arches work [1hdc, 1dc, 1tr, 1dtr, 1tr, 1dc, 1hdc], sl st into 2nd of 2ch at beg of round. Fasten off.

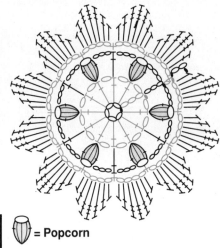

⬆ = Popcorn

III.2

Work as given for III.1 **but** working 1st and 2nd rounds in A and 3rd and 4th rounds in B.

3rd round: 3ch, into top of first bobble work [first bobble as at beg of previous round, 2ch, 1 bobble], 1ch, 1dc into next sc, 1ch, into same sc as last dc work [1dc, 1ch, 1dc], 1ch, *into top of next bobble work [1 bobble, 2ch, 1 bobble], 1ch, 1dc into next sc, 1ch, into same sc as last dc work [1dc, 1ch, 1dc], 1ch; rep from * 4 times more, sl st into top of first bobble.

4th round: 3ch, 1 bobble into first bobble as at beg of 2nd round, 2ch, 1 bobble into next 2ch sp, 2ch, 1 bobble into top of next bobble, 1ch, [1dc into next dc, 1ch] 3 times, *1 bobble into next bobble, 2ch, 1 bobble into next 2ch sp, 2ch, 1 bobble into next bobble, 1ch, [1dc into next dc, 1ch] 3 times; rep from * 4 times more, sl st into top of first bobble.

5th round: 3ch, 1 bobble into first bobble as at beg of 2nd round, 2ch, 1 bobble into next 2ch sp, 3ch, 1 bobble into next 2ch sp, 2ch, 1 bobble into next bobble, 1ch, [1dc into next dc, 1ch] 3 times, *1 bobble into next bobble, 2ch, 1 bobble into next 2ch sp, 3ch, 1 bobble into next 2ch sp, 2ch, 1 bobble into next bobble, 1ch, [1dc into next dc, 1ch] 3 times; rep from * 4 times more, sl st into first bobble. Fasten off.

III.3

Special Abbreviation

Bobble = work 5dc into next sc until 1 loop of each remains on hook, yo and through all 6 loops on hook.

Make 6ch, sl st into first ch to form a ring.

1st round: 1ch, work 12sc into ring, sl st into first sc.

2nd round: 3ch, work 4dc into same st as last sl st until 1 loop of each dc remains on hook, yo and through all 5 loops on hook (1 bobble made at beg of round), *5ch, skip 1sc, 1 bobble into next sc; rep from * 4 times more, 5ch, sl st into top of first bobble. Fasten off.

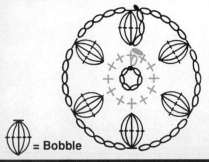

⬇ = Bobble

III.4

Special Abbreviation

Bobble = work 3dc into next st until 1 loop of each remains on hook, yo and through all 4 loops on hook.

Make 12ch, sl st into first ch to form a ring.

1st round: 4ch (count as 1dc, 1ch), into ring work [2dc, 1ch] 11 times, 1dc into ring, sl st into 3rd of 4ch at beg of round.

2nd round: Sl st into first ch sp, 3ch, into same sp work 2dc until 1 loop of each remains on hook, yo and through all 3 loops on hook (1 bobble made at beg of round), 3ch, 1sc into next ch sp, 3ch, [1 bobble into next ch sp, 3ch, 1sc into next ch sp, 3ch] 5 times, sl st into top of first bobble.

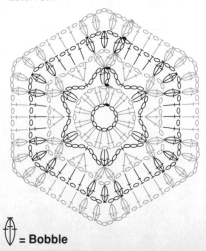

⬇ = Bobble

Abbreviations and Symbols on page 12

III.5

Special Abbreviations

4dc cluster = work 1dc into each of next 4dc until 1 loop of each remains on hook, yo and through all 5 loops on hook.

4dc bobble or 5dc bobble = work 4dc (or 5dc) into next ch until 1 loop of each remains on hook, yo and through all 5 (or 6) loops on hook.

Make 6ch, sl st into first ch to form a ring.

1st round: 3ch (count as 1dc), work 15dc into ring, sl st into 3rd of 3ch at beg of round.

2nd round: 3ch, 1dc into each of next 3dc, [7ch, 1dc into each of next 4dc] 3 times, 7ch, sl st into 3rd of 3ch at beg of round.

3rd round: 3ch, work 1dc into each of next 3dc until 1 loop of each remains on hook, yo and through all 4 loops on hook (1 cluster made at beg of round), 5ch, skip 3ch, into next ch work [1dc, 5ch, 1dc], 5ch, *4dc cluster over next 4dc, 5ch, skip 3ch, into next ch work [1dc, 5ch, 1dc], 5ch; rep from * twice more, sl st into top of first cluster.

4th round: 1ch, *1sc into top of cluster, 1sc into each of next 5ch, 1sc into next dc, 2ch, 4dc bobble into next ch, 5ch, skip 1ch, 5dc bobble into next ch, 5ch, skip 1ch, 4dc bobble into next ch, 2ch, 1sc into next dc, 1sc into each of next 5ch; rep from * 3 times more, sl st into first sc. Fasten off.

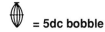 = 4dc cluster

= 4dc bobble   = 5dc bobble

III.6

Special Abbreviations

Popcorn = work 5tr into next ch, drop loop from hook, insert hook from the front into first of these tr, pick up dropped loop and draw through, 1ch to secure.

Picot = make 5ch, sl st into top of dc just worked.

Make 6ch, sl st into first ch to form a ring.

1st round: 6ch (count as 1dc, 3ch), into ring work [1dc, 3ch] 11 times, sl st into 3rd of 6ch at beg of round.

2nd round: 1 sl st into each of first 2ch of first arch, 4ch (count as 1tr), work 4tr into same ch as last sl st, drop loop from hook, insert hook from the front into 4th of 4ch, pick up dropped loop and draw through, 1ch to secure (popcorn made at beg of round), 5ch, 1sc into next 3ch arch, [5ch, skip 1ch of next 3ch arch, 1 popcorn into next ch, 5ch, 1sc into next 3ch arch] 5 times, 5ch, sl st into top of first popcorn.

3rd round: 4ch, into top of first popcorn work [3tr, 5ch, 4tr], 3ch, 1dc into next sc, 1 picot, 3ch, 1sc into top of next popcorn, 3ch, 1dc into next sc, 1 picot, 3ch, *into top of next popcorn work [4tr, 5ch, 4tr], 3ch, 1dc into next sc, 1 picot, 3ch, 1sc into top of next popcorn, 3ch, 1dc into next sc, 1 picot, 3ch; rep from * once more, sl st into 4th of 4ch at beg of round. Fasten off.

= Popcorn

III.7

Special Abbreviations

Popcorn = work 5hdc into next sc, drop loop from hook, insert hook from the front into top of first of these hdc, pick up dropped loop and draw through, 1ch to secure popcorn.

Picot = make 3ch, work 1sc into first of these ch.

Make 10ch, sl st into first ch to form a ring.

1st round: 1ch, work 16sc into ring, sl st into first sc.

2nd round: 2ch, work 4hdc into first sc, drop loop from hook, insert hook from the front into 2nd of 2ch, pick up dropped loop and draw through, 1ch to secure (1 popcorn made at beg of round), 2ch, 1 picot, 2ch, [skip 1sc, 1 popcorn into next sc, 2ch, 1 picot, 2ch] 7 times, sl st into top of first popcorn.

3rd round: 1ch, 1sc into same st as last sl st, [9ch, 1sc into top of next popcorn] 7 times, 4ch, 1dtr into first sc.

4th round: Sl st into arch just formed, 3ch (count as 1dc), work 4dc into same arch as last sl st, 4ch, 1sc into next 9ch arch, 4ch, *work [5dc, 5ch, 5dc] into next 9ch arch, 4ch, 1sc into next 9ch arch, 4ch; rep from * twice more, 5dc into same arch as first 5dc, 5ch, sl st into 3rd of 3ch at beg of round.

5th round: 7ch (count as 1dc, 4ch), *1sc into next 4ch arch, 6ch, 1sc into next 4ch arch, 4ch, work [5dc, 3ch, 5dc] into next 5ch arch, 4ch; rep from * 3 times more omitting 1dc and 4ch at end of last rep, sl st into 3rd of 7ch at beg of round. Fasten off.

= Popcorn    = Picot

III. Motifs

III.8

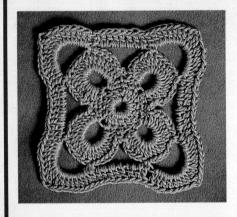

Make 6ch, sl st into first ch to form a ring.

1st round: 3ch (count as 1dc), work 15dc into ring, sl st into 3rd of 3ch at beg of round.

2nd round: 1ch, 1sc into same st as last sl st, 1sc into next dc, *[1sc, 7ch, 1sc] into next dc, 1sc into each of next 3dc; rep from * 3 times more omitting 2sc at end of last rep, sl st into first sc.

3rd round: 1ch, 1sc into same st as last sl st, *into next 7ch arch work [2hdc, 17dc, 2hdc] (1 shell made), skip 2sc, 1sc into next sc; rep from * 3 times more omitting 1sc at end of last rep, sl st into first sc.

4th round: Sl st into each of first 2hdc and 6dc of first shell, 1ch, 1sc into same st as last sl st, 9ch, skip 5dc, 1sc into next dc, *7ch, skip first 2hdc and 5dc on next shell, 1sc into next dc, 9ch, skip 5dc, 1sc into next dc; rep from * twice more, 7ch, sl st into first sc.

5th round: 3ch, *into next 9ch arch work [8dc, 1tr, 8dc], 1dc into next sc, 7dc into next 7ch sp, 1dc into next sc; rep from * 3

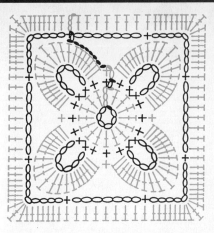

times more omitting 1dc at end of last rep, sl st into 3rd of 3ch at beg of round. Fasten off.

III.9

Special Abbreviation

Cluster = work 2dtr into next arch until 1 loop of each remains on hook, yo and through all 3 loops on hook.

1st round: Make 5ch, work 19tr into first ch, sl st into top of 5ch.

2nd round: 8ch (count as 1dtr, 3ch), [1dtr into next tr, 3ch] 19 times, sl st into 5th of 8ch at beg of round. 20 sps.

3rd round: Sl st into first arch, 5ch (count as 1dtr), work 1dtr into same arch as sl st, 6ch, [1 cluster into next arch, 6ch] 19 times, sl st into top of first dtr.

4th round: Work 1 sl st into each of first 3ch of first arch, 1ch, 1sc into same arch as sl sts, [8ch, 1sc into next 6ch arch] 19 times, 4ch, 1tr into first sc.

5th round: 1ch, 1sc into arch just formed, 9ch, [1sc into next 8ch arch, 9ch] 19 times, sl st into first sc. Fasten off.

↟↟↟ = Cluster

III.10

Special Abbreviation

Bobble = work 3dtr into ch until 1 loop of each remains on hook, yo and through all 4 loops on hook.

1st round: Make 6ch, work 2dtr into first ch until 1 loop of each remains on hook, yo and through all 3 loops on hook (bobble made at beg of round), into same ch work [5ch, 1 bobble] 7 times, 2ch, 1dc into top of first bobble.

2nd round: 1ch, work 1sc into arch just formed, 6ch, [1sc into next 5ch arch, 6ch] 7 times, sl st into first sc.

3rd round: Sl st into first 6ch arch, 3ch (count as 1dc), work 5dc into same arch, 3ch, [6dc into next 6ch arch, 3ch] 7 times, sl st into 3rd of 3ch at beg of round. Fasten off.

⬥ = Bobble

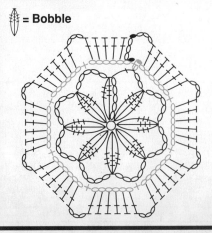

Abbreviations and Symbols on page 12

III.11

Make 10ch, sl st into first ch to form a ring.

1st round: 3ch (count as 1dc), work 23dc into ring, sl st into 3rd of 3ch at beg of round.

2nd round: 3ch (count as 1dc), 1dc into next dc, 2dc into next dc, [1dc into each of next 2dc, 2dc into next dc] 7 times, sl st into 3rd of 3ch at beg of round.

3rd round: 3ch, 2dc into next dc, 2ch, [1dc into each of next 3dc, 2dc into next dc, 2ch] 7 times, 1dc into each of last 2dc, sl st into 3rd of 3ch at beg of round.

4th round: 3ch, 1dc into each of next 2dc, 2ch, 1dc into next 2ch sp, 2ch, [1dc into each of next 5dc, 2ch, 1dc into next 2ch sp, 2ch] 7 times, 1dc into each of last 2dc, sl st into 3rd of 3ch at beg of round.

5th round: 3ch, 1dc into next dc, 5ch, skip 1dc, 1dc into next dc, [5ch, skip 1dc, 1dc into each of next 3dc, 5ch, skip 1dc, 1dc into next dc] 7 times, 5ch, skip 1dc, 1dc into last dc, sl st into 3rd of 3ch at beg of round.

III.12

Make 12ch, sl st into first ch to form a ring.

1st round: 1ch, work 24sc into ring, sl st into first sc.

2nd round: 12ch, skip next sc, 1sc into next sc, turn, *3ch (count as 1dc), 1dc into each of first 7ch of arch, turn, 3ch, skip first dc, 1dc into each of next 6dc, 1dc into top of 3ch**, (first block made). ★Skip next sc on ring, work 1tr into next sc, 8ch, skip 1sc, 1sc into next sc, turn and work from * to ** for next block. Rep from ★ 4 times more, sl st into 4th of 12ch at beg of round.

3rd round: Sl st to top of 3ch at corner of first block, 1ch, 1sc into top of 3ch, 13ch, [1sc into 3rd of 3ch at top of next block, 13ch] 5 times, sl st into first sc.

6th round: 11ch (count as 1dc, 8ch), skip next dc, 1dc into next dc, [8ch, skip 1dc, 1dc into next dc] 14 times, 8ch, sl st into 3rd of 11ch at beg of round. Fasten off.

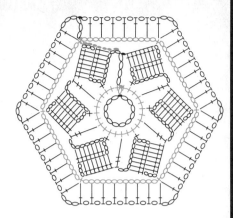

4th round: 6ch (count as 1dc, 3ch), 1dc into same st as last sl st, [1ch, skip 1ch, 1dc into next ch] 6 times, 1ch, *into next sc work [1dc, 3ch, 1dc], [1ch, skip 1ch, 1dc into next ch] 6 times, 1ch; rep from * 4 times more, sl st into 3rd of 6ch. Fasten off.

III.13

Make 9ch, sl st into first ch to form a ring.

1st round: 1ch, work 18sc into ring, sl st into first sc.

2nd round: 9ch, work 1sc into 4th ch from hook, 1hdc into each of next 2ch, 1dc into each of next 3ch, skip first 3sc on ring, sl st into next sc, *9ch, work 1sc into 4th ch from hook, 1hdc into each of next 2ch, 1dc into each of next 3ch, skip next 2sc on ring, sl st into next sc; rep from *4 times more placing last sl st into same st as sl st of previous round. Fasten off.

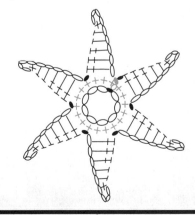

53

III. Motifs

III.14

Special Abbreviation

Cluster = work 1tr into each of next 5tr until 1 loop of each remains on hook, yo and through all 6 loops on hook.

Make 8ch, sl st into first ch to form a ring.

1st round: 9ch (count as 1tr, 5ch), into ring work [1tr, 5ch] 7 times, sl st into 4th of 9ch at beg of round.

2nd round: Sl st into first 5ch arch, 4ch (count as 1tr), work 6tr into same arch, work 7tr into each of next 7 arches, sl st into 4th of 4ch at beg of round.

3rd round: 4ch (count as 1tr), work 1tr into each of next 6tr, 5ch, [1tr into each of next 7tr, 5ch] 7 times, sl st into 4th of 4ch at beg of round.

4th round: Sl st into next tr, 4ch, 1tr into each of next 4tr until 1 loop of each remains on hook, yo and through all 5 loops on hook (1 cluster made at beg of round), 6ch, 1sc into next 5ch arch, [6ch, skip 1tr, work 1 cluster across next 5tr, 6ch, 1sc into next 5ch arch] 7 times, 3ch, 1dc into top of first cluster.

5th round: 1ch, 1sc into arch just formed, [8ch, 1sc into next 6ch arch] 15 times, 4ch, 1tr into first sc.

6th round: 1ch, 1sc into arch just formed, 9ch, [1sc into next 8ch arch, 9ch] 15 times, sl st into first sc. Fasten off.

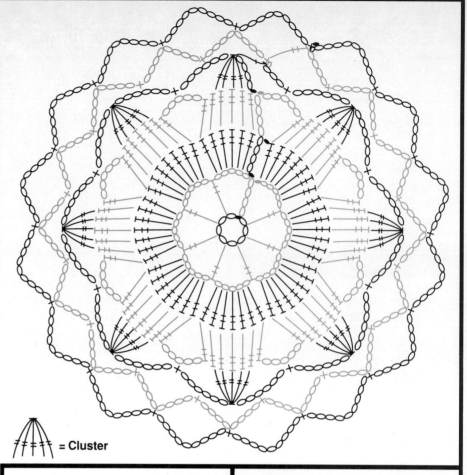

 = Cluster

Make 6ch, sl st into first ch to form a ring.

1st round: 3ch (count as 1dc), work 15dc into ring, sl st into 3rd of 3ch at beg of round.

2nd round: 5ch (count as 1dc, 2ch), 1dc into same st as last sl st, *1ch, skip 1dc, into next dc work [1dc, 2ch, 1dc]; rep from * 6 times more, 1ch, sl st into 3rd of 5ch at beg of round.

3rd round: Sl st into first 2ch sp, 3ch (count as 1dc), into same sp work [1dc, 2ch, 2dc], *1ch, into next 2ch sp work [2dc, 2ch, 2dc]; rep from * 6 times more, 1ch, sl st into 3rd of 3ch at beg of round.

4th round: Sl st into next dc and first 2ch sp, 3ch, work 6dc into same sp as last sl st, 1sc into next ch sp, [7dc into next 2ch sp, 1sc into next ch sp] 7 times, sl st into 3rd of 3ch at beg of round. Fasten off.

III.16

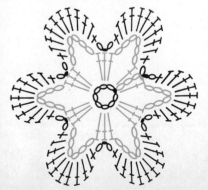

Make 8ch, sl st into first ch to form a ring.

1st round: 3ch (count as 1dc), into ring work 1dc, [6ch, 3dc] 5 times, 6ch, 1dc, sl st into 3rd of 3ch at beg of round.

2nd round: *1ch, into next 6ch arch work [1sc, 1hdc, 7dc, 1hdc, 1sc], 1ch, skip 1dc, 1 sl st into next dc; rep from * 5 times more placing last sl st into 3rd of 3ch at beg of previous round. Fasten off.

III.15

Abbreviations and Symbols on page 12

III.17

Make 8ch, sl st into first ch to form a ring.

1st round: 3ch (count as 1dc), work 19dc into ring, sl st into 3rd of 3ch at beg of round.

2nd round: [11ch, skip next dc, sl st into next dc] 9 times, 6ch, 1ttr into sl st of previous round.

3rd round: Sl st into loop just formed, 3ch, into same loop work [2dc, 3ch, 3dc], work [3dc, 3ch, 3dc] into each of next 9 loops, sl st into 3rd of 3ch at beg of round. Fasten off.

Note: After working 3rd round it may be necessary to ease the shells of [3dc, 3ch, 3dc] to center of loop formed in previous round.

III.18

Work as given for III.17 **but** working 1 round each in colors A, B and C.

III.19

Special Abbreviations

Petal = 1ch, 1tr into next sc, 2ch, work 1tr into stem of last tr two thirds of the way down, 2ch, into stem of last tr (two thirds of the way down as before) work [1dc, 2ch] twice, work 1dc two thirds of the way down stem of first tr, 1ch, 1sc into next dc.

3dc bobble = work 3dc into next sc until 1 loop of each remains on hook, yo and through all 4 loops on hook.

Make 8ch, sl st into first ch to form a ring.

1st round: 1ch, work 16sc into ring, sl st into first sc.

2nd round: 3ch, work 2dc into same st as last sl st until 1 loop of each dc remains on hook, yo and through all 3 loops, (1 bobble made at beg of round), [3ch, skip next sc, 1 bobble into next sc] 7 times, 3ch, sl st into 3rd of 3ch at beg of round.

3rd round: 6ch (count as 1dc, 3ch), 1sc into first 3ch arch, 3ch, [1dc into next bobble, 3ch, 1sc into next 3ch arch, 3ch] 7 times, sl st into 3rd of 6ch at beg of round.

4th round: 1ch, work 1sc into same st as last sl st, work 8 petals omitting sc at end of last petal, sl st into first sc. Fasten off.

 = Petal 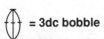 = 3dc bobble

III.20

Special Abbreviations

Tr2tog = work 2tr into ring until 1 loop of each remains on hook, yo and through all 3 loops on hook.

Cluster = work 3dc into sp until 1 loop of each remains on hook, yo and through all 4 loops on hook.

Make 10ch, sl st into first ch to form a ring.

1st round: 4ch, 1tr into ring, 2ch, into ring work [tr2tog, 2ch] 11 times, sl st into first tr.

2nd round: Sl st into 2ch sp, 3ch, into same 2ch sp as sl st, work 2dc until 1 loop of each remains on hook, yo and through all 3 loops on hook (first cluster made), 3ch, [1 cluster into next 2ch sp, 3ch] 11 times, sl st into top of first cluster.

3rd round: 5ch (count as 1hdc, 3ch), skip first 3ch arch, into next 3ch arch work [1 cluster, 2ch, 1 cluster, 4ch, 1 cluster, 2ch, 1 cluster], 3ch, *skip next 3ch arch, 1hdc into top of next cluster, 3ch, skip next 3ch arch, into next 3ch arch work [1 cluster, 2ch, 1 cluster, 4ch, 1 cluster, 2ch, 1 cluster], 3ch; rep from * twice more, sl st into 2nd of 5ch at beg of round.

4th round: 1ch, work 1sc into same st as last sl st, *3sc into next 3ch sp, 1sc into top of next cluster, 2sc into next 2ch sp, 1sc into next cluster, 5sc into next 4ch arch, 1sc into next cluster, 2sc into next 2ch sp, 1sc into next cluster, 3sc into next 3ch sp, 1sc into next hdc; rep from * 3 times more omitting 1sc at end of last rep, sl st into first sc. Fasten off.

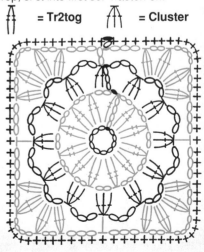 = Tr2tog = Cluster

III. Motifs

III.21

III.22

III.24

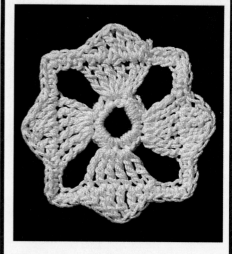

III.21

Special Abbreviations

Bobble = work 3dc into next st until 1 loop of each remains on hook, yo and through all 4 loops on hook.

Picot = make 3ch, sl st into first of these ch.

1st round: Make 2ch, work 12sc into first ch, sl st into first sc.

2nd round: 3ch (count as 1dc), skip first sc, 1dc into next sc, 3ch, [1dc into each of next 2sc, 3ch] 5 times, sl st into 3rd of 3ch at beg of round.

3rd round: Sl st into next dc and 3ch sp, 3ch (count as 1dc), into same 3ch sp work [2dc until 1 loop of each remains on hook, yo and through all 3 loops on hook (bobble made at beg of round), 3ch, 1 bobble], 7ch, *into next 3ch sp work [1 bobble, 3ch, 1 bobble], 7 ch; rep from * 4 times more, sl st into top of first bobble.

4th round: Work 2 sl sts into first 3ch arch, 1ch, 1sc into same arch, *into next 7ch arch work [6dc, 1 picot, 6dc], 1sc into next 3ch arch; rep from * 5 times more omitting sc at end of last rep, sl st into first sc. Fasten off.

⊓ = Bobble

⊖ = Picot

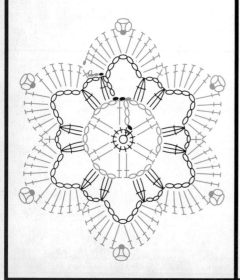

III.22

Work as given for III.21 **but** working 1st and 2nd rounds in A, 3rd round in B and 4th round in C.

III.23

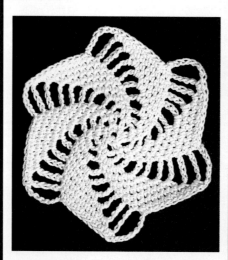

Note: This motif is worked as a continuous spiral, the size can therefore be increased or decreased as required.

1st round: Make 2ch, work 6sc into 2nd ch from hook, sl st into first sc.

Continue in a spiral as follows:
1ch, work 1sc into same st as last sl st, 3ch, [1sc into next sc, 3ch] 5 times, [1sc into next sc, 1sc into next sp, 3ch] 6 times, [skip 1sc, 1sc into next sc, 2sc into next sp, 3ch] 6 times, [skip 1sc, 1sc into each of next 2sc, 2sc into next sp, 4ch] 6 times, [skip 1sc, 1sc into each of next 3sc, 2sc into next 4ch sp, 4ch] 6 times, [skip 1sc, 1sc into each of next 4sc, 2sc into next 4ch sp, 5ch] 6 times, [skip 1sc, 1sc into each of next 5sc, 2sc into next 5ch sp, 5ch] 6 times, [skip 1sc, 1sc into each of next 6sc, 2sc into next 5ch sp, 6ch] 6 times, [skip 1sc, 1sc into each of next 7sc, 2sc into next 6ch sp, 6ch] 6 times, [skip 1sc, 1sc into each of next 8sc, 2sc into next 6ch sp, 7ch] 6 times, skip 1sc, sl st into next sc. Fasten off.

III.24

Make 8ch, sl st into first ch to form a ring.

1st round: 1ch, work 16sc into ring, sl st into first sc.

2nd round: 4ch (count as 1tr), work 2tr into first sc, 3tr into next sc, 5ch, [skip 2sc, 3tr into each of next 2sc, 5ch] 3 times, sl st into 4th of 4ch at beg of round.

3rd round: 1ch, 1sc into same st as last sl st, *[1hdc, 1dc] into next tr, 2tr into each of next 2tr, [1dc, 1hdc] into next tr, 1sc into next tr, 1sc into each of next 2ch, 3sc into next ch, 1sc into each of next 2ch, 1sc into next tr; rep from * 3 times more omitting 1sc at end of last rep, sl st into first sc. Fasten off.

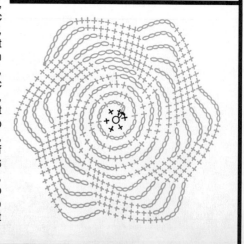

Abbreviations and Symbols on page 12

III.25

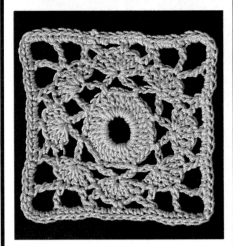

Special Abbreviation

Dc2tog = work 1dc into next dc until 2 loops remain on hook, skip 2dc, work 1dc into next dc until 3 loops remain on hook, yo and through all 3 loops on hook.

Make 10ch, sl st into first ch to form a ring.

1st round: 3ch (count as 1dc), work 31dc into ring, sl st into 3rd of 3ch at beg of round.

2nd round: [7ch, skip 3dc, sl st into next dc] 7 times, 3ch, 1tr into same st as last sl st of previous round.

3rd round: 3ch, work 6dc into top of tr, [7dc into 4th ch of next 7ch arch] 7 times, sl st into 3rd of 3ch at beg of round.

4th round: Sl st into next dc, 6ch (count as 1dc, 3ch), *skip 1dc, into next dc work [1tr, 5ch, 1tr], 3ch, skip 1dc, dc2tog, 3ch, skip 1dc, 1sc into next dc, 3ch, skip 1dc, dc2tog, 3ch; rep from * 3 times more omitting 1dc2tog and 3ch at end of last rep, skip 1dc, 1dc into next dc, sl st into 3rd of 6ch at beg of round.

5th round: 1ch, 1sc into same st as last sl st, *3sc into next 3ch sp, 1sc into next tr, 6sc into 5ch arch, 1sc into next tr, 3sc into next 3ch sp, 1sc into top of next dc2tog, 3sc into next 3ch sp, 1sc into next sc, 3sc into next 3ch sp, 1sc into top of next dc2tog; rep from * 3 times more omitting 1sc at end of last rep, sl st into first sc. Fasten off.

 = Dc2tog

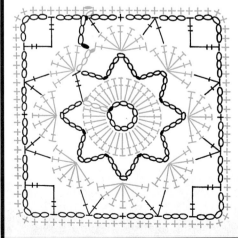

III.26

Work as given for III.25 **but** working 1 round in each of colors A, B and C, then work 4th and 5th rounds in A.

III.27

Special Abbreviation

3-Picot Cluster = work 4ch, sl st into first ch, [3ch, sl st into same ch as first sl st] twice.

Make 6ch, sl st into first ch to form a ring.

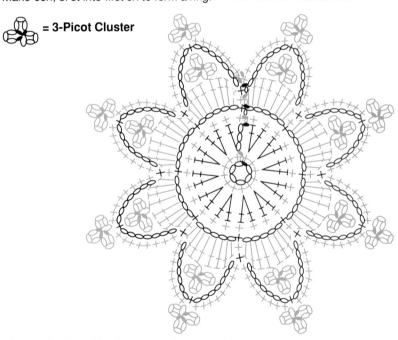 = 3-Picot Cluster

1st round: 1ch, work 12sc into ring, sl st into first sc.

2nd round: 3ch (count as 1dc), 1dc into same st as last sl st, work 2dc into each of next 11sc, sl st into 3rd of 3ch at beg of round.

3rd round: 1ch, 1sc into same st as last sl st, 1sc into each of next 23dc, sl st into first sc.

4th round: 1ch, 1sc into same sc as last sl st, 5ch, skip 2sc, [1sc into next sc, 5ch, skip 2sc] 7 times, sl st into first sc.

5th round: 1ch, 1sc into same st as last sl st, *into next 5ch arch work [1hdc, 3dc, 3-picot cluster, 3dc, 1hdc], 1sc into next sc; rep from * 7 times more omitting 1sc at end of last rep, sl st into first sc.

6th round: 1ch, 1sc into same st as last sl st, *7ch, 1sc into center picot of 3-picot cluster, 7ch, 1sc into next sc; rep from * 7 times more omitting 1sc at end of last rep, sl st into first sc.

7th round: Sl st into first 7ch arch, 1ch, [work 8sc into next 7ch arch, 3-picot cluster, 8sc into same 7ch arch] 8 times, sl st into first sc. Fasten off.

III.28

Work as given for III.27 **but** working 1st, 2nd and 3rd rounds in A, 4th and 5th rounds in B and 6th and 7th rounds in C.

III. Motifs

III.29

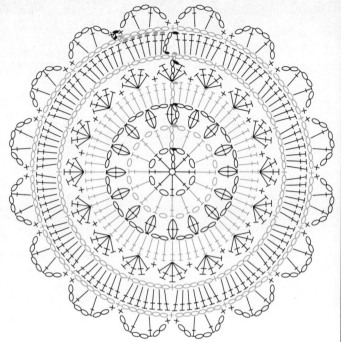

Special Abbreviations

Bobble = work 3dc into next st until 1 loop of each remains on hook, yo and through all 4 loops on hook.

Fan = into next dc work [1hdc, 3dc, 1hdc].

1st round: Make 5ch, work [1dc, 1ch] 7 times into first ch, sl st into 4th of 5ch.

2nd round: 4ch (count as 1dc, 1ch), work 1dc into first ch sp, 1ch, [1dc into next dc, 1ch, 1dc into next ch sp, 1ch] 7 times, sl st into 3rd of 4ch at beg of round.

3rd round: 3ch (count as 1dc), work 2dc into same st as last sl st until 1 loop of each remains on hook, yo and through all 3 loops on hook (1 bobble made at beg of round), 2ch, [1 bobble into next dc, 2ch] 15 times, sl st into top of first bobble.

4th round: 3ch, work 3dc into first 2ch sp, [1dc into next bobble, 3dc into next 2ch sp] 15 times, sl st into 3rd of 3ch at beg of round.

5th round: 3ch, work [1dc, 1hdc] into same st as last sl st, skip 1dc, 1sc into next dc, [skip 1dc, 1 fan into next dc, skip 1dc, 1sc into next dc] 15 times, skip last dc, work [1hdc, 1dc] into same st as sl st at end of previous round, sl st into 3rd of 3ch at beg of round.

6th round: 1ch, 1sc into same st as last sl st, 5ch, [1sc into center dc of next fan, 5ch] 15 times, sl st into first sc.

7th round: Sl st into first 5ch arch, 3ch, work 6dc into same arch as sl st, work 7dc into each of next 15 5ch arches, sl st into 3rd of 3ch at beg of round.

8th round: Sl st into each of first 6dc, 1ch, 1sc between last dc worked into and next dc, 6ch, [skip 7dc, 1sc between last dc skipped and next dc, 6ch] 14 times, skip 7dc, 1sc between last dc skipped and 3ch at beg of previous round, 6ch, sl st into first sc.

9th round: Sl st into first 6ch arch, 1ch, into each of next 16 6ch arches work [1sc, 2ch, 1dc, 2ch, 1dc, 2ch, 1sc], sl st into first sc. Fasten off.

 = Bobble   = Fan

III.30

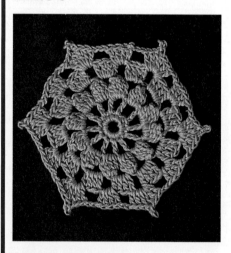

Special Abbreviations

Popcorn = work 5dc into next st, drop loop from hook, insert hook into top of first of these dc, pick up dropped loop and draw through, 1ch to secure popcorn.

Picot = 3ch, sl st into first of these ch.

Make 6ch, sl st into first ch to form a ring.

1st round: 1ch, work 12sc into ring, sl st into first sc.

2nd round: 5ch (count as 1dc, 2ch), skip first sc, [1dc into next sc, 2ch] 11 times, sl st into 3rd of 5ch at beg of round.

3rd round: Sl st into first 2ch sp, 3ch, 4dc into same sp as sl st, drop loop from hook, insert hook into top of 3ch, pick up dropped loop and draw through, 1ch to

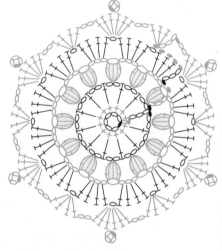

secure (1 popcorn made at beg of round), 3ch, [1 popcorn into next 2ch sp, 3ch] 11 times, sl st into top of first popcorn.

4th round: Sl st into first 3ch sp, 3ch (count as 1dc), 3dc into same sp as sl st, 1ch, [4dc into next 3ch sp, 1ch] 11 times, sl st into 3rd of 3ch at beg of round.

5th round: Sl st into each of next 3dc and into ch sp, 3ch, 3dc into same sp as last sl st, 2ch, into next ch sp work [3dc, 1 picot, 3dc], *2ch, work 4dc into next ch sp, 2ch, into next ch sp work [3dc, 1 picot, 3dc]; rep from * 4 times more, 2ch, sl st into 3rd of 3ch at beg of round. Fasten off.

 = Popcorn   = Picot

III.31

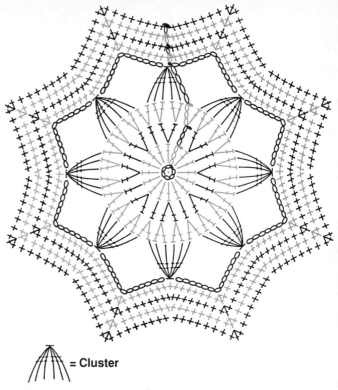

 = Cluster

Special Abbreviation

Cluster = work 1tr into each of next 6dc until 1 loop of each remains on hook, yo and through all 7 loops on hook.

Make 6ch, sl st into first ch to form a ring.

1st round: 3ch (count as 1dc), work 15dc into ring, sl st into 3rd of 3ch at beg of round.

2nd round: 3ch, 2dc into next dc, [1dc into next dc, 2dc into next dc] 7 times, sl st into 3rd of 3ch at beg of round.

3rd round: 3ch, work 2dc into each of next 23dc, 1dc into same st as sl st at end of previous round, sl st into 3rd of 3ch at beg of round.

4th round: 4ch, work 1tr into each of next 5dc until 1 loop of each remains on hook, yo and through all 6 loops on hook (1 cluster made at beg of round), 13ch, [1 cluster over next 6dc, 13ch] 7 times, sl st into top of first cluster.

5th round: 1ch, 1sc into same st as last sl st, *1sc into each of next 6ch, 3sc into next ch, 1sc into each of next 6ch, 1sc into top of next cluster; rep from * 7 times more omitting 1sc at end of last rep, sl st into first sc.

6th round: 1ch, skip first sc, 1sc into each of next 7sc, 3sc into next sc, 1sc into each of next 7sc, [skip 1sc, 1sc into each of next 7sc, 3sc into next sc, 1sc into each of next 7sc] 7 times, sl st into first sc at beg of round.

7th round: 1ch, skip first sc, 1sc into each of next 7sc, 3sc into next sc, 1sc into each of next 7sc, [skip 2sc, 1sc into each of next 7sc, 3sc into next sc, 1sc into each of next 7sc] 7 times, skip next sc, sl st into first sc.

8th round: As 7th round. Fasten off.

III.32

Special Abbreviation

3dc bobble or 4dc bobble = work 3 (or 4) dc into next st until 1 loop of each remains on hook, yo and through all 4 (or 5) loops on hook.

1st round: Make 4ch, work 11dc into first of these ch, sl st into 4th of 4ch at beg of round.

2nd round: 3ch, work 2dc into same st as last sl st until 1 loop of each remains on hook, yo and through all 3 loops on hook (3dc bobble made at beg of round), [1ch, 3dc bobble into next dc] twice, 5ch, *3dc bobble into next dc, [1ch, 3dc bobble into next dc] twice, 5ch; rep from * twice more, sl st into top of first bobble.

3rd round: Sl st into first ch sp, 3ch, into same ch sp as last sl st work 3dc until 1 loop of each remains on hook, yo and through all 4 loops on hook (4dc bobble made at beg of round), *1ch, 4dc bobble into next ch sp, 2ch, 5dc into 5ch arch, 2ch, work 4dc bobble into next ch sp; rep

from * 3 times more omitting bobble at end of last rep, sl st into top of first bobble.

4th round: Sl st into first ch sp, 3ch then complete first 4dc bobble as on 3rd round, *2ch, 1dc into 2ch sp, 1dc into each of next 2dc, 5dc into next dc, 1dc into each of next 2dc, 1dc into next 2ch sp, 2ch, 4dc bobble into next ch sp; rep from * 3 times more omitting bobble at end of last rep, sl st into top of first bobble.

5th round: 3ch, *2dc into next 2ch sp, 1dc into each of next 4dc, 3ch, skip 1dc, 4dc bobble into next dc, 3ch, skip 1dc, 1dc into each of next 4dc, 2dc into next 2ch sp, 1dc into top of next bobble; rep from * 3 times more omitting 1dc at end of last rep, sl st into 3rd of 3ch at beg of round.

6th round: 3ch, 1dc into each of next 6dc, *2ch, skip 2dc, 4dc bobble into next ch, 5ch, 4dc bobble into next ch, 2ch, 1dc into each of next 13dc; rep from * 3 times more omitting 7dc at end of last rep, sl st into 3rd of 3ch at beg of round. Fasten off.

〡 = 3dc bobble   〡 = 4dc bobble

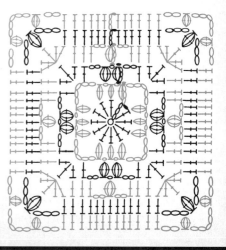

III. Motifs

III.33

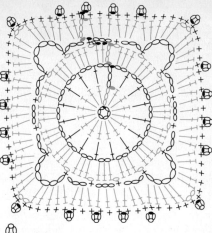

= Picot

Special Abbreviation

Picot = 3ch, sl st into side of last sc worked.

Make 6ch, sl st into first ch to form a ring.

1st round: 3ch (count as 1dc), work 15dc into ring, sl st into 3rd of 3ch at beg of round.

2nd round: 5ch (count as 1dc, 2ch), [1dc into next dc, 2ch] 15 times, sl st into 3rd of 5ch at beg of round.

3rd round: Sl st into first 2ch sp, 3ch (count as 1dc), work 2dc into first 2ch sp, 1ch, [3dc into next 2ch sp, 1ch] 15 times, sl st into 3rd of 3ch at beg of round.

4th round: Sl st into each of next 2dc, 1ch, 1sc into first ch sp, 3ch, 1sc into next ch sp, 6ch, *1sc into next ch sp, [3ch, 1sc into next ch sp] 3 times, 6ch; rep from * twice more, [1sc into next ch sp, 3ch] twice, sl st into first sc.

5th round: Sl st into first 3ch sp, 3ch, work 2dc into first 3ch sp, into next 6ch arch work [5dc, 2ch, 5dc], *3dc into each of next 3 3ch sps, into next 6ch arch work [5dc, 2ch, 5dc]; rep from * twice more, 3dc into each of last 2 3ch sps, sl st into 3rd of 3ch at beg of round.

6th round: 1ch, 1sc into same st as last sl st, 1sc into each of next 2dc, 1 picot, 1sc into each of next 5dc, into next 2ch sp work [1sc, 1 picot, 1sc], 1sc into each of next 5dc, *1 picot, [1sc into each of next 3dc, 1 picot] 3 times, 1sc into each of next 5dc, into next 2ch sp work [1sc, 1 picot, 1sc], 1sc into each of next 5dc; rep from * twice more, 1 picot, [1sc into each of next 3dc, 1 picot] twice, sl st into first sc. Fasten off.

III.34

Make 6ch, sl st into first ch to form a ring.

1st round: 3ch (count as 1dc), work 15dc into ring, sl st into 3rd of 3ch at beg of round.

2nd round: 3ch (count as 1dc), 2dc into same st as last sl st, 2ch, skip 1dc, 1dc into next dc, 2ch, skip 1dc, *3dc into next dc, 2ch, skip 1dc, 1dc into next dc, 2ch, skip 1dc; rep from * twice more, sl st into 3rd of 3ch at beg of round.

3rd round: 3ch, 5dc into next dc, *1dc into next dc, [2ch, 1dc into next dc] twice, 5dc into next dc; rep from * twice more, [1dc into next dc, 2ch] twice, sl st into 3rd of 3ch at beg of round.

4th round: 3ch, 1dc into each of next 2dc, 5dc into next dc, *1dc into each of next 3dc, 2ch, 1dc into next dc, 2ch, 1dc into each of next 3dc, 5dc into next dc; rep from * twice more, 1dc into each of next 3dc, 2ch, 1dc into next dc, 2ch, sl st into 3rd of 3ch at beg of round.

5th round: 3ch, 1dc into each of next 4dc, 5dc into next dc, *1dc into each of next 5dc, 2dc into next 2ch sp, 1dc into next dc, 2dc into next 2ch sp, 1dc into each of next 5dc, 5dc into next dc; rep from * twice more, 1dc into each of next 5dc, 2dc into next 2ch sp, 1dc into next dc, 2dc into last 2ch sp, sl st into 3rd of 3ch at beg of round. Fasten off.

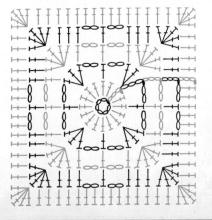

III.35

Special Abbreviation

Bobble = work 5dc into next st until 1 loop of each remains on hook, yo and through all 6 loops on hook.

1st round: Make 6ch and working into first of these ch work [1dc, 2ch] 7 times, sl st into 4th of 6ch at beg of round.

2nd round: 3ch (count as 1dc), work 2dc into same st as last sl st, 2ch, [3dc into next dc, 2ch] 7 times, sl st into 3rd of 3ch at beg of round.

3rd round: 3ch, 1dc into same st as last sl st, 1dc into next dc, 2dc into next dc, 2ch, [2dc into next dc, 1dc into next dc, 2dc into next dc, 2ch] 7 times, sl st into 3rd of 3ch at beg of round.

4th round: 5ch (count as 1dc, 2ch), skip next dc, 1 bobble into next dc, 2ch, skip 1dc, 1dc into next dc, 2ch, [1dc into next dc, 2ch, skip 1dc, 1 bobble into next dc, 2ch, skip 1dc, 1dc into next dc, 2ch] 7 times, sl st into 3rd of 5ch at beg of round.

5th round: 3ch, 1dc into same st as last sl st, 2dc into first 2ch sp, 1dc into top of next bobble, 2dc into next 2ch sp, 2dc into next dc, 2ch, [2dc into next dc, 2dc into next 2ch sp, 1dc into top of next bobble, 2dc into next 2ch sp, 2dc into next dc, 2ch] 7 times, sl st into 3rd of 3ch at beg of round. Fasten off.

= Bobble

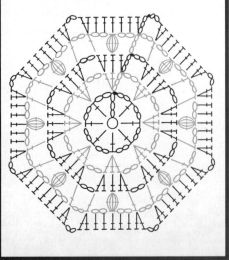

Abbreviations and Symbols on page 12

Irish Crochet

True Irish crochet is made by first working motifs and then creating a net or mesh background incorporating the motifs and forming the fabric which holds them in position. This is done by placing the motifs in the required position face down on paper or a scrap of fabric and temporarily securing them. The background or filling, is then worked progressively joining in the motifs, after the work is completed the paper or fabric is carefully removed.

Historically crochet is believed to have been introduced into Ireland in the early part of the 19th century by nuns, probably from Italy or France. It was evolved by them and convent-educated girls into an art-form in itself, reaching levels of complexity and delicacy not seen in other styles of crochet work.

Stitches and techniques were developed which are particular to Irish crochet. The use of padding threads which are held at the edge of the work, so that subsequent rows or rounds are worked over them to give a three-dimensional effect is one example, another is the Clones Knot, and both of these are described below.

Because of the difficulty of giving general instructions for the construction of true Irish crochet, and particularly since the various motifs can each be incorporated into almost any crocheted net background, we have simplified the following selection to give you a taste of Irish style crochet.

Padding Threads

Padding threads are used to give a three-dimensional appearance to some Irish crochet motifs. The thread used is usually the same as the thread used for the motif and the number of threads worked over determines the amount of padding. In this book we have usually worked over three thicknesses of thread.

The example below is for padding threads at the beginning of a motif, but they can also be used in other areas of motifs (see IV.11 on page 65).

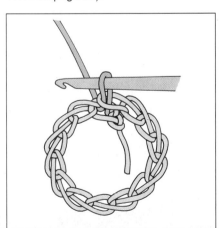

1. Make the required number of chain and join with a slip stitch.

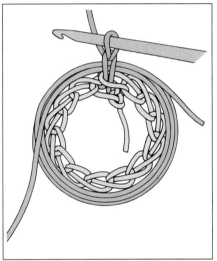

2. Wind a length of thread three or four times around the end of a pencil or finger and hold against the chain.

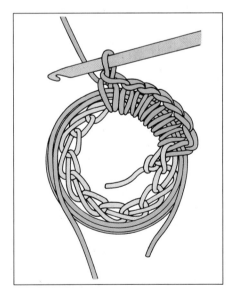

3. The stitches are then worked over the chain and 'padding' threads.

When the motif is complete the ends of the padding thread are pulled through several stitches and cut.

The instructions and diagrams of individual patterns indicate where it is appropriate to use padding threads. On the diagrams the padding thread is indicated with a thicker line.

Working into Base of Stitch

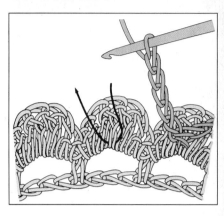

Insert the hook under two strands at the base of the stitch (this is indicated on the diagrams by red arrows see IV.17 on page 68). The diagram above shows work viewed from the back.

Clones Knot

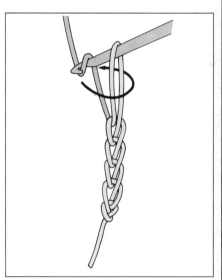

1. Draw up a chain. The length of the chain dictates the size of the Clones Knot.

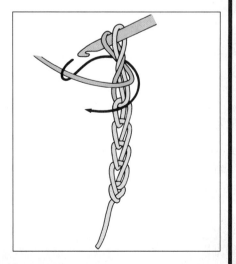

2. Holding chain in place, yarn over. Twist the hook over then under the loop.

IV. Irish Style Crochet

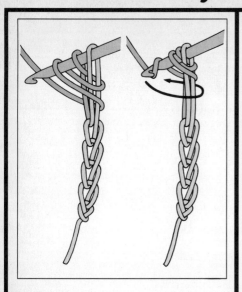

3. Pull the yarn back under the loop with the hook.

4. Repeat steps 2 and 3 until loop is completely covered.

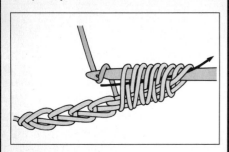

5. Yarn over, draw hook through all the loops.

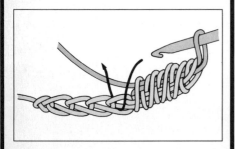

6. Secure knot by working a single crochet into the last chain worked before Clones Knot.

The Clones Knot can be secured in different ways, see individual pattern for instructions.

IV.1

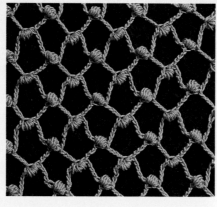

Starting chain: Multiple of 8 sts + 2.

Special Abbreviation

Clones Knot = draw up a chain to required length and hold it in place, *yarn over, twist hook over then under the loop, then pull the yarn back under the loop with the hook; rep from * until the loop is completely covered. Yo, draw hook through all loops on hook. To secure knot work 1sc into last ch before Clones Knot.

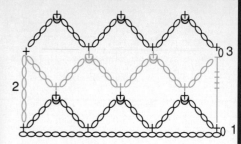

⊕ = **Clones Knot**

1st row (right side): Work 1sc into 2nd ch from hook, *4ch, 1 Clones Knot, 4ch, skip 7ch, 1sc into next ch; rep from * to end, turn.

2nd row: 10ch (count as 1ttr, 4ch), working behind first Clones Knot work 1sc into sc securing knot, *4ch, 1 Clones Knot, 4ch, 1sc into sc securing next Clones Knot as before; rep from * ending with 4ch, 1ttr into last sc, turn.

3rd row: 1ch, 1sc into ttr, *4ch, 1 Clones Knot, 4ch, working behind next Clones Knot work 1sc into sc securing knot; rep from * to end placing last sc into 6th of 10ch at beg of previous row, turn.

Rep 2nd and 3rd rows.

IV.2

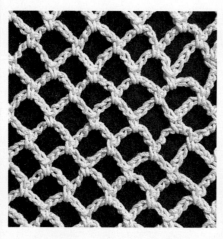

Starting chain: Multiple of 4 sts + 2.

1st row (right side): Work 1sc into 2nd ch from hook, *6ch, skip 3ch, 1sc into next ch; rep from * to end, turn.

2nd row: 8ch (count as 1dtr, 3ch), 1sc into first 6ch arch, *6ch, 1sc into next 6ch arch; rep from * to end, 3ch, 1dtr into last sc, turn.

3rd row: 1ch, 1sc into first dtr, *6ch, 1sc into next 6ch arch; rep from * to end placing last sc into 5th of 8ch at beg of previous row, turn.

Rep 2nd and 3rd rows.

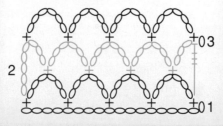

IV.3

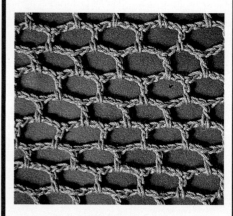

Starting chain: Multiple of 5 sts + 7.

1st row (right side): Work 1dc into 12th ch from hook, *4ch, skip 4ch, 1dc into next ch; rep from * to end, turn.

2nd row: 6ch (count as 1tr, 2ch), 1dc into next 4ch sp, *4ch, 1dc into next 4ch sp; rep from * to end, 2ch, 1tr into 5th ch, turn.

3rd row: 7ch (count as 1dc, 4ch), *1dc into next 4ch sp, 4ch; rep from * to last sp, 1dc into 4th of 6ch at beg of previous row, turn.

Rep 2nd and 3rd rows.

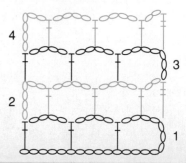

Abbreviations and Symbols on page 12

IV.4

Starting chain: Multiple of 7 sts + 6.

1st row (right side): Work 1sc into 6th ch from hook, 10ch, skip 6ch, *into next ch work [1sc, 4ch, 1sc], 10ch, skip 6ch; rep from * to last ch, into last ch work [1sc, 2ch, 1dc], turn.

2nd row: 11ch (count as 1ttr, 5ch), into next 10ch arch work [1sc, 4ch, 1sc], *10ch, into next 10ch arch work [1sc, 4ch, 1sc]; rep from * to end, 5ch, 1ttr into 3rd of 5ch at beg of previous row, turn.

3rd row: 5ch (count as 1dc, 2ch), 1sc into first arch, 10ch, *into next 10ch arch work [1sc, 4ch, 1sc], 10ch; rep from * to last arch, into last arch work [1sc, 2ch, 1dc], turn.

Rep 2nd and 3rd rows.

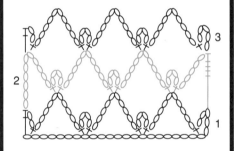

IV.5

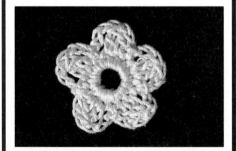

Special Abbreviation

Dc2tog = work 1dc into each of next 2sc until 1 loop of each remains on hook, yo and through all 3 loops on hook.

Make 6ch, sl st into first ch to form a ring.

1st round: 1ch, work 15sc into ring, sl st into first sc.

2nd round: [3ch, dc2tog over next 2sc, 3ch, sl st into next sc] 5 times placing last sl st into first sc of previous round.
Fasten off.

IV.6

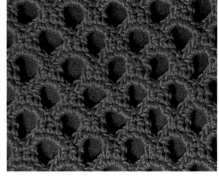

Starting chain: Multiple of 5 sts + 2.

1st row (right side): Work 1sc into 2nd ch from hook, 1sc into each ch to end, turn.

2nd row: 1ch, 1sc into each of first 2sc, *5ch, skip 2sc, 1sc into each of next 3sc; rep from * to end omitting 1sc at end of last rep, turn.

3rd row: 1ch, 1sc into first sc, *5sc into next 5ch arch, skip 1sc, 1sc into next sc; rep from * to end, turn.

4th row: 6ch (count as 1tr, 2ch), skip first 2sc, 1sc into each of next 3sc, *5ch, skip 3sc, 1sc into each of next 3sc; rep from * to last 2sc, 2ch, 1tr into last sc, turn.

5th row: 1ch, 1sc into first tr, 2sc into 2ch sp, skip 1sc, 1sc into next sc, *5sc into next 5ch arch, skip 1sc, 1sc into next sc; rep from * to last 2ch sp, 2sc into last sp, 1sc into 4th of 4ch at beg of previous row, turn.

6th row: 1ch, 1sc into each of first 2sc, *5ch, skip 3sc, 1sc into each of next 3sc; rep from * to end omitting 1sc at end of last rep, turn.

Rep 3rd to 6th rows.

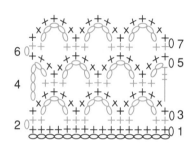

IV.7

Special Abbreviation

Bobble = work 3tr into next sc until 1 loop of each remains on hook, yo and through all 4 loops on hook.

Make 5ch, sl st into first ch to form a ring.

1st round: 1ch, work 12sc into ring, sl st into first sc.

2nd round: *4ch, work 1 bobble into next sc, 4ch, sl st into each of next 2sc; rep from * 3 times more omitting 1 sl st at end of last rep, 7ch, work 1sc into 2nd ch from hook, 1sc into each of next 5ch, sl st into first sc on first round. Fasten off.

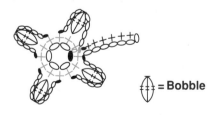

= Bobble

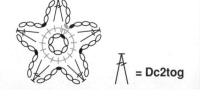

= Dc2tog

IV.8

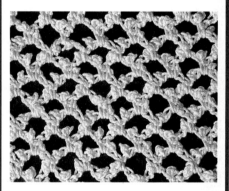

Starting chain: Multiple of 5 sts + 2.

1st row (right side): Work 1sc into 2nd ch from hook, *[4ch, 1sc into 3rd ch from hook] twice, 1ch, skip 4ch, 1sc into next ch; rep from * to end, turn.

2nd row: 9ch (count as 1dtr, 4ch), 1sc into 3rd ch from hook, 1ch, 1sc into center of first arch, *[4ch, 1sc into 3rd ch from hook] twice, 1ch, 1sc into center of next arch; rep from * to end, 4ch, 1sc into 3rd ch from hook, 1ch, 1dtr into last sc, turn.

3rd row: 1ch, 1sc into first dtr, *[4ch, 1sc into 3rd ch from hook] twice, 1ch, 1sc into center of next arch; rep from * to end placing last sc into 5th of 9ch at beg of previous row, turn.

Rep 2nd and 3rd rows.

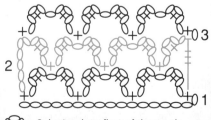

= 3ch, 1sc into first of these ch.

IV. Irish Style Crochet

IV.9

Line shows the direction of work for first two rows.

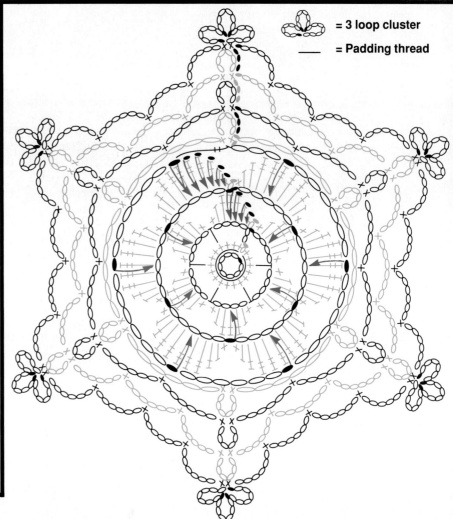

= 3 loop cluster

_____ = Padding thread

= sl st into next st, [7ch, sl st into same st as last sl st] 3 times.

The starting chain for this pattern forms part of the first row, and continues to form part of the second row.

1st row (right side): Make 16ch, sl st into 8th ch from hook, [7ch, sl st into same ch as last sl st] twice, *23ch, sl st into 8th ch from hook, [7ch, sl st into same ch as last sl st] twice; rep from * the number of times required, (one repeat is shown in the diagram), make 8ch and turn work ready for

2nd row: make 7 more ch, sl st into 8th ch from hook, 7ch, sl st into same ch as last sl st, 7ch, skip next 7ch loop, 1sc into next 7ch loop, *7ch, skip 7ch on previous row, sl st into next ch, [7ch, sl st into same ch as last sl st] 3 times, 7ch, skip next 7ch loop, 1sc into next 7ch loop; rep from * to last 8ch, 7ch, skip 7ch, into last ch work [1 sl st, 7ch, 1 sl st, 4ch, 1tr], turn.

3rd row: 1ch, 1sc into first tr, *7ch, 1 sl st into next sc, [7ch, 1 sl st into same sc as last sl st] 3 times, 7ch, skip next 7ch loop, 1sc into next 7ch loop; rep from * to end, turn.

4th row: [7ch, sl st into first sc] twice, 7ch, skip next 7ch loop, 1sc into next 7ch loop, *7ch, sl st into next sc, [7ch, sl st into same sc as last sl st] 3 times, 7ch, skip next 7ch loop, 1sc into next 7ch loop; rep from * to last sc, 7ch, into last sc work [1 sl st, 7ch, 1 sl st, 4ch, 1tr], turn.

Rep 3rd and 4th rows.

IV.10

Special Abbreviation

3 loop cluster = 7ch, sl st into first of these ch, [6ch, sl st into same ch as last sl st] twice.

Make 8ch, sl st into first ch to form a ring.

1st round: 1ch, working into ring and over

padding threads, work 18sc, sl st into first sc.

2nd round: 6ch (count as 1hdc, 4ch), skip first 3sc, 1hdc into next sc, [4ch, skip 2sc, 1hdc into next sc] 4 times, 4ch, sl st into 2nd of 6ch at beg of round.

3rd round: 1ch, work [1sc, 1hdc, 3dc, 1hdc, 1sc] into each of the 6 4ch arches, sl st into first sc. (6 petals).

4th round: Working behind each petal, sl st into base of each of first 4 sts, [5ch, skip next 6 sts, sl st into base of next dc] 6 times, working last sl st into base of same dc as sl st at beg of round.

5th round: 1ch, work [1sc, 1hdc, 1dc, 5tr, 1dc, 1hdc, 1sc] into each of the 6 5ch arches, sl st into first sc.

6th round: Working behind each petal, sl st into base of each of first 6 sts, [6ch, skip next 10 sts, sl st into base of next tr] 5 times, 3ch, skip next 10 sts, 1tr into base of next tr.

7th round: Sl st into arch just formed, into

same arch work [1sc, 6ch, 1sc], 6ch, *into next arch work [1sc, 6ch, 1sc], 6ch; rep from * 4 times more, sl st into first sc.

8th round: Sl st into each of first 3ch of 6ch loop, into same loop work [1sc, 6ch, 1sc], 6ch, 1sc into next 6ch arch, 6ch, *into next 6ch loop work [1sc, 6ch, 1sc], 6ch, 1sc into next 6ch arch, 6ch; rep from * 4 times more, sl st into first sc.

9th round: Sl st into each of first 3ch of 6ch loop, into same loop work [1sc, 6ch, 1sc], 6ch, [1sc into next 6ch arch, 6ch] twice, *into next 6ch loop work [1sc, 6ch, 1sc], 6ch, [1sc into next 6ch arch, 6ch] twice; rep from * 4 times more, sl st into first sc.

10th round: Sl st into each of first 3ch of first 6ch loop, into same loop work [1sc, 3 loop cluster, 1sc], 6ch, [1sc into next 6ch arch, 6ch] 3 times, *into next 6ch loop work [1sc, 3 loop cluster, 1sc], 6ch, [1sc into next 6ch arch, 6ch] 3 times; rep from * 4 times more, sl st into first sc. Fasten off.

Abbreviations and Symbols on page 12

IV.11

2nd round: *1ch, working into next 9ch loop and over **padding threads** work [2sc, 1hdc, 11dc, 1hdc, 2sc], 1ch, sl st into same ch as sl sts of first round; rep from * twice more.

3rd round: Sl st into each of first 9 sts of first loop, [16ch, skip first 8 sts on next loop, sl st into next dc] twice, 16ch, sl st into same dc as last sl st at beg of round.

4th round: 1ch, working over **padding threads**, work 1sc into same dc as last sl st of previous round, 19sc into first 16ch arch, [1sc into same dc as next sl st of previous round, 19sc into next 16ch arch] twice, sl st into first sc. 60sc.

5th round: 8ch (count as 1dc, 5ch), skip next 3sc, [1dc into next sc, 5ch, skip 3sc] 14 times, sl st into 3rd of 8ch at beg of round.

6th round: Sl st into first 3ch of first arch, 1ch, working over **padding threads** work 4sc into first arch, 7sc into each of next 14 arches, 3sc into same arch as first 4sc, sl st into first sc.

7th round: 6ch, [skip next 6sc, sl st into next sc] 14 times, 6ch, sl st into same sc as last sl st of previous round.

8th round: 1ch, into each 6ch arch and over **padding threads** work 2sc, [1 picot, 2sc] 3 times. Sl st into first sc and fasten off.

Special Abbreviation

Picot = make 3ch, sl st into first of these ch.

1st round: Make 10ch, sl st into first ch, [9ch, sl st into same ch as last sl st] twice (3 loops formed).

IV.12

Make 6ch, sl st into first ch to form a ring and continue as follows:

1ch, work [1sc, 12ch] 12 times into ring, sl st into first sc. Fasten off.

⬡ = **Picot**   —— = **Padding thread**

IV. Irish Style Crochet

IV.13

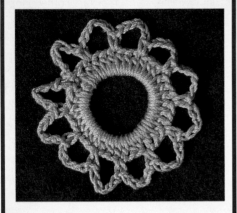

Make 16ch, sl st into first ch to form a ring.

1st round: 2ch (count as 1hdc), work 35hdc into ring and over **padding threads**, sl st into 2nd of 2ch at beg of round.

2nd round: 1ch, work 1sc into same st as last sl st, [5ch, skip 2hdc, 1sc into next hdc] 11 times, 5ch, sl st into first sc. Fasten off.

—— = **Padding thread**

IV.14

Special Abbreviation

Picot = make 3ch, sl st into first of these ch.

Make 15ch and work in a spiral as follows:

1sc into 2nd ch from hook, working 1 st into each ch work 1hdc, 3dc, 4tr, 3dc, 1hdc and 1sc, 3ch, then working 1 st into each ch on other side of starting chain work 1sc, 1hdc, 3dc, 4tr, 3dc, 1hdc, 1sc, 3ch, 1sc into first sc at beg of spiral, 1sc into next hdc, 1 picot, [1sc into each of next 2 sts, 1 picot] 6 times, into 3ch sp at point of leaf work [1sc, 4ch, sl st into 3rd ch from hook, 1ch, 1sc], [1 picot, 1sc into each of next 2 sts] 7 times, sl st into 3ch sp. Fasten off.

IV.15

IV.16

Make 5ch, sl st into first ch to form a ring.

1st round: 1ch, work 10sc into ring, sl st into first sc.

2nd round: 1ch, work 1sc into each sc, sl st into first sc.

3rd round: 2ch (count as 1hdc), skip first sc, work 2hdc into each of next 9sc, 1hdc into first sc, sl st into 2nd of 2ch.

4th round: *2ch, **working into front loop only** of each hdc work 2dc into each of next 3hdc, 2ch, sl st into next hdc; rep from * 4 times more placing last sl st into 2nd of 2ch at beg of previous round. (5 petals made).

5th round: Working behind each petal of previous round and **into back loop** of each hdc on 3rd round, sl st into first 2hdc, *4ch, work 2dtr into each of next 3hdc, 4ch, sl st into next hdc; rep from * 3 times more, 4ch, 2dtr into next hdc, 2dtr into 2nd of 2ch at beg of 3rd round, 2dtr into next hdc, 4ch, sl st into next hdc. Fasten off.

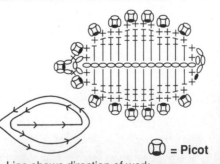

⊞ = **Picot**

Line shows direction of work.

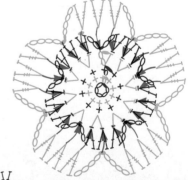

$\bigvee$ 2dc into **front loop only** of next st. On final round work into back loop only of hdc on 3rd round.

Abbreviations and Symbols on page 12

Make 7ch, sl st into first ch to form a ring.

1st round: 1ch, work 16sc into ring, sl st into first sc.

2nd round: 1ch, 1sc into first sc, [5ch, skip 1sc, 1sc into next sc] 7 times, 5ch, sl st into first sc.

3rd round: Sl st into first 5ch arch, 1ch, work [1sc, 5hdc, 1sc] into each 5ch arch to end, sl st into first sc. (8 petals).

4th round: 1ch, working behind each petal work 1sc into first sc on 2nd round, [6ch, 1sc into next sc on 2nd round] 7 times, 6ch, sl st into first sc.

5th round: Sl st into first 6ch arch, 1ch, work [1sc, 6hdc, 1sc] into each 6ch arch to end, sl st into first sc.

6th round: 1ch, working behind each pet-

al work 1sc into first sc on 4th round, [7ch, 1sc into next sc on 4th round] 7 times, 7ch, sl st into first sc.

7th round: Sl st into first 7ch arch, 1ch, work [1sc, 7hdc, 1sc] into each 7ch arch to end, sl st into first sc.

8th round: 1ch, working behind each petal work 1sc into first sc on 6th round, *[9ch, sl st into 6th ch from hook (1 picot made)] twice, 4ch, 1sc into next sc on 6th round, [13ch, sl st into 6th ch from hook (1 picot made)] twice, 8ch, 1sc into same sc as last sc, [9ch, sl st into 6th ch from hook] twice, 4ch, 1sc into next sc on 6th round; rep from * 3 times more omitting 1sc at end of last rep, sl st into first sc.

9th round: Sl st into each of first 3ch, behind first picot and into next ch of arch

between picots, 1ch, 1sc into same arch as sl st, **[10ch, sl st into 6th ch from hook] twice, 5ch, 1sc into corner loop between 2 picots, *[10ch, sl st into 6th ch from hook] twice, 5ch, 1sc into arch between 2 picots; rep from * once more; rep from ** 3 times more omitting 1sc at end of last rep, sl st into first sc.

10th round: Sl st into each of first 4ch, behind first picot and into next 2ch of arch between 2 picots, 1ch, 1sc into same arch between 2 picots, **[10ch, sl st into 6th ch from hook] twice, 5ch, 1sc into next sc at top of loop, *[10ch, sl st into 6th ch from hook] twice, 5ch, 1sc into next arch between 2 picots; rep from * twice more; rep from ** 3 times more omitting 1sc at end of last rep, sl st into first sc. Fasten off.

IV. Irish Style Crochet

IV.17

Make 8ch, sl st into first ch to form a ring.

1st round: 1ch, work 16sc into ring, sl st into first sc.

2nd round: 5ch (count as 1dc, 2ch), skip next sc, [1dc into next sc, 2ch, skip 1sc] 7 times, sl st into 3rd of 5ch at beg of round.

3rd round: Sl st into 2ch sp, 1ch, work [1sc, 1hdc, 1dc, 1hdc, 1sc] into each of the 8 2ch sps, sl st into first sc. (8 petals).

4th round: Working behind each petal, sl st into base of each of next 2 sts, 1ch, 1sc into base of same dc as last sl st, [3ch, skip 4 sts, 1sc into base of next dc] 7 times, 3ch, sl st into first sc.

5th round: Sl st into 3ch arch, 1ch, work [1sc, 1hdc, 3dc, 1hdc, 1sc] into each of the 8 3ch arches, sl st into first sc.

6th round: Working behind each petal, sl st into base of each of next 3 sts, 1ch, 1sc into base of same dc as last sl st, [5ch, skip 6 sts, 1sc into base of next dc] 7 times, 5ch, sl st into first sc.

7th round: Sl st into 5ch arch, 1ch, work [1sc, 1hdc, 5dc, 1hdc, 1sc] into each of the 8 5ch arches, sl st into first sc.

8th round: Working behind each petal, sl st into base of each of next 4 sts, 1ch, 1sc into base of same dc as last sl st, [7ch, skip 8 sts, 1sc into base of next dc] 7 times, 7ch, sl st into first sc.

9th round: Sl st into 7ch arch, 1ch, work [1sc, 1hdc, 7dc, 1hdc, 1sc] into each of the 8 7ch arches, sl st into first sc.

10th round: Working behind each petal, sl st into base of each of next 5 sts, 1ch, 1sc into base of same dc as last sl st, [9ch, skip 10 sts, 1sc into base of next dc] 7 times, 9ch, sl st into first sc.

11th round: Sl st into 9ch arch, 1ch, work [1sc, 1hdc, 9dc, 1hdc, 1sc] into each of the 8 9ch arches, sl st into first sc. Fasten off.

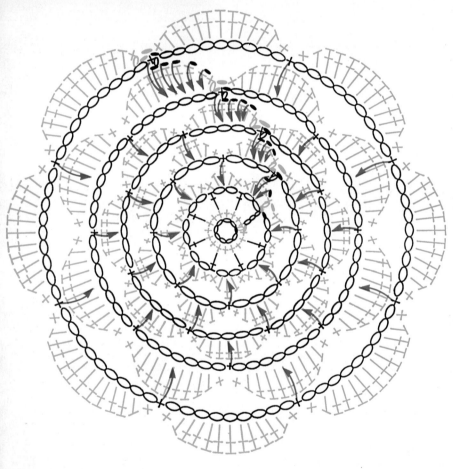

IV.18

Work as given for 1st to 7th round of IV.17. Fasten off.

IV.19

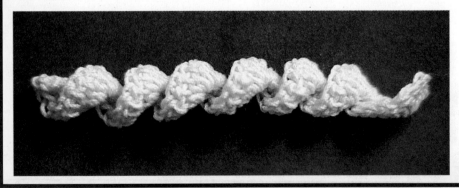

Starting chain: Any number of sts, plus 3.

Note: Sample photographed has starting chain of 31 sts.

Work 2dc into 4th ch from hook, 3dc into each ch to end. Fasten off.

Abbreviations and Symbols on page 12

IV.20

Make 6ch, sl st into first ch to form a ring.

1st round: 3ch (count as 1dc), work 17dc into ring and over **padding threads**, sl st into 3rd of 3ch at beg of round.

2nd round: 8ch (count as 1dc, 5ch), [1dc into next dc, 5ch] 17 times, sl st into 3rd of 8ch at beg of round.

3rd round: Sl st into each of next 3ch of first arch, 1ch, into same ch as last sl st work [1sc, 1ch, 1sc], *2sc into 2nd part of arch and 2sc into first part of next arch, into center ch of arch work [1sc, 1ch, 1sc]; rep from * 16 times more, 2sc into 2nd part of last arch, 2sc into first part of first arch, sl st into first sc.

4th round: Sl st into first ch sp, 1ch, into same sp as last sl st work [1sc, 1ch, 1sc], 1sc into each of next 6sc, *into next ch sp work [1sc, 1ch, 1sc], 1sc into each of next 6sc; rep from * 16 times more, sl st into first sc.

5th round: Sl st into first ch sp, 1ch, into same sp as last sl st work [1sc, 1ch, 1sc], 1sc into each of next 8sc, *into next ch sp work [1sc, 1ch, 1sc], 1sc into each of next 8sc; rep from * 16 times more, sl st into first sc.

6th round: Sl st into first ch sp, 1ch, into same sp as last sl st work [1sc, 1ch, 1sc], 1sc into each of next 10sc, *into next ch sp work [1sc, 1ch, 1sc], 1sc into each of next 10sc; rep from * 16 times more, sl st into first sc.

7th round: Sl st into first ch sp, 1ch, work 1sc into same sp as last sl st, 5ch, [1sc into next ch sp, 5ch] 17 times, sl st into first sc.

8th round: 1ch, 1sc into first sc of previous round, 3ch, 1sc into next 5ch arch, [3ch, 1sc into next sc, 3ch, 1sc into next 5ch arch] 17 times, 3ch, sl st into first sc.

9th round: Sl st into first ch of first 3ch arch, 1ch, 1sc into same arch as last sl st, *4ch, 1sc into next 3ch arch; rep from * to end, 4ch, sl st into first sc.

10th round: Sl st into each of first 2ch of first 4ch arch, 1ch, 1sc into same arch as last sl sts, *5ch, 1sc into next 4ch arch; rep from * to end, 5ch, sl st into first sc. Fasten off.

_____ = Padding thread

An enlargement of the area within the red frame showing in detail the stitches represented by the dotted lines on the main diagram.

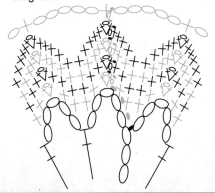

IV. Irish Style Crochet

IV.21

IV.22

Special Abbreviation

Picot = make 3ch, sl st into first of these ch.

Make 10ch, sl st into first ch to form a ring.

1st round: 1ch, into ring work 5sc, 1 picot, [8sc, 1 picot] twice, 3sc, sl st into first sc.

2nd round: 1ch, 1sc into same st as last sl st, *12ch, skip [4sc, 1 picot, 3sc], 1sc into next sc; rep from * once more, 12ch, sl st into first sc.

3rd round: Sl st into first 12ch arch, 1ch, into each of the 3 arches work [1sc, 1hdc, 2dc, 9tr, 2dc, 1hdc, 1sc], sl st into first sc.

4th round: *1ch, 1sc into next hdc, 1ch, [1dc into next st, 1ch] 13 times, 1sc into next hdc, 1ch, sl st into each of next 2sc; rep from * twice more omitting 1 sl st at end of last rep.

5th round: Sl st into each of first [sl st, ch sp, sc and ch sp], 1ch, into same ch sp as last sl st work [1sc, 4ch, 1sc], into each of next 13 ch sps work [1sc, 4ch, 1sc], *1ch, sl st into each of next [sc, ch sp, 2 sl sts, ch sp, sc and ch sp], 1ch, into same sp as last sl st work [1sc, 4ch, 1sc], into each of next 13 ch sps work [1sc, 4ch, 1sc]; rep from * once more, 1ch, sl st into each of last [sc, ch sp and sl st]. Fasten off.

Make 8ch, sl st into first ch to form a ring.

1st round: 1ch, work 15sc into ring, sl st into first sc.

2nd round: 5ch, skip first 3sc, [sl st into next sc, 5ch, skip 2sc] 4 times, sl st into sl st at end of previous round.

3rd round: Sl st into first 5ch arch, 1ch, into same arch and each of next 4 arches work [1sc, 1hdc, 5dc, 1hdc, 1sc], sl st into first sc. (5 petals).

4th round: 1ch, working behind each petal of previous round, work 1 sl st into last sl st on 2nd round, 8ch, [1 sl st into next sl st on 2nd round, 8ch] 4 times, sl st into same st as first sl st at beg of round.

5th round: Sl st into first 8ch arch, 1ch, into same arch and each of next 4 arches work [1sc, 1hdc, 8dc, 1hdc, 1sc], sl st into first sc.

6th round: 2ch, working behind each petal of previous round work 1 sl st into last sl st on 2nd round, 10ch, [1 sl st into next sl st on 2nd round, 10ch] 4 times, sl st into same st as first sl st at beg of round.

7th round: Sl st into first 10ch arch, 1ch, work 15sc into same arch and into each of next 4 arches, sl st into first sc.

8th round: Sl st into next sc, *[4ch, skip 1sc, sl st into next sc] 6 times, turn, work 2 sl sts into first 4ch arch, [4ch, sl st into next 4ch arch] 5 times, turn, work 2 sl sts into first 4ch arch, [4ch, sl st into next 4ch arch] 4 times, turn, work 2 sl sts into first 4ch arch, [4ch, sl st into next 4ch arch] 3 times, turn, work 2 sl sts into first 4ch arch, [4ch, sl st into next 4ch arch] twice, turn, work 2 sl sts into first 4ch arch, 4ch, sl st into next arch and fasten off*. [Turn, skip next 2sc on 7th round, rejoin yarn to next sc and rep from * to *] 4 times.

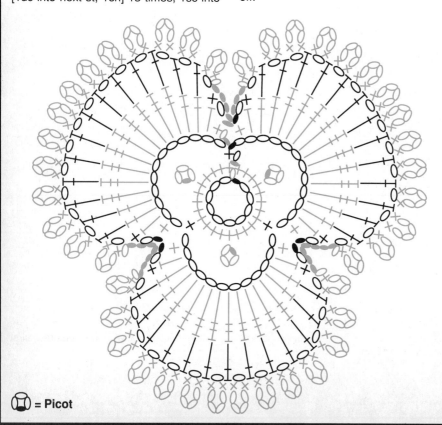

⬡ = Picot

Abbreviations and Symbols on page 12

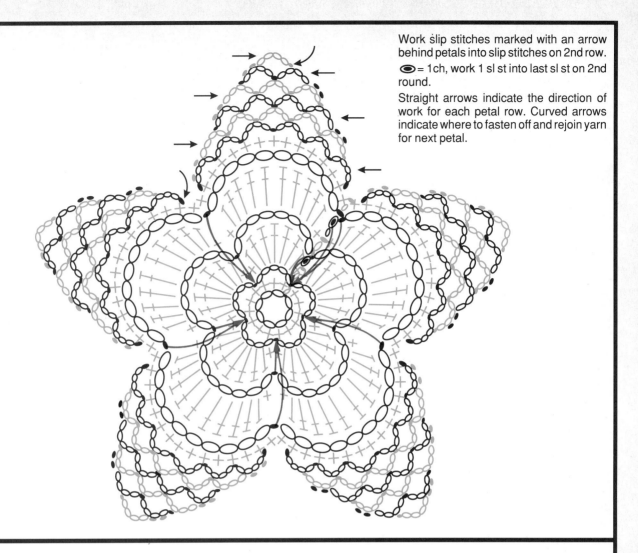

Work slip stitches marked with an arrow behind petals into slip stitches on 2nd row.

👁 = 1ch, work 1 sl st into last sl st on 2nd round.

Straight arrows indicate the direction of work for each petal row. Curved arrows indicate where to fasten off and rejoin yarn for next petal.

IV.23

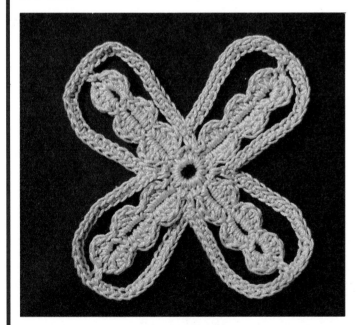

Make 6ch, sl st into first ch to form a ring.

1st round: 1ch, work 2sc into ring, *13ch, sl st into 6th ch from hook, 3ch, skip 3ch, sl st into next ch, 3ch, sl st into side of last sc worked, work 4sc into ring; rep from * 3 times more omitting 2sc at end of last rep, sl st into first sc. (4 points made).

2nd round: *Into each of first 2 sps on next point work [1sc, 3dc, 1sc], 1sc into top sp of same point, into same top sp work [3dc, 1sc] twice, then working on other side of loop work [1sc, 3dc, 1sc] into each of next 2 sps, 1 sl st into each of next 3sc on first round; rep from * 3 times more omitting 1 sl st at end of last rep.

3rd round: 1ch, work 1sc into same sc as last sl st, *16ch, 1sc into center sc at top of point, 16ch, 1sc into center sc between 2 points on first round; rep from * 3 times more omitting 1sc at end of last rep, sl st into first sc.

4th round: 1ch, *work 1sc into each of next 16ch, 1sc into next sc, 1sc into each of next 16ch, skip 1sc; rep from * 3 times more, sl st into first sc. Fasten off.

71

IV. Irish Style Crochet

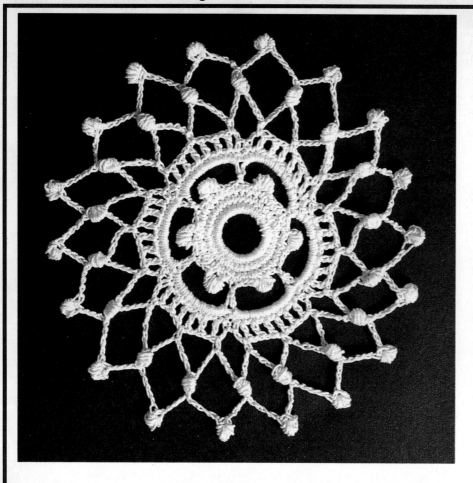

IV.24

Special Abbreviations

Clones Knot = ★draw up a chain to required length and hold it in place, *yarn over, twist hook over then under the loop, then pull the yarn back under the loop with the hook; rep from * until the loop is completely covered. Yo, draw hook through all loops on hook★. To secure knot work 1sc into last ch before Clones Knot.

Sc-Clones Knot = work as given for Clones Knot from ★ to ★. To secure knot work 1sc into last sc before Clones Knot.

Make 18ch, sl st into first ch to form a ring.

1st round: 1ch, working into ring and over **padding threads**, work 36sc, sl st into first sc.

2nd round: 1ch, work 1sc into same st as last sl st, 1sc into each of next 35sc, sl st into first sc.

3rd round: 1ch, work 1sc into same st as last sl st, 1sc into each of next 2sc, *into next sc work [1sc, 1Sc-Clones Knot], 1sc into each of next 5sc; rep from * 5 times more omitting 3sc at end of last rep, sl st into first sc.

4th round: 11ch, skip [first 3sc, 1Sc-Clones Knot, 2sc], sl st into next sc, *11ch, skip [2sc, 1Sc-Clones Knot, 2sc], sl st into next sc; rep from * 4 times more placing last sl st into first sc of previous round.

5th round: 1ch, work 15sc into each of the 6 arches and over **padding threads**, sl st into first sc.

6th round: 1ch, 1sc into next sc, 2ch, 1dc into next sc, [1ch, skip 1sc, 1dc into next sc] 5 times, 2ch, 1sc into next sc, *miss 2sc, 1sc into next sc, 2ch, 1dc into next sc, [1ch, skip 1sc, 1dc into next sc] 5 times, 2ch, 1sc into next sc; rep from * 4 times more, sl st into first sc.

7th round: Sl st into first ch, 1ch, 1sc into 2ch sp, *4ch, 1 Clones Knot, 4ch, skip 3dc, 1sc into next ch sp, [4ch, 1 Clones Knot, 4ch, 1sc into next 2ch sp] twice; rep from * 5 times more omitting 1sc at end of last rep, sl st into first sc.

8th round: Sl st into each ch to first Clones Knot, 1ch, [working behind Clones Knot work 1sc into sc securing Clones Knot, 4ch, 1 Clones Knot, 4ch] 18 times, sl st into first sc. Fasten off.

⤸ = Sc-Clones Knot

⤸ = Clones Knot

——— = Padding thread

Abbreviations and Symbols on page 12

IV.25

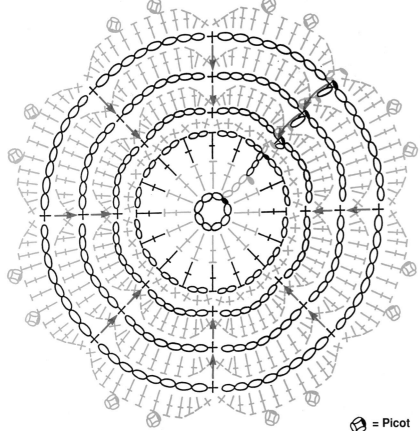

⊕ = Picot

Special Abbreviation

Picot = make 3ch, sl st into first of these ch.

Make 8ch, sl st into first ch to form a ring.

1st round: 3ch (count as 1dc), work 15dc into ring, sl st into 3rd of 3ch at beg of round.

2nd round: 5ch (count as 1dc, 2ch), [1dc into next dc, 2ch] 15 times, sl st into 3rd of 5ch at beg of round.

3rd round: 1ch, work 3sc into each of the 16 2ch sps, sl st into first sc.

4th round: 1ch, work 1sc into same sc as last sl st, *6ch, skip 5sc, 1sc into next sc; rep from * 6 times more, 6ch, sl st into first sc.

5th round: Sl st into first 6ch arch, 1ch, work [1sc, 1hdc, 6dc, 1hdc, 1sc] into each of the 8 6ch arches, sl st into first sc. (8 petals worked).

IV.26

1st round: Make 16ch, sl st into first ch (first loop formed), [15ch, sl st into same ch as last sl st] twice.

2nd round: 1ch, working over **padding threads** work [28sc into next loop, 1 sl st into same ch as sl sts of first round] 3 times.

3rd round: Sl st into each of first 3sc, 1ch, 1sc into same st as last sl st, 1sc into each of next 23sc, [skip 4sc, 1sc into each of next 24sc] twice, 17ch, working over **padding threads** work 1sc into 2nd ch from hook, 1sc into each of next 15ch, sl st into first sc. Fasten off.

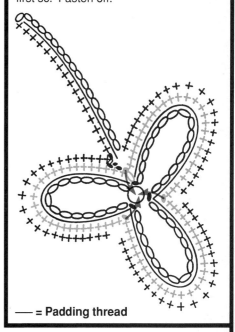

——— = Padding thread

6th round: 1ch, working behind each petal of previous round, work 1sc into first sc on 4th round, *7ch, 1sc into next sc on 4th round; rep from * 6 times more, 7ch, sl st into first sc.

7th round: Sl st into first 7ch arch, 1ch, work [1sc, 1hdc, 7dc, 1hdc, 1sc] into each of the 8 7ch arches, sl st into first sc.

8th round: 1ch, working behind each petal of previous round, work 1sc into first sc on 6th round, *8ch, 1sc into next sc on 6th round; rep from * 6 times more, 8ch, sl st into first sc.

9th round: Sl st into first 8ch arch, 1ch, work [1sc, 1hdc, 3dc, 1 picot, 3dc, 1 picot, 3dc, 1hdc, 1sc] into each of the 8 8ch arches, sl st into first sc. Fasten off.

V. Edgings and Trimmings

Using Edgings

Edgings are self evidently an addition to something which already exists. Household items such as table mats or cloths, handkerchiefs, towels and pillowcases are all enhanced when trimmed with a matching or toning crochet border.

All the written and diagramatic instructions in this section include the starting chain. If you are going to sew the border on to material you need this chain to work into. However in many cases it is preferable to omit the starting chain and work a row of single crochet directly into the folded edge of the fabric (see illustration of V.3 which has been worked in this way). If the first row of the design is a single crochet row the instructions as given do not need amending. If however this base is not included in the pattern it is recommended that you work a row of firm single crochet on to the folded edge of the material using the same multiple as given for the starting chain.

We have included a few examples of curved versions of some of the edgings (see V.5 opposite). These can be used as collar or neck edgings, or if worked or sewn on to a straight edge they will flute or form a frill.

The direction in which the edging is made can also vary. If a particularly long piece is required, as for example the border for a large table cloth, it may be advisable to choose one which is worked sideways like V.32 on page 84. The advantage of this is that you can pin or baste the border in position before it is finished, to ensure that the length you have worked is correct.

V.1

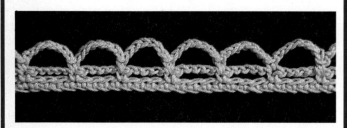

Starting chain: Multiple of 4 sts + 2.

1st row (right side): Work 1sc into 2nd ch from hook, 1sc into each ch to end, turn.

2nd row: 1ch, 1sc into first sc, *5ch, skip 3sc, 1sc into next sc; rep from * to end, turn.

3rd row: 1ch, 1sc into first sc, *7ch, 1sc into next sc; rep from * to end.

Fasten off.

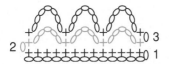

V.2

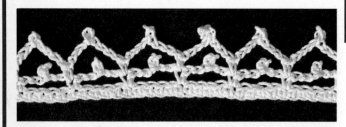

Starting chain: Multiple of 5 sts + 2.

1st row (right side): Work 1sc into 2nd ch from hook, 1sc into each ch to end, turn.

V.3

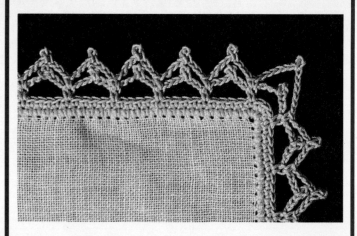

To make edging in rounds, make a starting chain of a multiple of 5 sts + 1 for each side + 1 for each of the 4 corners. Place a marker in last ch (4th corner ch) and in each of the other 3 corner ch. Sl st into first ch to form a ring.

1st round (right side): 1ch, work 1sc into same ch as last sl st, 1sc into each ch to first corner ch, [3sc into corner ch, 1sc into each ch to next corner ch] 3 times, 3sc into last corner ch, sl st into first sc.

2nd round: 1ch, work 1sc into same st as last sl st, *5ch, sl st into 3rd ch from hook, 3ch, skip 4sc, 1sc into next sc; rep from * to next corner, 6ch, sl st into 3rd ch from hook, 4ch, skip 3sc (corner scs), 1sc into next dc**; rep from * to ** 3 times more omitting 1sc at end of last rep, sl st into first sc.

3rd round: 1ch, work 1sc into same st as last sl st, *6ch, sl st into 3rd ch from hook, 4ch, 1sc into next sc; rep from * to next corner, 8ch, sl st into 3rd ch from hook, 6ch, 1sc into next sc**; rep from * to ** 3 times more omitting 1sc at end of last rep, sl st into first sc. Fasten off.

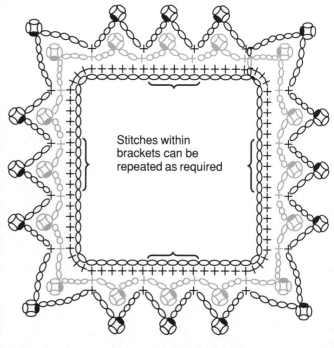

Stitches within brackets can be repeated as required

2nd row: 1ch, 1sc into first sc, *5ch, sl st into 3rd ch from hook, 3ch, skip next 4sc, 1sc into next sc; rep from * to end, turn.

3rd row: 1ch, 1sc into first sc, *6ch, sl st into 3rd ch from hook, 4ch, 1sc into next sc; rep from * to end. Fasten off.

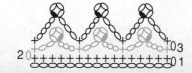

Abbreviations and Symbols on page 12

V.4

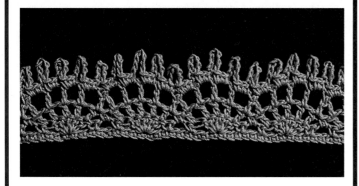

Starting chain: Multiple of 9 sts + 5.

Special Abbreviation

Dc2tog = work1dc into each of next 2dc until 1 loop of each remains on hook, yo and through all 3 loops on hook.

1st row (right side): Work 1sc into 2nd ch from hook, 1sc into each ch to end, turn.

2nd row: 1ch, 1sc into first sc, 2ch, skip 2sc, 1sc into next sc, *skip 2sc, 5dc into next sc, skip 2sc, 1sc into next sc, 2ch, skip 2sc, 1sc into next sc; rep from * to end, turn.

3rd row: 1ch, 1sc into first sc, 2ch, *1dc into next dc, [1ch, 1dc into next dc] 4 times, 1sc into next 2ch sp; rep from * to end omitting 1sc at end of last rep, 2ch, 1sc into last sc, turn.

4th row: 3ch (count as 1dc), [1dc into next dc, 2ch] 4 times, *dc2tog, 2ch, [1dc into next dc, 2ch] 3 times; rep from * to last dc, work 1dc into next dc until 2 loops remain on hook, 1dc into last sc until 3 loops remain on hook, yo and through all 3 loops, turn.

5th row: 1ch, 1sc into first st, 3sc into first 2ch sp, *7ch, 3sc into next 2ch sp; rep from * to end, 1sc into 3rd of 3ch at beg of previous row. Fasten off.

$\mathbb{A}$ = Dc2tog

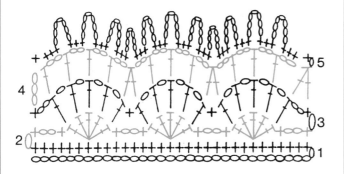

V.5

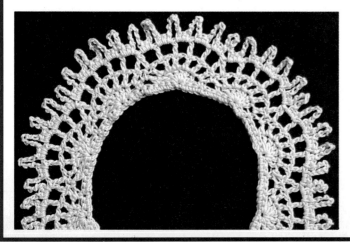

V.6

Starting chain: Multiple of 10 sts + 8.

1st row (wrong side): Work 1sc into 2nd ch from hook, 1sc into next ch, 6ch, skip 3ch, *1sc into each of next 7ch, 6ch, skip 3ch; rep from * to last 2ch, 1sc into each of last 2ch, turn.

2nd row: 1ch, 1sc into first sc, *into next 6ch arch work [1sc, 1hdc, 5dc, 1hdc, 1sc], 7ch; rep from * omitting 7ch at end of last rep, work 1sc into last sc, turn.

3rd row: 5ch, skip first 5 sts, work 1sc into next dc, [3ch, 1sc] 3 times into same st as last sc, *3ch, [1sc, 3ch, 1sc] into next 7ch arch, 3ch, skip next 4 sts, 1sc into next dc, [3ch, 1sc] 3 times into same st as last sc; rep from * to last 5 sts, 5ch, sl st into last sc. Fasten off.

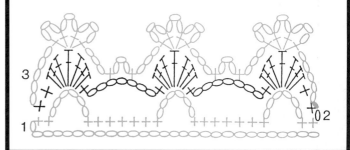

Starting chain: Multiple of 9 sts + 5.

Special Abbreviation

Dc2tog = work1dc into each of next 2dc until 1 loop of each remains on hook, yo and through all 3 loops on hook.

1st row (right side): Work 1sc into 2nd ch from hook, 1sc into each ch to end, turn.

2nd row: 1ch, 1sc into first sc, 2ch, skip 2sc, 1sc into next sc, *skip 2sc, 6dc into next sc, skip 2sc, 1sc into next sc, 2ch, skip 2sc, 1sc into next sc; rep from * to end, turn.

3rd row: 1ch, 1sc into first sc, 2ch, *1dc into next dc, [1ch, 1dc into next dc] 5 times, 1sc into next 2ch sp; rep from * to last 2sc, omitting 1sc at end of last rep, 2ch, 1sc into last sc, turn.

4th row: 3ch (count as 1dc), [1dc into next dc, 2ch] 5 times, *dc2tog, 2ch, [1dc into next dc, 2ch] 4 times; rep from * to last dc, work 1dc into next dc until 2 loops remain on hook, 1dc into last sc until 3 loops remain on hook, yo and through all 3 loops, turn.

5th row: 1ch, 1sc into first st, 3sc into first 2ch sp, *7ch, 3sc into next 2ch sp; rep from * to last 2dc, 1sc into 3rd of 3ch at beg of previous row. Fasten off.

$\mathbb{A}$ = Dc2tog

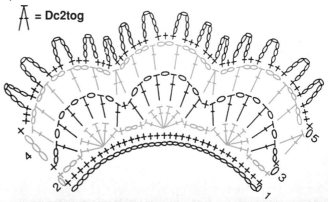

V. Edgings and Trimmings

V.7

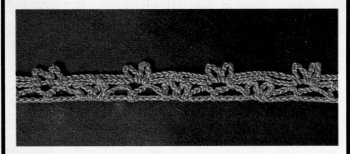

Starting chain: Multiple of 12 sts.

1st row (right side): Work 1sc into 2nd ch from hook, [5ch, skip 4ch, 1sc into next ch] twice, *[5ch, 1sc into next ch] twice, [5ch, skip 4ch, 1sc into next ch] twice; rep from * to end.

2nd row: 6ch (count as 1dc, 3ch), 1sc into first 5ch arch, *3ch, 1sc into next 5ch arch; rep from * to end, 3ch, 1dc into last sc, turn.

3rd row: 1ch, 1sc into first dc, *5ch, skip 1 arch, 1sc into next 3ch arch, into same arch as last sc work [5ch, 1sc] twice, 5ch, skip 1 arch, 1sc into next 3ch arch; rep from * to end working last sc into 3rd of 6ch at beg of previous row. Fasten off.

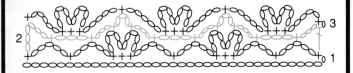

V.8

Starting chain: Multiple of 17 sts + 3.

Special Abbreviation

Bobble = work 3dc into next space until 1 loop of each remains on hook, yo and through all 4 loops on hook.

1st row (right side): Work 1sc into 2nd ch from hook, 1sc into each ch to end, turn.

2nd row: 1ch, work 1sc into each sc to end, turn.

3rd row: 1ch, work 1sc into each of first 8sc, *4ch, skip 3sc, 1sc into each of next 14sc; rep from * to last 11sc, 4ch, skip 3sc, 1sc into each of last 8sc, turn.

4th row: 3ch (count as 1hdc, 1ch), skip first 2sc, 1sc into each of next 3sc, 1ch, into next 4ch sp work [1dc, 1ch] 6 times, trskip 3sc, 1sc into each of next 3sc, *3ch, skip 2sc, 1sc into each of next 3sc, 1ch, into next 4ch sp work [1dc, 1ch] 6 times, skip 3sc, 1sc into each of next 3sc; rep from * to last 2sc, 1ch, 1hdc into last sc, turn.

5th row: 1ch, 1sc into first hdc, 2ch, [1 bobble into next ch sp, 2ch] 7 times, *1sc into next 3ch arch, 2ch, [1 bobble into next ch sp, 2ch] 7 times; rep from * to last 3ch, skip 1ch, 1sc into next ch, turn.

V.9

Starting chain: Multiple of 10 sts + 2.

Special Abbreviation

Bobble = work 3dc into next space until 1 loop of each remains on hook, yo and through all 4 loops on hook.

1st row (wrong side): Work 1sc into 2nd ch from hook, 1sc into each ch to end, turn.

2nd row: 5ch (count as 1tr, 1ch), work [1tr, 1ch] twice into first sc, skip 4sc, 1sc into next sc, *1ch, skip 4sc, into next sc work [1tr, 1ch] 5 times, skip 4sc, 1sc into next sc; rep from * to last 5sc, 1ch, work 1tr into last sc, 1ch, into same st as last tr work [1tr, 1ch, 1tr], turn.

3rd row: 1ch, 1sc into first tr, *2ch, into next sc work [1dtr, 2ch] 4 times, skip 2tr, 1sc into next tr; rep from * to end placing last sc into 4th of 5ch at beg of previous row, turn.

4th row: 1ch, 1sc into first sc, *4ch, skip next sp, 1 bobble into next 2ch sp, [3ch, 1 bobble into next 2ch sp] twice, 4ch, 1sc into next sc; rep from * to end. Fasten off.

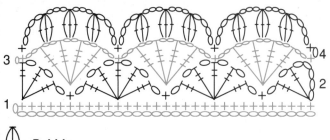

⏐⏐⏐ = Bobble

6th row: 1ch, 1sc into first sc, 2sc into first 2ch sp, 1sc into top of first bobble, 2sc into next 2ch sp, [3ch, 2sc into next sp] twice, 5ch, [2sc into next sp, 3ch] twice, 2sc into next sp, 1sc into top of next bobble, 2sc into next sp, *skip 1sc, 2sc into next sp, 1sc into top of next bobble, 2sc into next sp, [3ch, 2sc into next sp] twice, 5ch, [2sc into next sp, 3ch] twice, 2sc into next sp, 1sc into top of next bobble, 2sc into next sp; rep from * to last sc, 1sc into last sc. Fasten off.

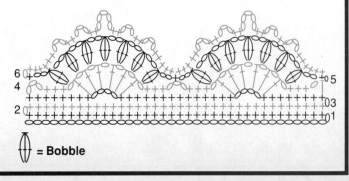

⏐⏐⏐ = Bobble

Abbreviations and Symbols on page 12

V.10

Starting chain: Multiple of 6 sts + 3.

1st row (wrong side): Work 1sc into 2nd ch from hook, 1sc into each ch to end, turn.

2nd row: 3ch (count as 1dc), skip first sc, 1dc into next sc, *1ch, skip 1sc, 1dc into each of next 2sc; rep from * to end, turn.

3rd row: 5ch (count as 1dc, 2ch), 1sc into next ch sp, *4ch, 1sc into next ch sp; rep from * to last 2 sts, 2ch, 1dc into 3rd of 3ch at beg of previous row, turn.

4th row: 1ch, 1sc into first dc, *work 5dc into next 4ch sp, 1sc into next 4ch sp; rep from * to end placing last sc into 3rd of 5ch at beg of previous row. Fasten off.

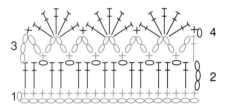

V.11

Starting chain: Multiple of 6 sts + 3.

Special Abbreviation

Picot = make 3ch, sl st into 3rd ch from hook.

1st row (wrong side): Work 1sc into 2nd ch from hook, 1sc into each ch to end, turn.

2nd row: 5ch (count as 1dc, 2ch), skip first 3sc, 1sc into next sc, work 3 picots, 1sc into next sc, *5ch, skip 4sc, 1sc into next sc, work 3 picots, 1sc into next sc; rep from * to last 3sc, 2ch, 1dc into last sc, turn.

3rd row: 1ch, 1sc into first dc, *8ch, 1sc into next 5ch arch; rep from * to end placing last sc into 3rd of 5ch at beg of previous row, turn.

4th row: 1ch, 1sc into first sc, *11sc into next 8ch arch, 1sc into next sc; rep from * to end. Fasten off.

 = Picot

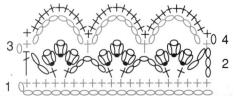

V.12

Starting chain: Multiple of 16 sts + 2.

Special Abbreviation

Bobble = work 4tr into arch until 1 loop of each remains on hook, yo and through all 5 loops on hook.

1st row (wrong side): Work 1sc into 2nd ch from hook, 1sc into each ch to end, turn.

2nd row: 1ch, 1sc into first sc, *3ch, skip 3sc, 1sc into next sc; rep from * to end, turn.

3rd row: 1ch, 1sc into first sc, 1ch, 1sc into first sp, *3ch, 1sc into next sp; rep from * to last sc, 1ch, 1sc into last sc, turn.

4th row: 6ch (count as 1dc, 3ch), skip first sc, 1sc into next sc, 3sc into next 3ch sp, 1sc into next sc, *6ch, 1sc into next sc, 3sc into next 3ch sp, 1sc into next sc; rep from * to last sc, 3ch, 1dc into last sc, turn.

5th row: 1ch, 1sc into first dc, *4ch, work 1 bobble into next 6ch arch, into same arch as last bobble work [3ch, 1 bobble] twice, 4ch, 1sc into next 6ch arch; rep from * to end placing last sc into 3rd of 6ch at beg of previous row, turn.

6th row: 7ch (count as 1tr, 3ch), *work 1 bobble into next 4ch arch, 3ch, [1 bobble into next 3ch arch, 3ch] twice, 1 bobble into next 4ch arch, 3ch, 1tr into next sc, 3ch; rep from * to end omitting 3ch at end of last rep, turn.

7th row: 1ch, 1sc into first tr, 1ch, [1sc into next arch, 3ch] twice, 4dc into next arch, *3ch, [1sc into next arch, 3ch] 4 times, 4dc into next arch; rep from * to last 2 arches, [3ch, 1sc into next arch] twice, 1ch, 1sc into 4th of 7ch at beg of previous row, turn.

8th row: 1ch, 1sc into first sc, 3ch, [1sc into next 3ch arch, 3ch] twice, skip 1dc, 1dc into each of next 2dc, *3ch, [1sc into next arch, 3ch] 5 times, skip 1dc, 1dc into each of next 2dc; rep from * to last 2 3ch arches, 3ch, [1sc into next arch, 3ch] twice, 1sc into last sc, turn.

9th row: 1ch, 1sc into first sc, work 3sc into each of next 3 arches, 1sc into next dc, 3ch, 1sc into next dc, *3sc into each of next 6 arches, 1sc into next dc, 3ch, 1sc into next dc; rep from * to last 3 arches, 3sc into each of last 3 arches, 1sc into last sc. Fasten off.

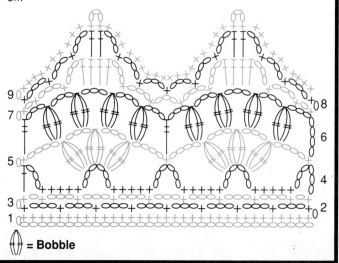

 = Bobble

V. Edgings and Trimmings

V.13

Starting chain: Multiple of 4 sts + 4.

1st row (right side): Work 1dc into 6th ch from hook, *1ch, skip 1ch, 1dc into next ch; rep from * to end, turn.

2nd row: 1ch, 1sc into first dc, *5ch, skip 1dc, 1sc into next dc; rep from * to last dc, 5ch, skip 1dc and 1ch, 1sc into next ch, turn.

3rd row: 1ch, 1sc into first sc, work 7sc into each 5ch arch to end, 1sc into last sc, turn.

4th row: 5ch (count as 1dc, 2ch), skip first 4sc, 1sc into next sc, *3ch, skip 6sc, 1sc into next sc; rep from * to last 4sc, 2ch, 1dc into last sc, turn.

5th row: 1ch, 1sc into first dc, 5ch, 1sc into 2ch sp, into each sp work [1sc, 5ch, 1sc] to end placing last sc into 3rd of 5ch at beg of previous row. Fasten off.

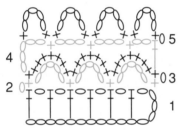

V.14

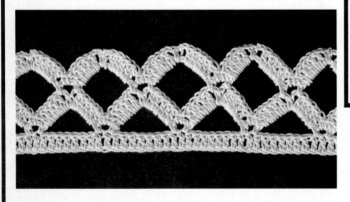

Starting chain: Multiple of 9 sts + 4.

1st row (right side): Work 1dc into 4th ch from hook, 1dc into each ch to end, turn.

2nd row: 1ch, 1sc into first dc, 1ch, 1sc into next dc, 9ch, skip 7dc, 1sc into next dc, *3ch, 1sc into next dc, 9ch, skip 7dc, 1sc into next dc; rep from * to end, 1ch, 1sc into top of 3ch, turn.

3rd row: 1ch, 1sc into first sc, 1sc into first ch sp, *5dc into next 9ch arch, 2ch, into same arch as last 5dc work [1sc, 2ch, 5dc], 1sc into next 3ch arch; rep from * to end placing last sc into last ch sp, 1sc into last sc, turn.

4th row: 9ch (count as 1dtr, 4ch), 1sc into next 2ch sp, 3ch, 1sc into next 2ch sp, *9ch, 1sc into next 2ch sp, 3ch, 1sc into next 2ch sp; rep from * to last 5dc, 4ch, 1dtr into last sc, turn.

V.15

Starting chain: Multiple of 10 sts + 2.

1st row (right side): Work 1sc into 2nd ch from hook, 1sc into each ch to end, turn.

2nd row: 3ch (count as 1dc), skip first sc, 1dc into each of next 3sc, *3ch, skip 3sc, 1dc into each of next 7sc; rep from * to end omitting 3dc at end of last rep, turn.

3rd row: 1ch, 1sc into each of first 4dc, 3sc into next 3ch sp, *1sc into each of next 7dc, 3sc into next 3ch sp; rep from * to last 4dc, 1sc into each of next 3dc, 1sc into 3rd of 3ch at beg of previous row, turn.

4th row: 1ch, 1sc into first sc, 2ch, skip 2sc, 1sc into next sc, 8ch, skip 3sc, 1sc into next sc, *5ch, skip 5sc, 1sc into next sc, 8ch, skip 3sc, 1sc into next sc; rep from * to last 3sc, 2ch, 1sc into last sc, turn.

5th row: 1ch, 1sc into first sc, 19dc into 8ch arch, *1sc into next 5ch sp, 19dc into next 8ch arch; rep from * to last 2ch sp, 1sc into last sc. Fasten off.

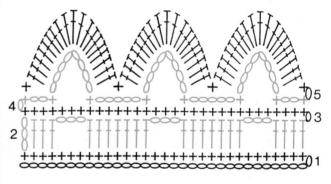

5th row: 3ch (count as 1dc), 5dc into 4ch arch, 1sc into next 3ch arch, *5dc into next 9ch arch, 2ch, into same arch as last 5dc work [1sc, 2ch, 5dc], 1sc into next 3ch arch; rep from * to last arch, 5dc into last arch, 1dc into 5th of 9ch at beg of previous row. Fasten off.

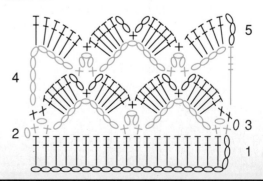

Abbreviations and Symbols on page 12

V.16

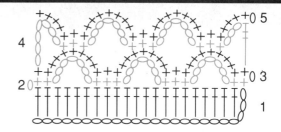

5th row: 1ch, 1sc into tr, 3sc into first arch, 1sc into each of next 3sc, *7sc into next 7ch arch, 1sc into each of next 3sc; rep from * to last arch, 3sc into last arch, 1sc into 4th of 7ch at beg of previous row. Fasten off.

Starting chain: Multiple of 7 sts + 3.

1st row (right side): Work 1dc into 4th ch from hook, 1dc into each ch to end, turn.

2nd row: 1ch, 1sc into each of first 2dc, *7ch, skip 4dc, 1sc into each of next 3dc, rep from * to end omitting 1sc at end of last rep and placing last sc into top of 3ch, turn.

3rd row: 1ch, 1sc into each of first 2sc, *7sc into 7ch arch, 1sc into each of next 3sc, rep from * to end omitting 1sc at end of last rep, turn.

4th row: 7ch (count as 1tr, 3ch), skip 4sc, 1sc into each of next 3sc, *7ch, skip 7sc, 1sc into each of next 3sc; rep from * to last 4sc, 3ch, 1tr into last sc, turn.

V.18

Starting chain: Multiple of 16 sts + 3.

Special Abbreviation

Cluster = work 2dtr into next st until 1 loop of each remains on hook, yo and through all 3 loops on hook.

1st row (right side): Work 1dc into 4th ch from hook, *1ch, skip 1ch, 1dc into next ch; rep from * to last ch, 1dc into last ch, turn.

2nd row: 3ch (count as 1dc), skip first dc, 1dc into each of next dc, ch sp and dc, 5ch, skip 2 sps, 1tr into next sp, 5ch, skip 2dc, 1dc into next dc, *[1dc into next sp, 1dc into next dc] 3 times, 5ch, skip 2 sps, 1tr into next sp, 5ch, skip 2dc, 1dc into next dc; rep from * to last 3 sts, 1dc into next sp, 1dc into next dc, 1dc into top of 3ch, turn.

3rd row: 3ch, skip first dc, 1dc into each of next 2dc, 7ch, 1sc into next tr, 7ch, *skip 1dc, 1dc into each of next 5dc, 7ch, 1sc into next tr, 7ch; rep from * to last 4 sts, skip 1dc, 1dc into each of next 2dc, 1dc into 3rd of 3ch at beg of previous row, turn.

4th row: 3ch, skip first dc, 1dc into next dc, 7ch, into next sc work [1sc, 5ch, 1sc], 7ch, *skip 1dc, 1dc into each of next 3dc, 7ch, into next sc work [1sc, 5ch, 1sc], 7ch; rep from * to last 3 sts, skip 1dc, 1dc into next dc, 1dc into 3rd of 3ch at beg of previous row, turn.

5th row: 6ch (count as 1dc, 3ch), *skip 7ch arch, work 1 cluster into 5ch arch then [1ch, 1 cluster] 4 times into same arch, 3ch, skip 1dc, 1dc into next dc, 3ch; rep from * to end omitting 3ch at end of last rep and placing last dc into 3rd of 3ch. Fasten off.

 = Cluster

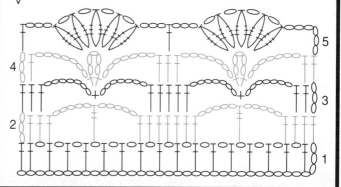

V.17

Starting chain: Multiple of 8 sts + 2.

1st row (right side): Work 1sc into 2nd ch from hook, 1sc into each ch to end, turn.

2nd row: 1ch, 1sc into each of first 4sc, into next sc work [1sc, 7ch, 1sc], *1sc into each of next 7sc, into next sc work [1sc, 7ch, 1sc]; rep from * to last 4sc, 1sc into each of last 4sc, turn.

3rd row: 3ch (count as 1dc), skip first sc, *1sc into next sc, 9sc into next arch, skip 3sc, 1sc into next sc, 1dc into next sc; rep from * to end, turn.

4th row: 1ch, 1sc into first dc, *4ch, skip 5sc, into next sc work [1sc, 5ch, 1sc], 4ch, skip 5sc, 1sc into next dc; rep from * to end placing last sc into 3rd of 3ch at beg of previous row, turn.

5th row: 1ch, 1sc into first sc, *3sc into next 4ch arch, 5sc into next 5ch arch, 3sc into next 4ch arch, 1sc into next sc; rep from * to end. Fasten off.

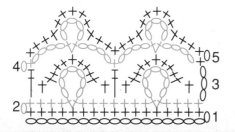

V. Edgings and Trimmings

V.19

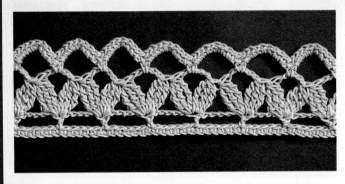

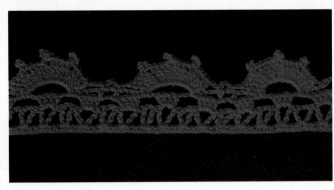

= Bobble

Starting chain: Multiple of 6 sts + 2.

Special Abbreviation

Bobble = work 3dtr into next st until 1 loop of each remains on hook, yo and through all 4 loops on hook.

1st row (right side): Work 1sc into 2nd ch from hook, 1sc into each ch to end, turn.

2nd row: 8ch (count as 1dc, 5ch), skip first 6sc, 1dc into next sc, *5ch, skip 5sc, 1dc into next sc; rep from * to end, turn.

3rd row: 6ch (count as 1tr, 2ch), work 1 bobble into first dc, *into next dc work [1 bobble, 5ch, 1 bobble]; rep from * to last dc, into 3rd of 3ch at beg of previous row work [1 bobble, 2ch, 1tr], turn.

4th row: 1ch, 1sc into first tr, *7ch, 1sc into next 5ch arch; rep from * to end placing last sc into 4th of 6ch at beg of previous row, turn.

5th row: 1ch, 1sc into first sc, *9sc into next 7ch arch, 1sc into next sc; rep from * to end. Fasten off.

V.20

Starting chain: Multiple of 9 sts + 5.

Special Abbreviation

Bobble = work 3dtr into sp until one loop of each remains on hook, yo and through all 4 loops on hook.

1st row (wrong side): Work 1dc into 8th ch from hook, *2ch, skip 2ch, 1dc into next ch; rep from * to end, turn.

2nd row: 3ch (count as 1dc), skip next sp, work 1 bobble into next sp, [6ch, 1dc into first of these ch] 3 times, 1 bobble into same sp as last bobble, *skip 2 sps, work 1 bobble into next sp, [6ch, 1dc into first of these ch] 3 times, 1 bobble into same sp as last bobble; rep from * to last sp, skip 2ch, 1dc into next ch. Fasten off.

= Bobble

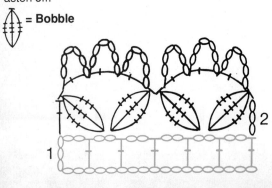

V.21

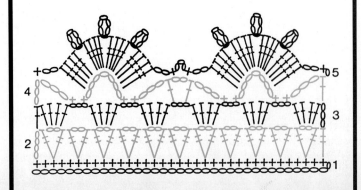

Starting chain: Multiple of 18 sts + 18.

1st row (right side): Work 1sc into 2nd ch from hook, 1sc into each ch to end, turn.

2nd row: 4ch (count as 1tr), *skip next 2sc, work [1tr, 2ch, 1tr] into next sc; rep from * to last 2sc, 1tr into last sc, turn.

3rd row: 3ch (count as 1dc), work 4dc into first 2ch sp, *3ch, skip 1 sp, 4dc into next sp; rep from * to end, 1dc into 4th of 4ch at beg of previous row, turn.

4th row: 6ch (count as 1dc, 3ch), 2sc into first 3ch sp, 7ch, 2sc into next sp, *3ch, into next sp work [1dc, 2ch, 1dc], 3ch, 2sc into next sp, 7ch, 2sc into next sp; rep from * to last 5 sts, 3ch, 1dc into 3rd of 3ch at beg of previous row, turn.

5th row: 1ch, 1sc into first dc, 2ch, into 7ch arch work 4tr and [5ch, sl st into first of these ch, 4tr] 3 times, 2ch, *skip 1 sp, into next 2ch sp work [1sc, 3ch, 1sc], 2ch, into 7ch arch work 4tr and [5ch, sl st into first of these ch, 4tr] 3 times; rep from * to last sp, 2ch, 1sc into 3rd of 6ch at beg of previous row. Fasten off.

Abbreviations and Symbols on page 12

V.22

Starting chain: Multiple of 10 sts + 3.

1st row (right side): Work 1dc into 4th ch from hook, 1dc into each ch to end, turn.

2nd row: 1ch, 1sc into each of first 3dc, *2ch, skip 2dc, into next dc work [2dc, 2ch] twice, skip 2dc, 1sc into each of next 5dc; rep from * to end omitting 2sc at end of last rep and placing last sc into top of 3ch at beg of previous row, turn.

3rd row: 1ch, 1sc into each of first 2sc, *3ch, skip next 2ch sp, into next 2ch sp work [3dc, 2ch, 3dc], 3ch, skip 1sc, 1sc into each of next 3sc; rep from * to end omitting 1sc at end of last rep, turn.

4th row: 1ch, 1sc into first sc, *4ch, skip next 3ch sp, into next 2ch sp work [4dc, 2ch, 4dc], 4ch, skip 1sc, 1sc into next sc; rep from * to end, turn.

5th row: 1ch, 1sc into first sc, *5ch, skip next 4ch sp, into next 2ch sp work [4dc, 2ch, 4dc], 5ch, 1sc into next sc; rep from * to end. Fasten off.

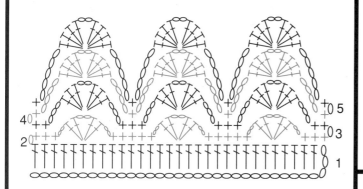

V.23

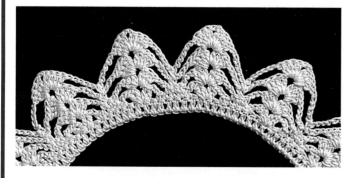

Starting chain: Multiple of 8 sts + 3.

1st row (right side): Work 1dc into 4th ch from hook, 1dc into each ch to end, turn.

2nd row: 1ch, 1sc into each of first 3dc, *2ch, skip 1dc, into next dc work [2dc, 2ch] twice, skip 1dc, 1sc into each of next 5dc; rep from * to end omitting 2sc at end of last rep and placing last sc into top of 3ch at beg of previous row, turn.

V.24

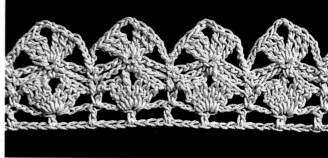

Starting chain: Multiple of 8 sts + 6.

1st row (right side): Work 1dc into 10th ch from hook, *3ch, skip 3ch, 1dc into next ch; rep from * to end, turn.

2nd row: 1ch, 1sc into first dc, *2ch, into next dc work [3tr, 3ch, 3tr], 2ch, 1sc into next dc; rep from * to end placing last sc into 4th ch, turn.

3rd row: 1ch, 1sc into first sc, *5ch, 1sc into next 3ch sp, 5ch, 1sc into next sc; rep from * to end, turn.

4th row: 1ch, 1sc into first sc, *4ch, 1sc into next sc; rep from * to end, turn.

5th row: 1ch, 1sc into first sc, *3ch, into next sc work [3tr, 3ch, 3tr], 3ch, 1sc into next sc; rep from * to end. Fasten off.

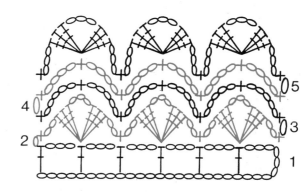

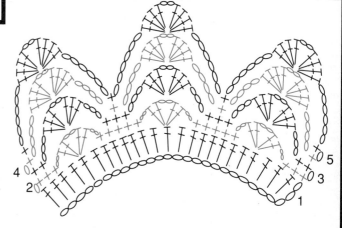

3rd row: 1ch, 1sc into each of first 2sc, *3ch, skip next 2ch sp, into next 2ch sp work [3dc, 2ch, 3dc], 3ch, skip 1sc, 1sc into each of next 3sc; rep from * to end omitting 1sc at end of last rep, turn.

4th row: 1ch, 1sc into first sc, *4ch, skip next 3ch sp, into next 2ch sp work [4dc, 2ch, 4dc], 4ch, skip 1sc, 1sc into next sc; rep from * to end, turn.

5th row: 1ch, 1sc into first sc, *6ch, skip next 4ch sp, into next 2ch sp work [4dc, 2ch, 4dc], 6ch, 1sc into next sc; rep from * to end. Fasten off.

V. Edgings and Trimmings

V.25

Starting chain: Multiple of 6 sts + 6.

Special Abbreviation

Bobble = work 4dtr into ch until 1 loop of each remains on hook, yo and through all 5 loops on hook.

1st row (right side): Work 1sc into 2nd ch from hook, 1sc into each ch to end, turn.

2nd row: 6ch (count as 1dc, 3ch), skip 4sc, 1dc into next sc, *1ch, skip 1sc, 1dc into next sc, 3ch, skip 3sc, 1dc into next sc; rep from * to end, turn.

3rd row: 1ch, 1sc into first dc, *4ch, skip 1ch, 1 bobble into next ch, 4ch, 1sc into next dc, 1ch, 1sc into next dc; rep from * to end, omitting last ch and sc and working final sc into 3rd of 6ch at beg of previous row. Fasten off.

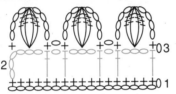

 = Bobble

V.26

Starting chain: Multiple of 11 sts + 3.

Special Abbreviation

Bobble = Work 3dtr into 3ch loop until 1 loop of each remains on hook, yo and through all 4 loops on hook.

1st row (right side): Work 1dc into 4th ch from hook, 1dc into each ch to end, turn.

2nd row: 1ch, 1sc into first dc, *9ch, sl st into 3rd ch from hook, 7ch, skip 10dc, 1sc into next dc; rep from * to end placing last sc into top of 3ch, turn.

3rd row: 5ch, *work 1 bobble into next 3ch loop, 5ch, into same loop as last bobble work [1 bobble, 5ch, 1 bobble], 1dtr into next sc; rep from * to end. Fasten off.

 = Bobble

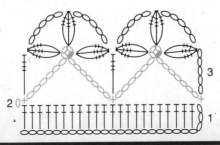

V.27

Starting chain: Multiple of 8 sts + 2.

Special Abbreviation

Triple loop = sl st into next sc, [7ch, 1 sl st] 3 times into same sc.

1st row (wrong side): Work 1sc into 2nd ch from hook, 1sc into each ch to end, turn.

2nd row: 1ch, work 1sc into each sc to end, turn.

3rd row: 1ch, 1sc into each of first 3sc, *9ch, skip 3sc, 1sc into each of next 5sc; rep from * to end omitting 2sc at end of last rep, turn.

4th row: 1ch, 1sc into each of first 2sc, *5ch, 1sc into next 9ch arch, 5ch, skip 1sc, 1sc into each of next 3sc; rep from * to end omitting 1sc at end of last rep, turn.

5th row: 1ch, 1sc into first sc, *5ch, skip 1sc, 1sc into next sc; rep from * to end, turn.

6th row: 1ch, 1sc into first sc, *5ch, work 1 triple loop into next sc, 5ch, 1sc into next sc; rep from * to end. Fasten off.

= **Triple loop**

V.28

Starting chain: Multiple of 5 sts + 1.

Special Abbreviation

Popcorn = work 4dc into next sc, drop loop from hook, insert hook from the front into top of first of these dc, pick up dropped loop and draw through dc, 1ch to secure popcorn.

1st row (right side): Work 1sc into 2nd ch from hook, 1sc into each ch to end, turn.

2nd row: 4ch (count as 1hdc, 2ch), skip first 2sc, 1sc into next sc, *5ch, skip 4sc, 1sc into next sc; rep from * to last 2sc, 2ch, 1hdc into last sc, turn.

3rd row: 1ch, 1sc into first hdc, 3ch, 1 popcorn into next sc, 3ch, *1sc into next 5ch arch, 3ch, 1 popcorn into next sc, 3ch; rep from * to last sp, 1sc into 2nd of 4ch at beg of previous row. Fasten off.

 = Popcorn

Abbreviations and Symbols on page 12

V.29

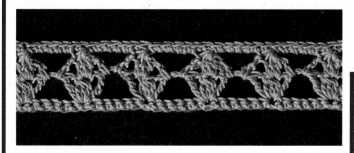

Starting chain: Multiple of 6 sts + 4.

Special Abbreviations

Bobble = work 3dc into next st until 1 loop of each remains on hook, yo and through all 4 loops on hook.

Cluster = work 1tr into next ch sp until 2 loops remain on hook, 3dc into top of next bobble until 1 loop of each remains on hook (5 loops on hook), skip 1ch sp, 1tr into next ch sp until 6 loops remain on hook, yo and through all 6 loops on hook

1st row (wrong side): Work 1sc into 2nd ch from hook, 1sc into each ch to end, turn.

2nd row: 4ch (count as 1dc, 1ch), skip first 4sc, 1tr into next sc, work [1ch, 1 bobble, 1ch, 1tr] into same st as last tr, 1ch, *skip 5sc, 1tr into next sc, work [1ch, 1 bobble, 1ch, 1tr] into same st as last tr, 1ch; rep from * to last 4sc, 1dc into last sc, turn.

3rd row: 6ch (count as 1dc, 3ch), *1 cluster, 5ch; rep from * to end working first tr of each cluster into same ch sp as last tr of previous cluster and omitting 2ch at end of last rep, 1dc into 3rd of 4ch at beg of previous row, turn.

4th row: 1ch, 1sc into first dc, 3sc into first 3ch sp, 1sc into top of first cluster, *5sc into next 5ch sp, 1sc into top of next cluster; rep from * to last sp, 3sc into last sp, 1sc into 3rd of 6ch at beg of previous row. Fasten off.

V.30

Starting chain: Multiple of 4 sts + 2.

1st row (right side): Work 1sc into 2nd ch from hook, 1sc into each ch to end, turn.

2nd row: 6ch (count as 1dc, 3ch), skip first 4sc, 1dc into next sc, *3ch, skip 3sc, 1dc into next sc; rep from * to end.

3rd row: 1ch, 1sc into first dc, *3ch, 1dc into next sp, 3ch, work 7dc over stem of dc just worked, 1sc into next dc; rep from * to end placing last sc into 3rd of 6ch at beg of previous row. Fasten off.

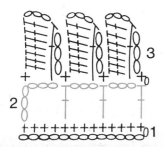

 = Bobble

 = Cluster

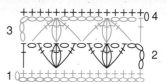

V.31

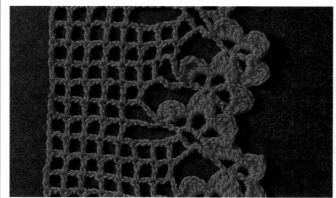

Worked lengthways.

1st row (right side): Make 31ch, work 1dc into 7th ch from hook, [2ch, skip 2ch, 1dc into next ch] 8 times, turn. (9 sps).

2nd row: 5ch (count as 1dc, 2ch), skip first dc, 1dc into next dc, [2ch, 1dc into next dc] 3 times, 5ch, skip next 4 sps, 1dc into next sp, work [3ch, 1dc] 3 times into same sp as last dc, turn.

3rd row: 1ch, 1sc into first dc, into first 3ch sp work [1hdc, 1dc, 1tr, 1dc, 1hdc, 1sc], into next 3ch sp work [1sc, 1hdc, 1dc, 1tr, 1dc, 1hdc, 1sc], into next 3ch sp work [1sc, 1hdc, 1dc, 1tr, 1dc, 1hdc], 1sc into next dc, 5ch, 1dc into next dc, [2ch, 1dc into next dc] 4 times placing last dc into 3rd of 5ch at beg of previous row, turn.

4th row: 5ch (count as 1dc, 2ch), skip first dc, [1dc into next dc, 2ch] 4 times, 1dc into 5ch sp, 7ch, skip first group of 7 sts, work 1dc into tr at center of next group of 7 sts, [3ch, 1dc] 3 times into same st as last dc, turn.

5th row: 1ch, 1sc into first dc, into first 3ch sp work [1hdc, 1dc, 1tr, 1dc, 1hdc, 1sc], into next 3ch sp work [1sc, 1hdc, 1dc, 1tr, 1dc, 1hdc, 1sc], into next 3ch sp work [1sc, 1hdc, 1dc, 1tr, 1dc, 1hdc], 1sc into next dc, 5ch, 1dc into 7ch sp, [2ch, 1dc into next dc] 6 times placing last dc into 3rd of 5ch at beg of previous row, turn.

6th row: 5ch (count as 1dc, 2ch), skip first dc, [1dc into next dc, 2ch] 6 times, 1dc into 5ch sp, 7ch, skip first group of 7 sts, work 1dc into tr at center of next group of 7 sts, [3ch, 1dc] 3 times into same st as last dc, turn.

7th row: 1ch, 1sc into first dc, into first 3ch sp work [1hdc, 1dc, 1tr, 1dc, 1hdc, 1sc], into next 3ch sp work [1sc, 1hdc, 1dc, 1tr, 1dc, 1hdc, 1sc], into next 3ch sp work [1sc, 1hdc, 1dc, 1tr, 1dc, 1hdc], 1sc into next dc, 5ch, 1dc into 7ch sp, [2ch, 1dc into next dc] 8 times placing last dc into 3rd of 5ch at beg of previous row, turn.

Rep 2nd to 7th rows ending with a 7th row.

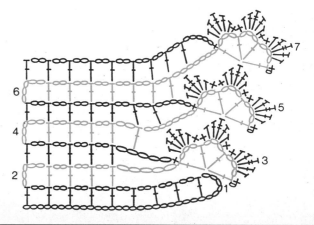

V. Edgings and Trimmings

V.32

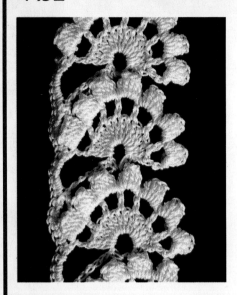

Worked lengthways.

Special Abbreviations

Popcorn at beg of row = 3ch, work 6dc into first sp, drop loop from hook, insert hook from the front into top of 3ch, pick up dropped loop and draw through, 1ch to secure.

7dc Popcorn = work 7dc into next sp, then complete as for popcorn at beg of row inserting hook into top of first of these dc.

V.33

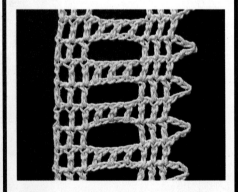

Worked lengthways.

1st row (wrong side): Make 20ch, work 1dc into 6th ch from hook, *1ch, skip 1ch, 1dc into next ch; rep from * to end, turn.

2nd row: 7ch, 1dc into first dc, [1ch, 1dc into next dc] twice, 7ch, skip 3dc, [1dc into next dc, 1ch] twice, skip 1ch, 1dc into next ch, turn.

3rd row: 4ch (count as 1dc, 1ch), skip first dc, 1dc into next dc, 1ch, 1dc into next dc, [1ch, skip 1ch, 1dc into next ch] 3 times, [1ch, 1dc into next dc] 3 times.

Rep 2nd and 3rd rows.

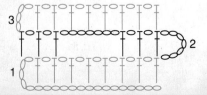

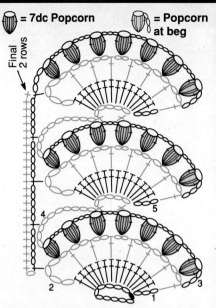

= 7dc Popcorn   **= Popcorn at beg**

Make 10ch and join into a ring with a sl st.

1st row (right side): 3ch (count as 1dc), work 14dc into ring, turn.

2nd row: 5ch (count as 1dc, 2ch), skip first 2dc, 1dc into next dc, [2ch, skip 1dc, 1dc into next dc] 6 times placing last dc into 3rd of 3ch at beg of previous row, turn.

3rd row: Work 1 popcorn at beg of row, [3ch, 1 7dc popcorn into next 2ch sp] 6 times, turn.

4th row: 10ch, skip first 2 sps, work [1sc, 5ch, 1sc] into next 3ch sp, turn.

5th row: 3ch (count as 1dc), work 14dc into 5ch sp, turn.

Rep 2nd to 5th rows until edging is required length ending with a 3rd row. Do not turn work but continue along side edge as follows:

1st Final row: 3ch, 1sc into sp formed at beg of 2nd row of pattern, *5ch, 1sc into sp formed at beg of 4th row of pattern, 5ch, 1sc into sp formed at beg of 2nd row of pattern; rep from * to end, turn.

2nd Final row: 1ch, 1sc into first sc, *5sc into 5ch sp, 1sc into next sc; rep from * to end. Fasten off.

V.34

Worked lengthways.

1st row (wrong side): Make 4ch (count as 1dc, 1ch), work 2dc into first of these ch, 2ch, 3dc into same ch as last 2dc, turn.

V.35

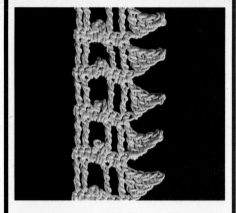

Worked lengthways.

1st row (right side): Make 14ch, work 1sc into 3rd ch from hook, 1hdc into next ch, 1dc into next ch, 1tr into next ch, [1ch, skip 1ch, 1tr into next ch] twice, 2ch, skip 2ch, 1tr into each of last 2ch, turn.

2nd row: 1ch, 1sc into each of first 2tr, 1sc into 2ch sp, 4ch, 1sc into same sp as last sc, 1sc into next tr, 1sc into ch sp, 1sc into next tr, turn.

3rd row: 7ch, work 1sc into 3rd ch from hook, 1hdc into next ch, 1dc into next ch, 1tr into next ch, 1ch, 1tr into next sc, 1ch, skip 1sc, 1tr into next sc, 2ch, skip 2sc, 1tr into each of last 2sc, turn.

Rep 2nd and 3rd rows.

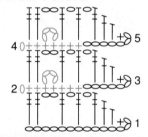

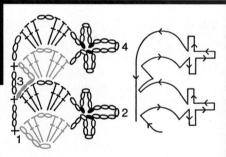

2nd row: 8ch, sl st into 6th ch from hook, 7ch, sl st into same ch as last sl st, 5ch, sl st into same ch as last 2 sl sts, 2ch, 3dc into 2ch sp, 2ch, 3dc into same sp as last 3dc, turn.

3rd row: Sl st into each of first 3dc, 3ch (count as 1dc), 2dc into 2ch sp, 2ch, 3dc into same sp as last 2dc, turn.

Rep 2nd and 3rd rows until edging is required length ending with a 2nd row. Do not turn work but continue along side edge as follows:

Final row: *3ch, 1sc into top of 3ch at beg of next fan, 3ch, 1sc into first sl st at beg of next fan; rep from * to last fan, 1sc into top of 4ch at beg of 1st row. Fasten off.

Abbreviations and Symbols on page 12

Afghan Crochet

Afghan or Tunisian crochet is worked with a long hook available in the same range of thicknesses as traditional crochet hooks. The hooks are longer than crochet hooks as they are required to hold the loops created on the first (Forward) half of the row before working them off on the return half.

The fabric produced by this technique can be dense and thick. It is important to use a suitable size of hook in relation to the yarn. This is usually at least two sizes larger than would be used when working ordinary crochet with the same yarn.

Each row is worked in two parts. The first or 'Forward' part of the row involves working from right to left and pulling up loops or stitches on to the hook. On the second or 'Return' part of the row these loops are worked off again as the hook travels back from left to right. Afghan crochet is nearly always made without turning, therefore the right side is always facing.

Holding the Hook

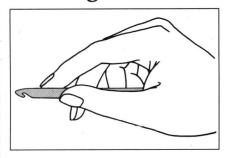

The hook should be held in the center with the hand as shown in the diagram.

Starting Chain

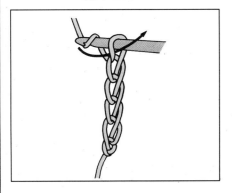

Make the number of chains needed to correspond with the number of stitches required in the first row.

Tip

When working a large piece it is sensible to start with more chains than necessary as it is simple to undo the extra chains if you have miscounted.

Although there are exceptions, Afghan stitch patterns usually begin with the same initial forward and return row - referred to as: **Basic Forward and Return row.**

Forward

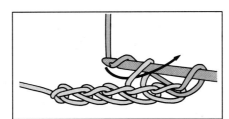

1. Working into back loop only of each chain, insert hook into second chain from hook, yarn over, draw loop through and leave on hook.
2. Insert hook into next chain, yarn over, draw loop through and leave on hook.

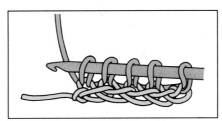

Repeat this in each chain to end. Do not turn.

The number of loops on hook should equal the number of stitches required for first row.

Note: Because the fabric produced in Afghan crochet is usually firmer than in ordinary crochet we recommend that the hook is inserted into the back loop only of the starting chain as this produces a firmer edge.

Return

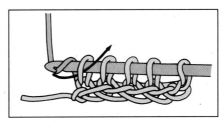

1. Yarn over, draw through one loop. (This chain forms the edge stitch).

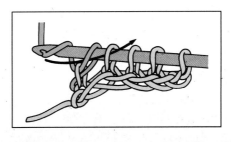

2. Yarn over, and draw through two loops.

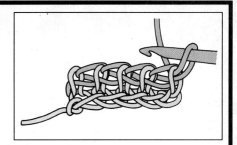

3. Repeat step 2 until one loop remains on hook. Do not turn. The loop remaining on the hook becomes the first stitch of the following row.

The Basic Stitches

These are produced by varying the technique of picking up loops on the Forward row.

Tunisian Simple Stitch (Tss ⌐|)

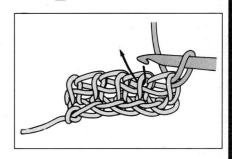

1. Insert hook from right to left behind single vertical thread.

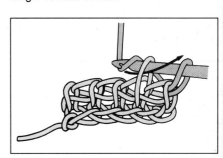

2. Yarn over hook.

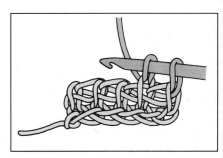

3. Draw loop through and leave on hook. Unless otherwise stated, the hook is always inserted in this way. For example, Afghan half double crochet and double crochet are usually worked from this position.

VI. Afghan (Tunisian) Crochet

Making Afghan (Tunisian) Fabric

Make chain as required and work a Basic Forward and Return row. Generally the single loop on the hook at the end of each Return row counts as the first stitch in the next Forward row and so the first stitch is skipped. (As shown in first diagram for Tunisian simple stitch).

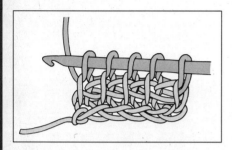

Next row: Pick up loop in each stitch (Tss or as required) including edge stitch.

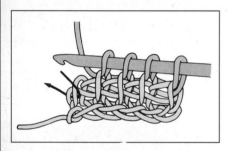

If you require a firmer edge at this end of the row you can work through two loops of the last stitch.

Return as Basic Return row.

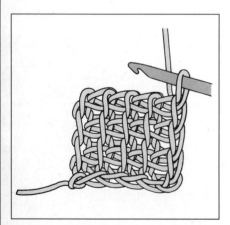

Repeat Forward and Return row as required. It is important to understand how to produce basic Afghan fabric before attempting pattern stitches.

Finishing Off

It is possible simply to finish with a Return row, cutting yarn and threading it through the remaining stitch to secure. However the following method leaves a neater edge and is useful where the Afghan fabric is complete in itself - as for a mat or rug for example.

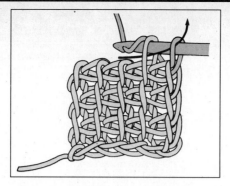

1. Finish with Return row. Insert hook into next stitch, yarn over.

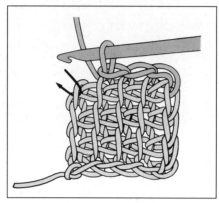

2. Draw through two loops.
Repeat steps 1 and 2 to end. Fasten off remaining loop.
Note: The hook can be inserted as if working Tunisian simple, Tunisian knit or Tunisian purl stitches so that stitches can be finished off in pattern.

Tunisian Knit Stitch (Tks ⟨ ⟩)

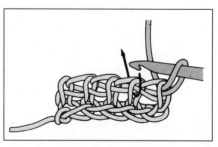

1. Insert hook from front to back through fabric and below chains formed by previous Return row, to right of front vertical thread but to left of corresponding back thread.

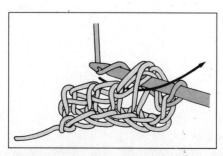

2. Yarn over, draw loop through and leave on hook.

3. Repeat steps 1 and 2 into each stitch to end. At the last stitch of each Forward row work under two loops, return as Basic Return row.

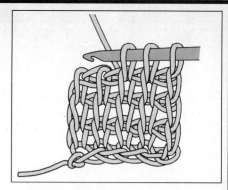

Tunisian Purl Stitch (Tps ⟨~⟩)

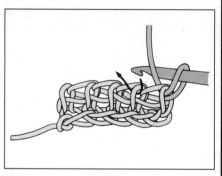

1. Bring yarn to front, insert hook as for Tunisian simple stitch.

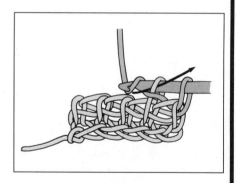

2. Take yarn to back of work and over hook (yo). Draw loop through and leave on hook.

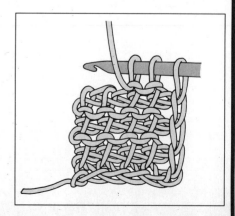

Repeat steps 1 and 2 in each stitch to end, return as Basic Return row.

Increasing

Inc 1Tss

1. To increase one stitch on a Forward row, insert hook under the back loop between two stitches, yarn over and draw loop through.

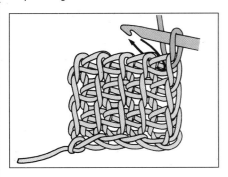

2. Work next stitch in the normal way.

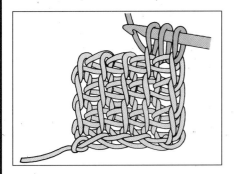

Two loops are to be worked off on Return row.

Decreasing

Tss2tog

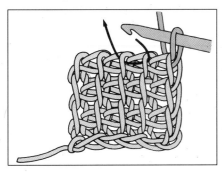

1. To decrease one stitch on a Forward row, insert hook through two stitches.
2. Yarn over and draw through loops. One loop to be worked off on Return row.

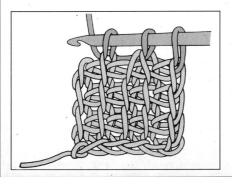

Note: Tss2tog is often worked in conjunction with a yarn over to create a lacy effect. For example:

Yo, Tss2tog

Tss2tog, yo

Two loops are then worked off on the Return row.

Tss3tog

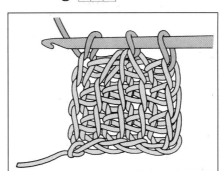

To decrease two stitches on a Forward row work as Tss2tog but insert hook through next three stitches.

Changing Color

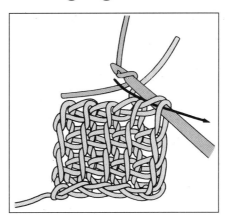

1. When a color change is required at the beginning of a Forward row, yarn over in the new color when two loops remain on the hook at the end of previous Return row.

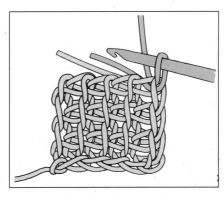

2. Draw through both loops.

To change color at the beginning of a Return row change yarn and continue to work as normal.

Stitch Variations

Tunisian Double Crochet (Tdc   )

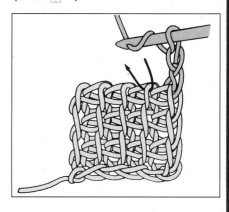

1. Make two chain for the first stitch at beginning of the row. Yarn over and insert hook into the next stitch as if working a Tunisian simple stitch.

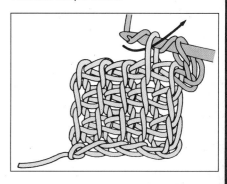

2. Yarn over and draw loop through.

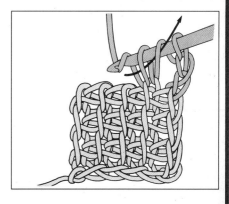

3. Yarn over and draw through two loops on hook.

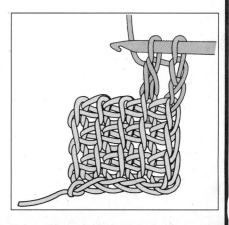

4. Leave remaining loop on hook.

VI. Afghan (Tunisian) Crochet

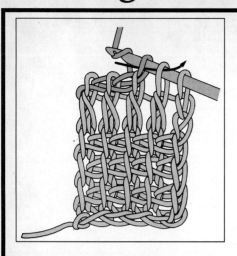

5. Double crochet is completed when Return row is worked.

Tunisian half double crochet (Thdc), Tunisian treble (Ttr), Tunisian double treble (Tdtr) etc. are also used frequently within Afghan patterns. As with Tunisian double crochet these stitches are worked in the same way as for crochet. Refer to introduction on pages 5 and 6 for detailed instructions of how to work these stitches. When working Afghan fabric, unless otherwise stated, the hook should be inserted as if working a Tunisian simple stitch and the stitch then worked as for crochet until one loop remains on the hook. Stitches are completed on the Return row. Turning chains are made at the beginning of Forward rows and are usually one chain less than for ordinary crochet. (Refer to individual pattern instructions).

Working between stitches

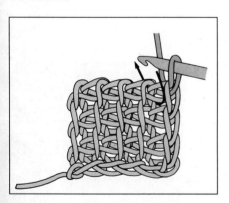

1. Insert hook between vertical loops that form stitches.
2. Yarn over and draw loop through.

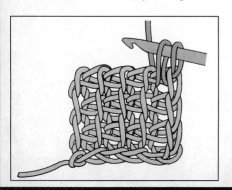

Thdc, Tdc, Ttr etc. can also be worked between stitches.

Tunisian Slipped Stitch (Tsl st ⱴ)

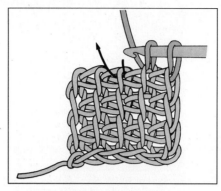

1. Insert hook into stitch as if working Tunisian simple stitch but do not pull yarn through.

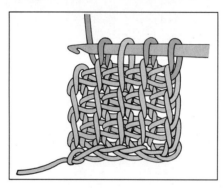

2. Continue working leaving slipped stitch on hook.

Twisted Tunisian Simple Stitch (TwTss ⸯ)

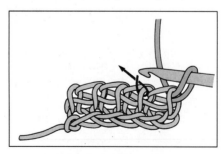

1. Insert hook into stitch from left to right.

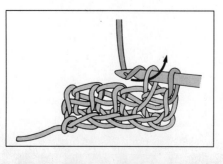

2. Yarn over and draw loop through.

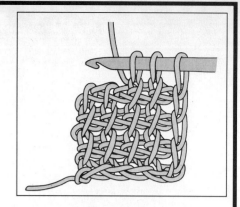

3. Finish stitch with Basic Return row.

Tunisian Bobbles

The following instructions are for a frequently used bobble. However individual pattern instructions should be followed.

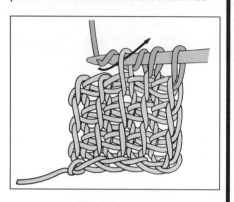

1. Yarn over and insert hook into next stitch as if working Tunisian simple stitch, yarn over and draw loop through.

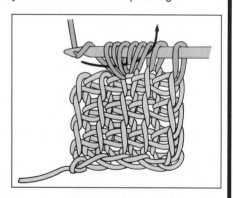

2. Repeat step 1 twice more into same stitch as before.

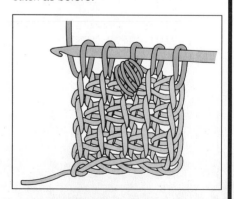

3. Yarn over and draw through all six loops. Remaining loop is worked off on Return row.

Surface Decoration

The evenness of Tunisian simple stitch makes it ideal to add surface decoration. The fabric in the photograph above has been embroidered using cross stitch. The diagram below indicates where to position the crosses in relation to the threads of the fabric.

It is also possible to use many other embroidery stitches in a similar way.

Following Afghan Pattern Instructions

All Afghan patterns are given in the form of written instructions and stitch diagrams. Much of the information about following pattern instructions, pattern repeats, tension etc. given on pages 10 to 12 apply equally to Afghan crochet. The stitch diagrams however are given on a grid where one rectangle represents one stitch worked over a Forward and Return row.

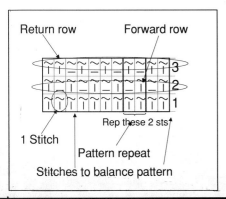

Stitches within dark lines form the pattern repeat. Compare stitch diagrams with written instructions if you have difficulty following the pattern.

Abbreviations and Symbols
Abbreviations

Beg = beginning, **ch** = chain, **dec** = decrease, **inc** = increase, **rep** = repeat, **sp** = space, **st(s)** = stitch(es), **tog** = together, **Tdc** = Tunisian double crochet, **Tdtr** = Tunisian double treble, **Thdc** = Tunisian half double crochet, **Tks** = Tunisian knit stitch, **Tps** = Tunisian purl stitch, **Tsl st** = Tunisian slipped stitch, **Tss** = Tunisian simple stitch, **Ttr** = Tunisian treble, **TwTss** = Twisted Tunisian simple stitch, **yo** = yarn over, **yf** = yarn forward, **yb** = yarn back.

Common Symbols

Note: All symbols represent a completed stitch; the lower part of the symbol is worked on the Forward row where the loops are held on the hook, the upper part (or swash ⁓) is worked on the Return row when the loops are worked off.

= Tunisian simple stitch (Tss)

= Tunisian purl stitch (Tps)

= Tunisian knit stitch (Tks)

= Tunisian slipped stitch (Tsl st)

= Twisted Tunisian simple stitch (TwTss)

= Tss worked under chain loop and between two vertical loops of previous row

= Tss worked into back loop only of stitch in previous row

= Tunisian half double crochet (Thdc)

= Tunisian double crochet (Tdc)

= Tunisian double crochet worked between stitches

= Increase one Tunisian simple stitch (Inc 1Tss)

= Tunisian simple stitch two together (Tss2tog)

= Tunisian simple stitch three together (Tss3tog)

= Make Bobble (MB)

= Yo, Tss2tog

= Tss2tog, yo

= Yo, tss3tog, yo

VI.1

Note: Because this pattern incorporates a slipped stitch it should be worked on a hook which is at least 2 sizes (1mm) larger than usual.

Multiple of 2 sts + 3.

1st row: Using A, as Basic Forward and Return row, changing to B when 2 loops remain at end of return.

2nd row: Using B, with 1 loop on hook, *1Tss into next st, 1Tsl st into next st; rep from * to last 2 sts, 1Tss into each of next 2 sts. Return, changing to A when 2 loops remain.

3rd row: Using A, with 1 loop on hook, *1Tsl st into next st, 1Tss into next st; rep from * to end. Return, changing to B when 2 loops remain.

Rep 2nd and 3rd rows.

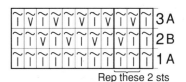

Rep these 2 sts

VI.2

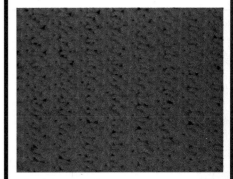

Multiple of 2 sts + 1.

1st row: As Basic Forward and Return row.

2nd row: With 1 loop on hook, *1TwTss into next st, 1Tss into next st; rep from * to end. Return.

Rep 2nd row.

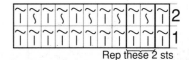

Rep these 2 sts

VI. Afghan (Tunisian) Crochet

VI.3

Any number of sts.

Note: Check the number of sts after each Forward row. It will be easier to keep the number of sts correct and the edges of the material straight if you take care to alternate the placing of the first Tss, as given on 2nd and 3rd rows.

1st row: As Basic Forward and Return row.

2nd row: With 1 loop on hook, work 1Tss into space between 2nd and 3rd sts, 1 Tss into each sp to end, 1Tss into last st. Return.

3rd row: With 1 loop on hook, work 1Tss into sp between first and 2nd sts, 1Tss into each sp to last sp, skip last sp, work 1Tss into last st. Return.

Rep 2nd and 3rd rows.

Rep this stitch

VI.4

Multiple of 2 sts + 3.

1st row: As Basic Forward and Return row.

2nd row: With 1 loop on hook, *1Tps into next st, 1Tss into next st; rep from * to end. Return.

3rd row: With 1 loop on hook, *1Tss into next st, 1Tps into next st; rep from * to last 2 sts, 1Tss into each of last 2 sts. Return.

Rep 2nd and 3rd rows.

Rep these 4 sts

VI.5

Multiple of 4 sts + 3.

1st row: Using A, as Basic Forward and Return row, changing to B when 2 loops remain.

2nd row: Using B, with 1 loop on hook, *1Tsl st into next st, work 1Tss into each of next 3 sts; rep from * to last 2 sts, 1Tsl st into next st, work 1Tss into last st. Return, changing to A when 2 loops remain.

3rd row: Using A with 1 loop on hook work 1Tss into each st to end. Return, changing to B when 2 loops remain.

4th row: Using B, with 1 loop on hook, work 1Tss into each of next 2 sts, *1Tsl st into next st, 1Tss into each of next 3 sts; rep from * to end. Return, changing to A when 2 loops remain.

5th row: As 3rd row.

Rep 2nd to 5th rows.

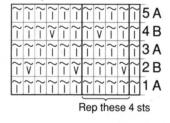

Rep these 4 sts

VI.6

Note: It is recommended that this stitch is worked using a hook 1 or 2 sizes (0.5mm or 1mm) larger than usual.

Multiple of 2 sts + 3.

VI.7

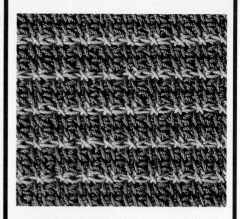

Multiple of 2 sts + 2.

Special Abbreviation

Cross 2 = skip next st, 1Tss into next st, 1Tss into skipped st.

Note: The crossed stitches appear 1 row below the row on which the cross 2 is worked.

1st row: Using A, as Basic Forward and Return row.

2nd row: Using A, with 1 loop on hook, 1Tss into each st to end. Return.

3rd row: Using B, as 2nd row.

4th row: Using A, with 1 loop on hook, *cross 2; rep from * to last st, 1Tss into last st. Return.

Rep 2nd to 4th rows.

Rep these 4 sts

Special Abbreviation

Sl 1 fwd = yf, insert hook into next st without working it, yb.

1st row: Using A, as Basic Forward and Return row.

2nd row: Using B, with 1 loop on hook, *sl 1 fwd, 1Tss into next st; rep from * to end. Return, changing to A when 2 loops remain.

3rd row: Using A, with 1 loop on hook, *1Tss into next st, sl 1 fwd; rep from * to last 2 sts, 1Tss into each of last 2 sts. Return, changing to B when 2 loops remain.

Rep 2nd and 3rd rows.

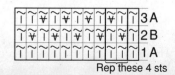

Rep these 4 sts

Abbreviations and Symbols on page 89

VI.8

Multiple of 14 sts + 7.

1st row: As Basic Forward and Return row.

2nd row: With 1 loop on hook, work 1Tss into each of next 6 sts, *work 1Tps into each of next 7 sts, work 1Tss into each of next 7 sts; rep from * to end. Return.

3rd to 7th rows: Rep 2nd row 5 times more.

8th row: With 1 loop on hook, work 1Tps into each of next 6 sts, *work 1Tss into each of next 7 sts, work 1Tps into each of next 7 sts; rep from * to end. Return.

9th to 13th rows: Rep 8th row 5 times more.

Rep 2nd to 13th rows.

VI.10

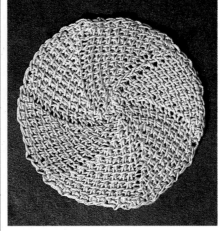

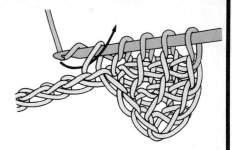

Using B, rep these 11 rows but working into sts of previous color instead of ch. Continue working segments in alternate colors until **6** segments in all have been worked. Fasten off last st.

Join seam.

Using A make 12ch.

1st row: With 1 loop on hook, work 1Tss into next ch. Return.

2nd row: With 1 loop on hook, work 1Tss into next st, then work 1Tss into next ch (3 loops on hook). Return.

3rd row: With 1 loop on hook, work 1Tss into each of next 2 sts, then work 1Tss into next ch (4 loops on hook). Return.

Continue working in this manner until all 12ch have been picked up (12 loops on hook). Return, changing color when 2 loops remain.

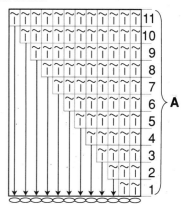

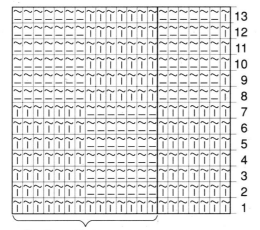

Rep these 14 sts

VI.11

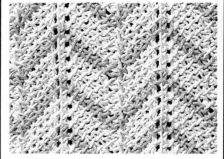

Work as VI.9 **but** working 3 rows in color A and 1 row in color B throughout **or** work using random colors as illustrated below.

VI.9

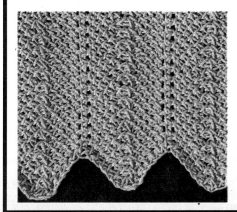

Multiple of 14 sts + 1.

1st row: As Basic Forward and Return row.

2nd row: With 1 loop on hook, *inc 1Tss, work 1Tss into each of next 4 sts, Tss3tog, work 1Tss into each of next 5 sts, inc 1Tss; rep from * to end. Return.

Rep 2nd row.

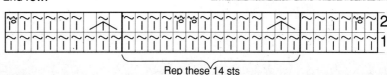

Rep these 14 sts

VI. Afghan (Tunisian) Crochet

VI.12

Multiple of 2 sts + 3.

Special Abbreviation

⟆ **Long Tdc** (worked on Forward rows) = loosely work 1Tdc into next st 2 rows below.

1st row: As Basic Forward and Return row.

2nd row: With 1 loop on hook, work 1Tss into each st to end. Return.

3rd row: With 1 loop on hook, *1 long Tdc, 1Tss into next st; rep from * to end. Return.

4th row: With 1 loop on hook, *1Tss into next st, 1 long Tdc; rep from * to last 2 sts, 1Tss into each of last 2 sts. Return.

Rep 3rd and 4th rows.

Rep these 2 sts

VI.13

Work as VI.12 **but** working 1 row each in colors A and B throughout.

VI.14

Multiple of 8 sts + 4.

1st row: As Basic Forward and Return row.

2nd row: With 1 loop on hook, work 1Tss into each of next 3 sts, *work 1Tps into each of next 4 sts, work 1Tss into each next 4 sts; rep from * to end. Return.

Rep 2nd row.

VI.15

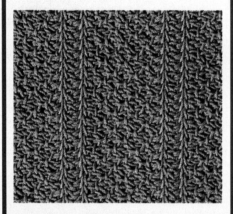

Multiple of 10 sts + 11.

1st row: As Basic Forward and Return row.

2nd row: With 1 loop on hook, 1Tps into next st, 1Tss into each of next 2 sts, *1TwTss into next st, 1Tss into next st, 1TwTss into next st, 1Tps into next st, [1Tss into next st, 1Tps into next st] twice, 1Tss into each of next 2 sts; rep from * to last 7 sts, 1TwTss into next st, 1Tss into next st, 1TwTss into next st, [1Tps into next st, 1Tss into next st] twice. Return.

3rd row: With 1 loop on hook, 1Tss into next st, 1Tps into next st, 1Tss into next st, *[1TwTss into next st, 1Tss into next st] twice, [1Tps into next st, 1Tss into next st] 3 times; rep from * to last 7 sts, [1TwTss into next st, 1Tss into next st] twice, 1Tps into next st, 1Tss into next st, 1Tps into last st. Return.

Rep 2nd and 3rd rows.

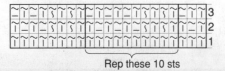

Rep these 10 sts

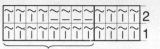

Rep these 8 sts

VI.16

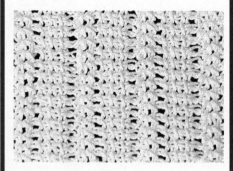

Multiple of 6 sts + 3.

Special Abbreviations

⟆ **Basic Group 3** = first part worked as Basic Forward row, on return row work 1ch, yo, draw hook through 4 loops, 1ch.

⟆ **Group 3** = on Forward row insert hook under next ch, yo, draw loop through, insert hook into loop over the group 3 on previous row, yo, draw loop through, insert hook under next ch, yo, draw loop through. On Return row work 1ch, yo, draw hook through 4 loops, 1ch.

1st row: As Basic Forward row. Return as follows: Yo, draw hook through 1 loop, [yo, draw hook through 2 loops] twice, *basic group 3, [yo, draw through 2 loops] 3 times; rep from * to end.

2nd row: With 1 loop on hook, work 1Tss into each of next 2 sts, *group 3, work 1Tss into each of next 3 sts; rep from * to end. Return as follows: Yo, draw hook through 1 loop, [yo, draw hook through 2 loops] twice, *group 3, [yo, draw through 2 loops] 3 times; rep from * to end.

Rep 2nd row.

Rep these 6 sts

VI.17

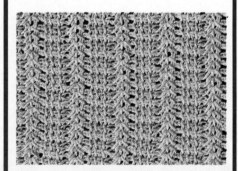

Work as given for VI.16 **but** working 1 row in A and 1 row in B throughout.

Abbreviations and Symbols on page 89

VI.18

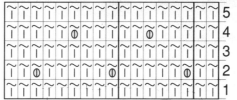

Rep thes 6 sts

Multiple of 6 sts + 5.

Special Abbreviation

⦿ **MB (Make Bobble)** = using color B [yo, insert hook into next st, yo and draw loop through] 3 times into same st, yo and draw through 6 loops, see Note.

Note: Pattern is worked in color A on every row. Color B is used for bobbles only and is carried **loosely** across back of work on 2nd and 4th rows. Cut and rejoin color B at beginning of each bobble row.

1st row: As Basic Forward and Return row.

2nd row: With 1 loop on hook, work 1Tss into next st, MB into next st, *1Tss into each of next 5 sts, MB into next st; rep from * to last 2 sts, Tss into each of last 2 sts. Return using A only.

3rd row: With 1 loop on hook, 1Tss into each st to end. Return.

4th row: With 1 loop on hook, 1Tss into each of next 4 sts, *MB into next st, 1Tss into each of next 5 sts; rep from * to end. Return using A only.

5th row: As 3rd row.

Rep 2nd to 5th rows.

VI.19

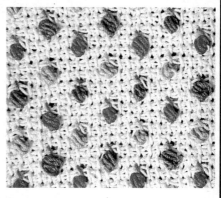

Work as given for VI.18 **but** working 1 row of bobbles each in colors B, C and D.

VI.20

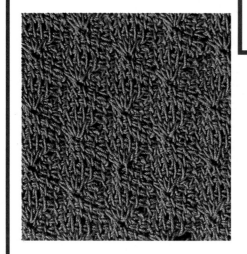

Multiple of 10 sts + 7.

Special Abbreviation

5Tdc fan = skip next 2 sts, work 5 **loose** Tdc round stem of next st 3 rows below, skip next 2 sts (see diagrams).

1st row: As Basic Forward and Return row.

2nd row: With 1 loop on hook, 1Tss into each st to end. Return.

3rd and 4th rows: Rep 2nd row twice.

5th row: With 1 loop on hook, work 5Tdc fan, *1Tss into each of next 5 sts, work 5Tdc fan; rep from * to last st, 1Tss into last st. Return.

6th and 7th rows: Rep 2nd row twice.

8th row: With 1 loop on hook, *1Tss into each of next 5 sts, work 5Tdc fan; rep from * to last 6 sts, 1Tss into each of last 6 sts. Return.

Rep 3rd to 8th rows.

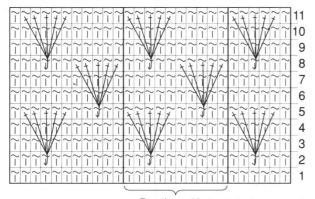

Rep these 10 sts

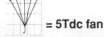
= 5Tdc fan

Tunisian 5 Double Crochet Fan

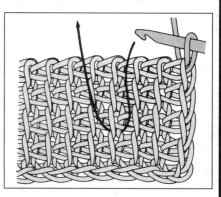

1. Skip two stitches. Loosely work a Tunisian double crochet into the next stitch three rows below (inserting hook as indicated).

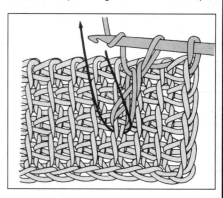

2. Loosely work four more Tunisian double crochet into the same stitch.

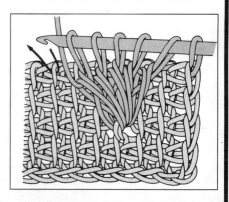

3. Skip two stitches and continue working.

VI. Afghan (Tunisian) Crochet

VI.21

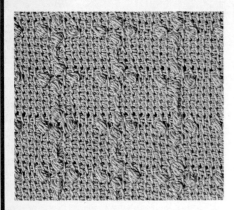

Multiple of 8 sts + 7.

Special Abbreviations

Long Tdc (worked on Forward rows) = loosely work 1Tdc into vertical loop above bobble 3 rows below.

MB (Make Bobble) = [yo, insert hook into next st, yo and draw loop through] 3 times into same st, yo, draw yarn through 6 loops.

VI.22

Multiple of 3 sts + 3.

Note: Color is changed after each **Forward** row. Work first ch of each Return row in new color.

Special Abbreviation

Cross 2 = skip next st, 1Tss into next st, 1Tss into skipped st.

Make chain in color A.

1st row: Using color A as Basic Forward row. Using color B Return.

2nd row: Using B, with 1 loop on hook, *1Tps into next st, cross 2; rep from * to last 2 sts, 1Tps into next st, 1Tss into last st. Using A Return.

3rd row: Using A, with 1 loop on hook, *1Tps into next st, cross 2; rep from * to last 2 sts, 1Tps into next st, 1Tss into last st. Using B Return.

Rep 2nd and 3rd rows.

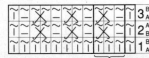

Rep these 3 sts

1st row: As Basic Forward and Return row.

2nd row: With 1 loop on hook, work 1Tss into each of next 2 sts, *MB into next st, 1Tss into each of next 7 sts; rep from * to last 4 sts, MB, 1Tss into each of last 3 sts. Return.

3rd row: With 1 loop on hook, *MB into next st, 1Tss into each of next 3 sts; rep from * to last 2 sts, MB, 1Tss into last st. Return.

4th row: As 2nd row.

5th row: With 1 loop on hook work 1Tss into each st to end. Return.

6th row: As 5th row.

7th row: With 1 loop on hook, work 1Tss into each of next 2 sts, *work long Tdc, 1Tss into each of next 7 sts; rep from * to last 4 sts, work long Tdc, 1Tss into each of last 3 sts. Return.

Rep 2nd to 7th rows.

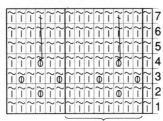

Rep these 8 sts

VI.23

Multiple of 2 sts + 3.

Special Abbreviation

MB (Make Bobble) = work [yo, insert hook into next st, yo and draw loop through] 3 times into same st, yo, draw yarn through 6 loops.

1st row: As Basic Forward and Return row.

2nd row: With 1 loop on hook, work 1Tss into next st, *MB into next st, 1Tss into next st; rep from * to last st, 1Tss into last st. Return.

3rd row: With 1 loop on hook, *MB into next st, 1Tss into next st; rep from * to end. Return.

Rep 2nd and 3rd rows.

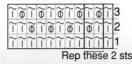

Rep these 2 sts

VI.24

Multiple of 3 sts + 2.

Special Abbreviation

Long Ttr (worked on Forward rows) = loosely work 1Ttr into vertical loop of next st 2 rows below.

1st row: As Basic Forward and Return row.

2nd row: With 1 loop on hook, 1Tps into next st, *1Tdc into next st, 1Tps into each of next 2 sts; rep from * to end. Return.

3rd row: With 1 loop on hook, work 1Tss into each st to end. Return.

4th row: With 1 loop on hook, 1Tps into next st, *work 1 long Ttr, 1Tps into each of next 2 sts; rep from * to end. Return.

Rep 3rd and 4th rows.

Rep these 3 sts

VI.25

Multiple of 2 sts + 1.

1st row: As Basic Forward and Return row.

2nd row: With 1 loop on hook, *1Tdc into next st, 1Tps into next st; rep from * to end. Return.

3rd row: With 1 loop on hook, *work 1Tps into next st, 1Tdc into next st; rep from * to end. Return.

Rep 2nd and 3rd rows.

Rep these 2 sts

Abbreviations and Symbols on page 89

VI.26

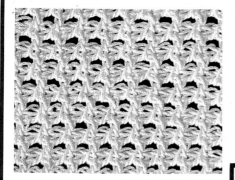

Multiple of 2 sts + 3.

1st row: As Basic Forward and Return row.

2nd row: With 1 loop on hook, *Tss2tog, yo; rep from * to last 2 sts, 1Tss into each of last 2 sts. Return.

3rd row: With 1 loop on hook, *1Tss into next vertical loop, 1Tss under ch loop of next st; rep from * to last 2 sts, 1Tss into each of last 2 sts. Return.

Rep 2nd and 3rd rows.

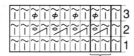

Rep these 2 sts

VI.27

Multiple of 7 sts + 7.

Special Abbreviation

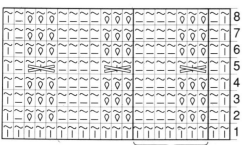 **T3st cable** = skip next 2 sts, work 1Tks into 3rd st, work 1Tks into 2nd st, work 1Tks into first st.

1st row: As Basic Forward and Return row.

2nd row: With 1 loop on hook 1Tps into next st, *1Tks into each of next 3 sts, 1Tps into each of next 4 sts; rep from * to last 5 sts, 1Tks into each of next 3 sts, 1Tps into next st, 1Tss into last st. Return.

3rd and 4th rows: Rep 2nd row twice.

5th row: With 1 loop on hook 1Tps into next st, *T3st cable, 1Tps into each of next 4 sts; rep from * to last 5 sts, T3st cable, 1Tps into next st, 1Tss into last st. Return.

6th to 11th rows: Rep 2nd row 6 times.

Rep 5th to 11th rows.

VI.28

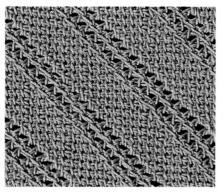

Multiple of 11 sts + 2.

Note: When working Tss2tog work through diagonal loop of yo of previous row where applicable.

1st row: As Basic Forward and Return row.

2nd row: With 1 loop on hook, 1Tss into each of next 3 sts, [yo, Tss2tog] twice, *1Tss into each of next 7 sts, [yo, Tss2tog] twice; rep from * to last 5 sts, 1Tss into each of last 5 sts. Return.

3rd row: With 1 loop on hook, 1Tss into each of next 3 sts, 1Tss under ch loop of next st, [yo, Tss2tog] twice, *1Tss into each of next 6 sts, 1Tss under ch loop of next st, [yo, Tss2tog] twice; rep from * to last 4 sts, 1Tss into each of last 4 sts. Return.

4th row: With 1 loop on hook, 1Tss into each of next 4 sts, 1Tss under ch loop of next st, [yo, Tss2tog] twice, *1Tss into each of next 6 sts, 1Tss under ch loop of next st, [yo, Tss2tog] twice; rep from * to last 3 sts, 1Tss into each of last 3 sts. Return.

5th row: With 1 loop on hook, 1Tss into each of next 5 sts, 1Tss under ch loop of next st, [yo, Tss2tog] twice, *1Tss into each of next 6 sts, 1Tss under ch loop of next st, [yo, Tss2tog] twice; rep from * to last 2 sts, 1Tss into each of last 2 sts. Return.

6th row: With 1 loop on hook, *1Tss into each of next 6 sts, 1Tss under ch loop of next st, [yo, Tss2tog] twice; rep from * to last st, 1Tss into last st. Return.

7th row: With 1 loop on hook, 1Tss into each of next 7 sts, 1Tss under ch loop of next st, *[yo, Tss2tog] twice, 1Tss into each of next 6 sts, 1Tss under ch loop of next st; rep from * to last 4 sts, yo, Tss2tog, 1Tss into each of last 2 sts. Return.

8th row: With 1 loop on hook, yo, Tss2tog, 1Tss into each of next 6 sts, 1Tss under ch loop of next st, *[yo, Tss2tog] twice, 1Tss into each of next 6 sts, 1Tss under ch loop of next st; rep from * to last 3 sts, yo, Tss2tog, 1Tss into last st. Return.

9th row: With 1 loop on hook, 1Tss under ch loop of next st, yo, Tss2tog, 1Tss into each of next 6 sts, 1Tss under ch loop of next st, *[yo, Tss2tog] twice, 1Tss into each of next 6 sts, 1Tss under ch loop of next st; rep from * to last 2 sts, 1Tss into each of last 2 sts. Return.

10th row: With 1 loop on hook, [yo, Tss2tog] twice, *1Tss into each of next 6 sts, 1Tss under ch loop of next st, [yo, Tss2tog] twice; rep from * to last 8 sts, 1Tss into each of last 8 sts. Return.

11th row: With 1 loop on hook, *1Tss under ch loop of next st, [yo, Tss2tog] twice, 1Tss into each of next 6 sts; rep from * to last st, 1Tss into last st. Return.

12th row: With 1 loop on hook, 1Tss into next st, *1Tss under ch loop of next st, [yo, Tss2tog] twice, 1Tss into each of next 6 sts; rep from * to end. Return.

13th row: With 1 loop on hook, 1Tss into each of next 2 sts, 1Tss under ch loop of next st, [yo, Tss2tog] twice, *1Tss into each of next 6 sts, 1Tss under ch loop of next st, [yo, Tss2tog] twice; rep from * to last 5 sts, 1Tss into each of last 5 sts. Return.

Rep 3rd to 13th rows.

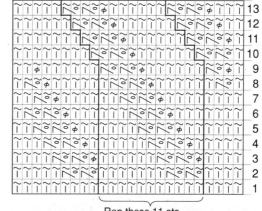

Rep these 11 sts

8
7
6
5
4
3
2
1

Rep these 7 sts

Diagram only: Rep 2nd to 8th rows.

VI. Afghan (Tunisian) Crochet

VI.29

Multiple of 6 sts + 7.

Special Abbreviation

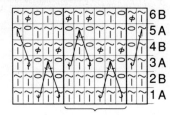 **3 st triangle** = on Forward row work 1Tdc into previous st 2 rows below, work 1Tss into next st, work 1Tdc into next st 2 rows below, yo, draw through 3 loops. Return as follows: Yo, draw through 2 loops.

1st row: Using A, as Basic Forward and Return row.

2nd row: Using B, with 1 loop on hook, work 1Tss into next st, *skip 1 st, work 1Tss into next st, skip 1 st, work 1Tss into each of next 3 sts; rep from * to last 5 sts, skip next st, work 1Tss into next st, skip next st, work 1Tss into each of last 2 sts. Return as follows: Yo, draw hook through 1 loop, yo, draw hook through 2 loops, *1ch, yo, draw hook through 2 loops, 1ch, [yo, draw hook through 2 loops] 3 times; rep from * until 4 loops remain on hook, 1ch, yo, draw hook through 2 loops, 1ch, [yo, draw hook through 2 loops] twice.

3rd row: Using A, with 1 loop on hook, work 1Tss into next st, skip next sp, work 3 st triangle, skip next sp,* work 1Tss into each of next 3 sts, skip next sp, work 3 st triangle, skip next sp; rep from * to last 2 sts, work 1Tss into each of last 2 sts. Return as follows: Yo, draw hook through 1 loop, yo, draw hook through 2 loops, *1ch, yo, draw hook through 2 loops, 1ch, [yo, draw hook through 2 loops] 3 times; rep from * until 4 loops remain on hook, 1ch, yo, draw hook through 2 loops, 1ch, [yo, draw hook through 2 loops] twice.

4th row: Using B, with 1 loop on hook, *skip next st, 1Tss under ch loop of next st, 1Tss into next st, 1Tss under ch loop of next st, skip 1 st, 1Tss into next st; rep from * to end. Return as follows: Yo, draw hook through 1 loop, *1ch, [yo, draw hook through 2 loops] 3 times, 1ch, yo, draw hook through 2 loops; rep from * to end.

5th row: Using A, with 1 loop on hook, work 1Tdc into next vertical loop 2 rows below, yo, draw hook through 2 loops, skip next sp, 1Tss into each of next 3 sts, skip next sp, *work 3 st triangle, skip next sp, 1Tss into each of next 3 sts, skip next sp; rep from * to last st, work 1Tdc into

previous st 2 rows below, 1Tss into last st, yo and through 2 loops. Return as follows: Yo, draw hook through 1 loop, *1ch, [yo, draw hook through 2 loops] 3 times, 1ch, yo, draw hook through 2 loops; rep from * to end.

6th row: Using B, with 1 loop on hook, *work 1Tss under ch loop of next st, skip next st, 1Tss into next st, skip next st, 1Tss under ch loop of next st, 1Tss into next st; rep from * to end. Return as follows: Yo, draw hook through 1 loop, yo, draw hook through 2 loops, *1ch, yo, draw hook through 2 loops, 1ch, [yo, draw hook through 2 loops] 3 times; rep from * until 4 loops remain on hook, 1ch, yo, draw hook through 2 loops, 1ch, [yo, draw hook through 2 loops] twice.

Rep 3rd to 6th rows always working Tdc into sts 2 rows below.

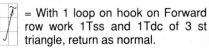

Rep these 6 sts

◯ = On Forward rows skip 1 st or space, on Return rows work 1ch.

⟋ = With 1 loop on hook on Forward row work 1Tss and 1Tdc of 3 st triangle, return as normal.

⟍ = On Forward row work 1Tdc of 3 st triangle and 1Tss, Return as normal.

VI.30

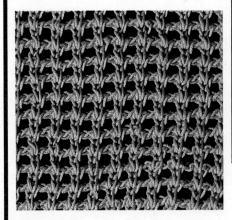

Multiple of 2 sts + 1.

1st row: As Basic Forward and Return row.

2nd row: With 1 loop on hook, 2ch, *skip next st, yo, 1Tks into next st, 2ch; rep from * to end. Return.

3rd row: With 1 loop on hook, 2ch, *skip next sp, yo, 1Tks into upper of 2ch of previous Forward row, 2ch; rep from * to end. Return.

Rep 3rd row.

VI.31

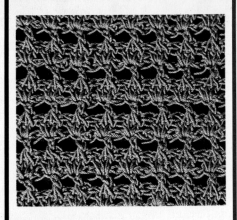

Multiple of 3 sts + 2.

Special Abbreviations

 **Fan** = work 3Tdc into center of upper of 2ch in previous Forward row.

Lace 3tog = insert hook through next 3 vertical loops, yo, draw loop through, 2ch (on Return row 1ch, yo, draw hook through 2 loops, 1ch).

Note: Only count sts after 3rd row.

1st row: As Basic Forward and Return row.

2nd row: With 1 loop on hook, 2ch, *Lace 3tog; rep from * to last st, 1Tss into last st, 2ch. Return as follows: Yo, draw hook through 1 loop, 1ch, *yo, draw hook through 2 loops, 2ch; rep from * until 3 loops remain on hook, yo draw hook through 2 loops, 1ch, yo, draw hook through 2 loops.

3rd row: With 1 loop on hook, 2ch, *work 1 Fan; rep from * to last st, 1Tdc into upper ch of last st. Return.

Rep 2nd and 3rd rows.

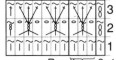

Rep these 3 sts

⧈ = With 1 loop on hook at beginning of Forward row work 2ch. 1 loop to be worked off on Return row.

⧊ = Into last st of Forward row work 1Tss, 2ch. On Return row work yo and through 1 loop.

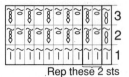

Rep these 2 sts

⧈ = With 1 loop on hook at beginning of Forward row work 2ch.

⧊ = Skip next st, yo on Forward row, (1 loop to be worked off on Return row).

⧈ = 1Tks, 2ch on Forward row, (1 loop to be worked off on Return row). **Note:** On 3rd and every following Forward row work 1Tks into the upper of 2ch of previous Forward row.

Abbreviations and Symbols on page